THE SONG WRITING Sourcebook

How to turn chords into great songs
by RIKKY ROOKSBY

THE SONGWRITING SOURCEBOOK

by Rikky Rooksby

Additional material for this revised edition by Rod Fogg

Dedicated to Alan Slutsky, in recognition of his outstanding effort to illuminate and preserve the legacy of the musicians who recorded for the Motown label during the 1960s and 70s.

A BACKBEAT BOOK
This new second edition 2011
First edition 2003
Published by Backbeat Books
An imprint of Hal Leonard Corporation
7777 West Bluemound Road,
Milwaukee, WI 53213
www.backbeatbooks.com

Designed and produced for Backbeat Books by
Outline Press Ltd
2A Union Court, 20-22 Union Road,
London SW4 6JP, England
www.jawbonepress.com

ISBN 978-0-87930-959-6

DESIGN: Paul Cooper Design
EDITOR: Jim Roberts

Printed by Regent Publishing Services Limited, China

11 12 13 14 15 6 5 4 3 2

contents

PREFACE

Picture a table, a cooling cup of coffee, a pen, a few sheets of paper, and a figure lost in thought. Sitting at a piano or holding a guitar, someone presses the keys or fingers the strings. Music is heard, half-formed, repeating. A tapping foot on the wooden floor sets the beat. Something invisible takes shape as a chord change. The mood flickers from happy to sad as a major chord gives way to a minor. The chain of chords slowly lengthens as each finds a place that feels right. A few letter names are scribbled for memory's sake. Soon the chords are settled enough in their sequence and character for the songwriter to start humming, trying out notes for a melody. Thus, from the cloud of unformed grace, emotion, and recollected experience which is inspiration, a song comes into being.

The simplest method for writing a song is to put some chords together in a musically pleasing, expressive progression. Many people find this an effective way to stimulate a mood and a context in which a melody and a lyric can be written. This is successfully done by writers whose guitar technique is very limited, but that doesn't matter. It only takes a handful of common chords to lay the foundation of a great song.

*The Songwriting Sourceboo*k is both a method and a resource. It shows you how to link chords into the kinds of chord progression that occur in almost all popular songs, whatever their genre. It begins with simple three-chord progressions. Then gradually, section by section, it explains how to add chords and create sequences with four, five, six, and more chords. It also provides no less than 100 techniques that explain the finer points of song structure and chord movement, so you can get the most out of the chords you put together. As a resource it provides scores of ready-made song fragments.

All the sequences are presented in a style which means you won't be reading any conventional music, and there are chord boxes with the examples to remind you of the necessary shapes on the guitar. *The Songwriting Sourcebook* is also equipped with a 20-track CD of song sequences illustrating in audio many of the techniques analysed in the book. You can practise your chord-changing by playing along with these tracks.

Have you ever wanted to write a song but not known where to begin? Have you ever wondered how songwriters use chords? Or maybe you've been writing songs for a while and need some new ideas? This revised edition of *The Songwriting Sourcebook* will open new doors to the wonderful world of harmony and composing songs.

RIKKY ROOKSBY 2010

HOW TO USE THIS BOOK

If you already write songs *The Songwriting Sourcebook* does not have to be read sequentially, so dip straight into any section of interest. If you are a beginner, and haven't read any of my other songwriting titles – such as *How To Write Songs On Guitar* – it would be sensible to read the book from the start so you grasp the initial techniques described in **Section One** where there are only three chords to be concerned about. Before that the **Introduction** provides an overview of factors that influence some of the choices people make when they write songs, and some necessary preliminary information about song structure at its most general.

The Songwriting Sourcebook has 10 sections. **Section One** explains the three-chord trick song and shows how chord sequences are built from simple two and four-bar ideas into larger 12 and 16-bar verses. Examples in this section use only three easy guitar chords: G, C, and D. It also reveals how to make these chords go further by using their inversions (G/B, G/D, C/E, C/G, D/F♯, and D/A) which are also easy guitar shapes.

Section Two goes on one step to the four-chord song, when minor chords are brought in to combine with the major chords of **Section One**. It describes devices such as the 'secondary' three-chord trick, inverted minor chords, and the powerful songwriting device I call the 'turnaround', the class of progression that drives many hit songs to commercial success. It also features fully mapped-out four-chord song sequences, which show how a small number of chords can be distributed in a song's intro, verse, chorus, and bridge.

The number of available chords to work with rises to five and six in **Section Three**. New musical avenues dramatically open up in **Section Four**, with the possibility of going beyond the limit of six standard major-key chords to the three 'flat degree chords'. These are chords which do not strictly belong in key, but songwriters can use them to give their sequences extra colour. The same is true of the category of chords I term 'reverse polarity' explained in **Section Five**. Any songwriter who knows how to use these effectively has made a big step forward in their available harmonic raw material.

For blue moods and rainy days, **Section Six** describes how to write a song in a minor key, and presents a number of popular sequences that are constantly re-used by songwriters. **Section Seven** focuses on another important facet of songwriting, knowing how to change the type of chord in a progression for a specific mood or style. This is where you can find information about whether a G chord in one of your song ideas would be better voiced as G7, Gmaj7, Gsus2, Gadd9, or G6, etc. **Section Eight** opens up the amazing possibilities which keys and key-changes offer to the songwriter, and **Section Nine** gathers together a miscellany of other techniques.

Finally, **Section 10** of *The Songwriting Sourcebook* lays out the full-length song examples heard, in a variety of styles, on the 20-track CD. These audio tracks comprise strummed chord sequences, with intros, verses, prechoruses, choruses, bridges and codas. Each audio example includes a number of broader songwriting tips. More at-a-glance information is featured in the appendices, including tables and a glossary.

This book was the fourth in my multi-volume series on songwriting, which commenced publication in 2000. To find out more on chord sequences, melody, guitar chords, and guitar tunings, get *How To Write Songs On Guitar* (2000, revised 2009), *How To Write Songs In Altered Guitar Tunings* (2010), *Chord Master* (2004), *Melody* (2005), *How To Write Songs On Keyboards* (2005), and *Lyrics* (2006). *Riffs* (2002, revised 2010) is the most encyclopaedic study ever published about them. To learn more about the elements that make a magic recording, 100 songs from 1960 to the present go under the microscope in *Inside Classic Rock Tracks* (2001). Tips on the art of instrumentation, and how to arrange and record your songs more effectively, can be found in *Arranging Songs* (2008). Information about these titles is at www.backbeatbooks.com and www.rikkyrooksby.com.

INTRODUCTION

The Songwriting Sourcebook is a book about chords, but it isn't a chord dictionary. A chord dictionary is a book of box diagrams that tell guitarists where to put their fingers on the fretboard in order to play various types of chords, from majors and minors to sevenths, ninths, etc. The Songwriting Sourcebook is something different.

This is a book about the chord sequences that run through the intros, verses, choruses and bridges of all the songs you have ever heard, ever written and ever will write; of all the hits that were, are and will be. It is about how the chords in, say, a dictionary like *Every Chord You Ever Wanted To Play But Were Afraid To Even Imagine Existed* are used by songwriters. And it's not just for guitarists. Guitar chord-boxes are given at the foot of the page, but *The Songwriting Sourcebook* is just as relevant for people who write songs on keyboards. Whether a song is composed on guitar or keyboard makes no difference to the centrality of the chord sequence to the song. This book is about how chord progressions are made. It is also a sourcebook of popular progressions.

WHAT'S SO IMPORTANT ABOUT CHORD SEQUENCES?

A song consists of four basic elements: melody, lyrics, rhythm – comprising the time signature, the speed (tempo) and other rhythmic elements – and harmony. Harmony means the chords that support and colour the melody. Each section of a song will usually have chords.

A song can be written starting from any one of these four elements. A songwriter collaborating with a lyricist, for example, will have a sheet of words to set to music. A songwriter with access to recording equipment might start with the rhythm by creating a drum loop and building the song from that. Sometimes a tune will occur to the songwriter – a melody for which words, chords and rhythms could be found later.

But the most common method is to start by combining chords into a sequence ("chord changes"). This is a popular method because it happens naturally when someone strums a guitar or plays chords at a piano. Just by casually linking one chord to another, a mood is often established. This mood leads the songwriter to look for other chords that will sustain it. Eventually the emotion evoked by the chords may inspire a melody and/or words – perhaps a title that fixes the mood in the memory and evokes a theme. Someone who enjoys playing an instrument is more likely to drift into writing a song this way than by trying to pen a lyric on a sheet of paper (which is initially a word-oriented activity, not a musical one) or by trying to construct a melody out of thin air (although some songwriters "grow" a melody as they link the chords).

Of the four elements of a song, it is harmony which provides the quickest route to an initial structure that will inspire the others. Rhythm quickly follows, because as soon as a songwriter plays a chord sequence he or she has to decide how many chords will go in a bar, how many beats each will take, how many times each will be struck, and how fast or slow the sequence will be.

Chords make up the harmony, and the harmony has a profound effect on the emotion the song will communicate. It colours both the words and the melody to which the words are sung. *The Songwriting Sourcebook* is a practical course in the harmony of popular song, whatever genre you want to write in. There have been many books about harmony, but most were written to explain the harmony in "classical" music, whose rules and procedures contrast with popular music. *The Songwriting Sourcebook* is different because it's grounded in popular songs and the craft of popular songwriters.

WHAT DO I NEED TO KNOW ABOUT CHORD SEQUENCES?

Many songs are composed intuitively. People without any technical knowledge of music simply put together chords that sound good to their ears. There's nothing wrong with that. The history of popular music is full of performers who knew almost nothing about what they were doing. A combination of inspiration, creative drive, sheer luck and sometimes genius led to great songs. But it can be a hit-or-miss affair. What happens if inspiration doesn't strike? What happens if you come up with a fine sequence and then get stuck because you don't know how to develop it? What do you do if all your songs sound the same? What do you do if the songs you write are not exciting the audiences who hear them?

Music is about inspiration and feeling. Unfortunately, they are not automatically available when you want them. A songwriter with even limited experience soon realizes that although it would be great to be able to push a button and be guaranteed a classic song every time he or she picked up the guitar, it doesn't happen that way. This is not ideal if the Abscess Records Corp expects the band – let's call them Mike Magma & The Meltdown – to record their next album in six weeks and there are still 14 new songs to write, two of which will be singles and therefore have to be commercial.

HOW DO I FIND INSPIRATION?

I am often asked if there is anything a songwriter can do to summon inspiration. It certainly can't be forced to visit, but it can be *encouraged* – in the same way that running around in a thunderstorm dressed like Iron Man somewhat increases your chance of being struck by lightning! To extend the electrical metaphor, inspiration is out there and you need to increase your conductivity or receptivity. This is achieved partly by becoming a better all-round musician. Love music, and listen attentively to as broad a range of music as you can. Learn your instrument; learn the craft of songwriting. Knowledge about songwriting is like the lightning rod that transfers the power of the storm safely to earth – "earth" in this metaphor being the finished song. And sometimes inspiration strikes not at the beginning of the creative process but in the *middle*.

Most experienced songwriters have at least one anecdote about a time when they sat down to write a song – either because they wanted to, or because they *had* to – without the compelling "it just came to me" feeling of true inspiration. Despite the lack of inspiration, they used their knowledge of chord sequences and song structure to gradually bolt together a song. After a while, unexpectedly, the parts suddenly fitted together, and what seemed a moment ago merely workmanlike now sparked and crackled with life. The song felt inspired, twice as good as it had sounded a few minutes back. To change our electrical metaphor to a chemical one, it is as if chord sequence W combined with chord sequence X at tempo Y in the key of Z caused a reaction which fused the separate substances into a new compound. In some ways, this can be an even more striking experience than writing a song that seems to arrive in a single piece.

Receptivity to inspiration is also related to how you live. The songwriter and the person are one, even if the songs are not autobiographical. Grow in awareness of yourself, of others and of the wider world. To cite an old songwriter's trick, every newspaper is full of unwritten songs because it is full of human stories.

For the hapless Mike Magma, with 14 songs to write in six weeks, inspiration may not be his to command, but craft could save the day. Music isn't just about inspiration; it's also about knowledge that can be acquired and put to use when it's needed. A little knowledge can do a lot, from getting you out of musical blind alleys to making the best of inspiration when it strikes to getting those 14 songs written. And even if you don't have the guys from Abscess Records breathing down your neck, ask yourself if there are things you would like to know how to do. Would you like to put together chords in new ways? Use inversions? Write a middle eight? Change key? Broaden your style? Or maybe you've simply never written a song but would like to. Read on …

LIKE AN ARTIST MIXING PAINT: THE COLOURS OF HARMONY

The Songwriting Sourcebook lays out how to combine chords into satisfying sequences. It shows which chords sound good together and how to use them to build the parts of a song. It presents, in an easy-to-play format, scores of classic chord sequences that have repeatedly proved their artistic and commercial appeal in thousands of hit records and album tracks. These are the chord patterns that songwriters have employed for over 50 years in all styles of popular music. They will take the "impress" of your musical personality just as they have that of the famous. They are inexhaustible.

What this book can't do is write melodies and lyrics over these sequences for you. A chord sequence is the harmonic skeleton of a song. You have to put flesh on those bones. Only when you have chosen a tempo, a rhythm, and then a melody, and written a lyric (to change metaphor) will the universal musical currency of these song fragments take on the specific identity of being part of a particular song by you. So if you play some of these examples and think, 'well, that doesn't sound like a song' you now know why. The rest is up to you. If you need help with melodies and words, have a look at my books on *Melody* and *Lyrics*.

The Songwriting Sourcebook works from simple songs to complex ones. It starts with the most popular song type, the "three-chord trick", and the most popular song structure, the 12-bar. In each section, new opportunities are gradually introduced. The book shows you how to write four-, five-, six- and seven-chord songs. It explains which chords will naturally combine in a given key. The songwriter, like an artist, moves from a few simple, bold colours to an increasingly subtle palette of harmony that evokes more shades of feeling. You will learn about "exotic" chords and how they can be combined with the more usual ones. The different song sections are examined, and the book shows how to make chord sequences in major and minor keys, how to change key, how to write short songs and epics. Also here are many tips and tricks of the songwriting trade – the little touches of artistry that make songs more interesting and individual. No one can guarantee that you will write great songs or successful songs. But if you are creative, or have the potential to be creative, this book provides an essential grounding in songwriting harmony. With a secure knowledge of chords and song sections, you have the best possible foundation for your melody and words.

WHAT KIND OF SONG DO YOU WANT TO WRITE?

This may seem an odd question to ask, but it does have a powerful bearing on how a songwriter goes about writing songs. Mike Magma probably has, at least, a good idea of what kind of song he's trying to write to please himself, his band and Abscess Records. So before tackling the three-chord trick, let's consider how this question affects the song to be written. There are two major aspects to consider – the first is genre.

GENRE: WHERE ARE YOU COMING FROM?

Be it rock, pop, HM (heavy metal), folk, soul, indie, dance, disco, punk, MOR (middle of the road), blues, reggae or something else, each genre of popular music has its own conventions and forms, and to write within a genre convincingly you need to know these. If you write an HM number with a complicated harmony, it probably won't sound very heavy. Conversely, not many Burt Bacharach ballads have power chords in them! Songwriters usually start writing songs that sound like the genre(s) they listen to, so the beginner doesn't need to worry too much about this – his or her ears will, to some extent, be "self-correcting". If you like punk rock, you probably won't write six-minute epics with four key changes and diminished-seventh chords – even if you know how.

UNDERGROUND/OVERGROUND: WHERE ARE YOU GOING?

The other aspect concerns the distinction between the "artistic" (underground) and "commercial" (overground) poles. These labels are approximate and oversimplify the issue, but they will do for now. It is not that they are incompatible, like matter and anti-matter. The great songwriters of popular music have created many recordings whose commercial appeal does not cancel out their artistic achievement. But a budding songwriter should be aware of the different expectations these poles signify. This distinction is tied up with an awareness of your intended audience: for whom are you writing?

THE MANY/THE FEW: YOUR AUDIENCE

There is one audience for whom there are no rules and no limitations when it comes to songwriting. The most obscure lyrics, the longest intros, the most disconcerting chord changes, the strangest rhythms, the most convoluted melodies, the weirdest endings … all alike are tolerated by this particular listener. In fact, not just tolerated but positively enjoyed. This listener puts up with anything. No songwriting twist or turn will dent his/her admiration. This person is the ideal audience because you can do exactly what you want with the songs you play and write. He or she can tolerate complete artistic freedom. Who is this ideal audience?

IT'S YOU.

If you write songs purely for your own pleasure, to express your thoughts, feelings and experiences, then you can do whatever you like. Your songwriting is shaped by your own taste, the limits of your musical knowledge and songcraft, and your own self-criticism (or lack of it). The issue of the potential conflict between artistic ambition and commercial necessity does not arise.

But as soon as you play for other people, your songs are evaluated by other people's sensibilities and standards. Family and friends tolerate what they might consider imperfections in your songs because it's you presenting them. They will generally be supportive of your music. Venture further afield and this may change.

WHEN SONGS COLLIDE: THE GIG

Imagine you decide to try out some of your songs in public – as a solo performer in a coffeehouse or folk club, or perhaps in a bar band. In such environments you cannot take people's attention for granted. You must fight to get their attention and – if you do get it – fight to hold onto it. Now your songs are put to the test … and things may sound different. That six-minute ballad now seems two minutes too long. The fourth verse in that blues sounds redundant. The first chorus in the set-opener went by too quickly. That throw-away soul take-off that you don't really like gets people's feet tapping. A couple get up and dance. But the next tune is long and complicated, with unpredictable tempo changes. The dancing couple sit down halfway through it. Many of the lyrics that seem to you to speak volumes about the human condition now sound obscure or rambling. People don't grasp what you're singing about. Their attention wanders … the background hubbub of talking increases …

This is a common experience among songwriters starting out. This is not to say that the audience is necessarily right in its initial response. Some of the songs they don't 'get' are as good as you think they are. But it may also be that the artistic strength of the songs renders them ineffective to an audience that hasn't heard them before. In front of a concert hall of devotees who have memorized every word and nuance of your previous three albums, the same problem doesn't arise. But you're not there yet. To reach that level of success, you may need to give yourself a fighting chance by reshaping some of your songs to make them accessible to an audience hearing them for the first time.

So you go home and cut that six-minute ballad to four minutes, and you write another throw-away soul tune. You have now experienced and acknowledged the potential conflict between the artistic and the commercial poles in songwriting.

This experience is important, because the way you balance these forces in your songwriting has a concrete effect on many creative decisions made during the writing of a song. You are no longer just pleasing yourself. You're writing with an audience in mind – one that hears your music live, or on the radio or Web. You want to help them get into your music. You want to lay paths and stepping stones. In songwriting this expresses itself in precise details: Shall I use this chord or that one? Shall I have a solo? What shall I call this song? How long should the intro be? Should I start with a chorus or a verse? Should I cut the second verse in half to get to the second chorus earlier? How shall I end it? And so on.

IMMEDIACY: SAY IT NOW, SAY IT CLEAR, SAY IT ONE MORE TIME

The essence of commercial appeal is *immediacy*. Songs stand a greater chance of communicating fastest with the largest number of people when they can be immediately grasped in terms of their sound and their emotion. This type of immediate song is characterised by:

- having a very limited number of musical ideas, often popular formulas
- presentation of these ideas with the maximum of repetition and the minimum of distraction
- a strong hook – whether lyric, melodic, rhythmic or harmonic – that you can't forget even after one listen. The song is constructed around this hook.
- an obvious, easy-to-follow structure
- no unusual changes of chord, key or tempo
- lyrics that deal with the simplest of emotions in cliches and predictable rhymes.

Herein lies a Faustian bargain. Sell the soul of your songwriting to this concept and you might (with a lot of luck) make money, but the songs could end up bland, formulaic, and monotonous. The challenge is to walk near the edge but not topple over into the abyss.

RESISTANCE: FINDING HIDDEN GOLD

By contrast, what does the 'artistic' pole require? Its watchword is *resistance*. That is, resistance to being thoroughly grasped on a first hearing. A song written to fulfil artistic ideals might not be immediate overall, although some parts of it might connect straight away. But it leaves a feeling that the song's depth hasn't been revealed on a first listen. Such a song can:

- have a hook that is less obvious
- use some repetition but in a way that disguises this
- have elements of the unexpected in its structure and harmony
- create an expectation in the listener that is not satisfied in a straightforward way
- take a musical cliché and use it ironically
- change key, or time, or tempo
- have a 'false' intro that isn't part of the main song
- have a lyric that deals with emotional ambiguity or contrasting points of view

- use unusual chord changes that are not immediately appealing but grow on the listener with repeated plays.

There are good and bad commercial songs, as well as good and bad artistic songs. The two are not mutually exclusive. We are not talking about a rigid divide but degrees of emphasis. As a songwriter, where you place yourself between those poles is up to you. It may change from time to time, from project to project. As you gain experience as a songwriter you learn how a particular artistic choice will take a song in one direction or the other, and so be able to adjust accordingly. The important thing is to be aware of these competing pulls. For a variety of reasons, *The Songwriting Sourcebook* leans toward song techniques that help you write songs that fit some of the expectations of the commercial popular song: brevity, immediacy, repetition, hooks. It focuses on well-known methods of building a song from recognizable sections.

THE STRUCTURE OF SONGS: FILLING THE MOULD

The Songwriting Sourcebook provides information about two essential parts of songwriting: chord sequences and the moulds into which those sequences are put, namely song sections. In most popular music, a song has three main sections: the verse, the chorus and the bridge.

The chorus

The chorus is the most important section. It is usually the most memorable element in the song. It is the part the audience remember the longest and enjoy singing the most. It is often the part of the song where the dominant emotion is strongest. If the song makes a statement of some kind, this is where you find it. The success of a commercial song usually rests on its chorus. If you have ideas for two chord sequences, the stronger one should be the chorus, as long as it isn't too long or complicated. Choruses tend to simplify musically to achieve greater focus.

The verse

The verse is the section that leads to a chorus or links choruses. It often maps out the emotional territory of the song and the basic situation described by the lyric. If the chorus is the house, the verse is the plot of land on which it's built. A good verse not only holds interest in its own right but prepares for the chorus, both lyrically and musically. It may describe a situation so the chorus can comment on it. A verse may say, in a love song, that X is in love with Y but Y is in love with Z. In the chorus X will declares his position: that he will pursue Y or walk away.

The bridge

As James Brown cried in 'Sex Machine', "Shall I take it to the bridge?" Most songwriters feel that once you have had two verses and two choruses, it is time for something new. The function of the bridge is to contrast with the verse and the chorus, to introduce new musical content, to take the song somewhere else. For the lyric, this is a chance to imagine an alternative to the events and emotions previously described. Various musical devices, such as different chords or a key change, can enhance this sense of contrast. In some songs the bridge leads straight to the final chorus. The bridge is also known as the "middle eight" – because it comes in the middle of the song and is often eight bars long. A bridge can be complemented or replaced by an instrumental solo. The solo could be the bridge itself, or it could come before or after the bridge. A more complex song structure might have a bridge and later on a solo over the same chords.

Verse, chorus, and bridge are the three *primary* sections of a song. If a songwriter gets these right, the rest of the song usually falls into place. Often the first ideas a songwriter has become a verse or chorus. Songs also have what might be termed *secondary* parts. These include the intro, the outro (coda), the prechorus, short link passages and possibly solo sections.

The intro

Although a song could begin at bar 1 of a verse or chorus, most have some kind of introduction. The intro's job is to set the scene. It signals to the listener what type of song to expect. It establishes the dynamics (loud to soft), the tempo (fast to slow), the beat (4/4, waltz, shuffle, etc), the instrumentation, the key, and most importantly the atmosphere - much of which depends on the initial harmony. Major chords can provide an upbeat intro; minor chords evoke unhappiness or loss. A clutch of sevenths could give the intro a jazzy or bluesy feel (see Section 7).

The link

If a song moved straight from verse to chorus and back to verse, it might sound too hurried. Without pauses in the melody and lyric, a song could seem 'gabbled'. The link creates breathing space for both singer and listener. Links are often short - four bars - and usually instrumental. They can recycle a chord sequence from another part of the song, such as the verse or intro. They can be given extra interest by placing instrumental hooks in them, such as a guitar riff or a memorable melodic figure played on another instrument.

The prechorus

Sometimes a verse has two sections. The first part is lyrically different (and possibly musically altered) each time a verse comes round, but the second part remains the same. This is a prechorus. A prechorus is a powerful signal that the song is heading for the chorus, because the same words heard before chorus 1 are the ones heard before chorus 2. It is like sending the message: hold on, the chorus is coming. A good prechorus can be something of a hook in itself.

The outro (coda)

This covers everything after the last chorus, assuming that the song doesn't just repeat the last chorus and fade. A variation on this is to repeat the basic structure of the chorus but simplify it in some way. For example, you could play a solo over the chorus's chord sequence while the singer ad libs. A coda may also have a new sequence, which might suggest that the situation described in the song has now been changed in some way. If the intro is recycled as the coda, the song will possess a strong circularity; this can be satisying if it fits the lyric. Always remember to consider if the theme of your lyric implies one structure more than others.

These are the basic elements of song structure. They are the moulds into which harmony is poured. So now to those chord sequences … and perhaps your first song.

the songwriting sourcebook

SECTION 1
THE THREE-CHORD SONG

The chord sequence of a song supports and colours the melody and words. When you strum chords on a guitar or play them on the piano, you generate harmony. This first section looks at the harmony generated by three chords – but not just any three chords. These are three special chords that sound great together.

The chords in a song, its melody and its sense of key are derived from the major scale. There are other types of scale, but none as important to songwriting as this. The major scale is a sequence of eight notes. The gaps between these notes make this pattern of intervals: tone, tone, semitone, tone, tone, tone, semitone (whole-step, whole-step, half-step, whole-step, whole-step, whole-step, half-step).

Pick any note on any guitar string below the fifth fret and play up the string using the fret distances 2 2 1 2 2 2 1. That will create a major scale beginning on the first note. On the piano, find the note C and play up the white keys until you arrive at C an octave higher. That is a C major scale.

Seven magic numbers

Putting aside the eighth note (which has the same letter name as the first), the scale has seven different notes. The chords built upon these notes are designated with Roman numerals: I, II, III, IV, V, VI, and VII. At the moment, it is not important to know how the chords are formed. These seven chords sound good together and generate the sense of a key. *The Songwriting Sourcebook* will introduce all of them … but not just yet!

The Roman numerals signify harmonic function – that is, possible tonal 'roles' that a chord of a given pitch and type can play. This means that a single chord such as C major can play the role of I, IV, or V depending on the key in which it occurs (see tables 1–4 in the Appendix for examples).

The three 'magic' chords we need for our song occur on the first, fourth and fifth notes of the scale. These chords are called I, IV, and V regardless of their pitch name (A, C, D, F♯, etc). To play a specific example it is necessary to choose a key, which will give these Roman-numeral chords a pitch. Let's use a guitar-friendly key in which I, IV, and V are easy shapes: G major. In G major, chord I is G, chord IV is C, and chord V is D.

I	II	III	IV	V	VI	VII
G			C	D		

Chord I is the most important chord. Imagine a key as a solar system: chord I is the Sun in the centre, giving light and energy to everything else, and offering a point of gravity and stability. Each time a chord sequence returns to chord I, the listener feels some sense of having arrived 'home'. No wonder, then, that songs often end on chord I, as this gives the strongest sense of having finished, of reaching completion.

The next most important chord is chord V. This is like a 'gas giant' planet. It might be also be compared to a pillar that helps to support the arch of the scale. Chord V is also vital in creating the powerful feeling of 'returning home' whenever it is placed before chord I. A songwriter must respect these two mighty players in the musical system. Among the subtleties of songwriting is knowing where to place these chords, when to hold them back, when to stop them from coming into contact, how to create certain moods by their careful positioning. We will look at examples later on.

After chords I and V, there is chord IV. If chord I is like the Sun and chord V is like Jupiter, then chord IV is like Saturn. Chord IV isn't quite such a stabilising force as chord V, but it is still important for supporting the scale and key. In some contexts, it offers a softer effect than chord V.

IS IT POSSIBLE TO WRITE A SONG WITH ONLY ONE OR TWO CHORDS?

Yes – but it is not easy to do this successfully. You might think it would be easier to have fewer chords in a song. But therein lies the challenge. The one- or two-chord song always runs the risk of harmonic monotony. The ear tires of the sameness, and the effect can be curiously static. If the song has a theme that mirrors such an impression, then it might work. The Beatles' 'Tomorrow Never Knows' is essentially a one-chord song that is trying to convey the timelessness of the psychedelic experience. By comparison, Bruce Springsteen's 'Born In The USA' is a two-chord song that works because of its sheer driving power and the stark emotions evoked by the lyric. The success of one- and two-chord songs depends less on those chords and more on how they are performed, arranged and recorded. The verse of Robert Plant's 'Slow Dancer' has only two main chords but is compelling because of the guitar riff and Cozy Powell's heavy drums. Similarly, it is the slinky, understated menace of the arrangement which lets the verse of The Police's 'Wrapped Around Your Finger' ride on an Am-G chord change.

Technique #1: the primary three-chord trick

Thousands of songs have been written using only these three chords, many in the key of G and other guitar-friendly keys such as F, C, D, A, and E. A guitar-friendly key is one in which many of the chord shapes are open-string chords, avoiding the need for tiring barre-chords. With only these three chords, we can try our hand at putting together some progressions. Here's the simplest of song fragments using three chords. Repeated four times, it might make a verse or chorus. The diagram is typical of those used throughout *The Songwriting Sourcebook* so you don't need to read any music.

Two-bar idea in G

I		IV		V				x4
G	/	C	/	‖D	/	/	/	:‖

In this example (and throughout the book), the Roman numeral appears over the pitch name. With familiarity, this designation will allow you to change any sequence in the book into any key by referring to tables 5 and 6 in the Appendix. Most of the examples in this book assume a 4/4 time signature, since this is the most common in popular music of all genres. It means there are four beats in a bar. The dashes represent the chord played on a beat. It could be any strumming pattern on a guitar, as long as there are four beats.

How often do chords change? In popular music it is unusual to find chords changing on every beat, as is the case in hymn tunes and the classical 'art-music' song tradition. The coda to Coldplay's 'Violet Hill' is a beautiful exception. Once or twice a bar is the typical rate. Set your own speed – play at a tempo that enables you to change chords with ease but keep a regular beat.

Four-bar idea in G

I				IV				V				I				
G	/	/	/	‖C	/	/	/	‖D	/	/	/	‖G	/	/	/	:‖

This is a possible intro and verse for a short song. The song could begin on this progression without any singing. Provided the tempo is slow enough, it would be possible to sing a short line for each of bars 1–3. The vocal line could finish in bar 4, followed by several beats with no singing as a 'breather' before starting again. The four bars could be repeated to make an eight, 12, or 16-bar verse. Clearly, these three chords sound effective together.

Here are the same chords placed in two eight-bar structures, suitable for either a verse or chorus. In the second eight-bar idea listen for the effect of staying on D in bar 8 rather than changing to C as happened in bar 4. You can find a similar eight-bar three-chord idea in Marshall Crenshaw's 'Who Stole That Train'.

Eight-bar idea in G

I				I				I				I				
G	/	/	/	‖G	/	/	/	‖G	/	/	/	‖G	/	/	/	‖

IV				V				I				I				
C	/	/	/	‖D	/	/	/	‖G	/	/	/	‖G	/	/	/	‖

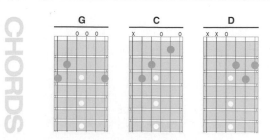

Another eight-bar idea in G

I				IV				V				IV			
G	/	/	/	C	/	/	/	D	/	/	/	C	/	/	/

I				IV				V				V			
G	/	/	/	C	/	/	/	D	/	/	/	D	/	/	/

This example places a return to chord I in bar 3:

Variation in G

I				IV				I				IV			
G	/	/	/	C	/	/	/	G	/	/	/	C	/	/	/

I				IV				V				V			
G	/	/	/	C	/	/	/	D	/	/	/	D	/	/	/

Here's a verse idea which is harmonically static in that chord I is played in six of the eight bars:

Eight-bar idea in G

I				I				I				I			
G	/	/	/	G	/	/	/	G	/	/	/	G	/	/	/

IV				V				I				I			
C	/	/	/	D	/	/	/	G	/	/	/	G	/	/	/

It's not hard to find examples of songs that use chords I, IV, and V. They are the most likely chords to be used in any style, but they tend to be particularly common in country music, folk music, and classic rock. Here are some song examples that use these chords in four and eight-bar patterns. Van Morrison based almost all of 'Brown Eyed Girl', including the intro, verse, and "sha la la" singalong, on G-C-G-D in a four-bar pattern with each chord sounding for one bar. Another repeated four-bar idea can be found in Christina Aguilera's 'The Voice Within' which begins G-G-C-D. The static intro is two bars of G. The Beatles' 'Hey Jude' has an eight-bar verse as follows: G-D-D-G-C-G-D-G. (The song is recorded in the key of F, and so uses F, Bb, and C chords. Refer to table 5 in the Appendix to discover how to transpose these chords to other keys.)

Two chords can be plenty for an eight-bar verse: Blondie's 'Dreaming' has an eight-bar intro and an eight-bar verse, both of which are based only on chords I and IV in the key of D: D-D-G-G-D-D-G-G. Just to show how economical it is possible to be, these same eight bars then re-appear as the chorus.

THE THREE-CHORD SONG

Technique #2: playing with expectation

Even with only three chords, you can introduce a touch of surprise into a chord sequence by setting up a repeating change and then breaking the pattern. In this example, bars 1–4 create two expectations – one general and one specific. The general expectation is that every bar has a chord change. The specific expectation is that bar 5 will be a G. Instead, bar 5 breaks the pattern and defeats both expectations by remaining on chord IV:

Eight-bar idea in G

I				IV				I				IV			
G	/	/	/	C	/	/	/	G	/	/	/	C	/	/	/

IV				V				I				I			
C	/	/	/	D	/	/	/	G	/	/	/	G	/	/	/

Technique #3: the 12-bar

Song sections tend to be dominated by the number four and its multiples (8, 12, 16, etc) – what I term the 'tyranny of four'. An example would be the 12-bar structure, one of the most frequently used in the history of popular music. It is found in a huge number of blues songs. From the blues it passed to 1950s rock'n'roll and can be heard in many songs by Chuck Berry, Elvis Presley, Little Richard, Jerry Lee Lewis, and other artists. From them it passed to 1960s pop and soul, regaining its blues roots during the British Blues Boom and the heavy, psychedelic rock that was influenced by the blues revival (Hendrix, Cream, Free, Led Zeppelin). It then featured in 1970s glam rock and continues to be used to this day.

The 12-bar implies not only a verse length but a certain order for chords I, IV, and V. Here is a traditional example. Note that chord I fills bars 1–4:

12-bar in G

I				I				I				I			
G	/	/	/	G	/	/	/	G	/	/	/	G	/	/	/

IV				IV				I				I			
C	/	/	/	C	/	/	/	G	/	/	/	G	/	/	/

V				V				I				I			
D	/	/	/	D	/	/	/	G	/	/	/	G	/	/	/

The 12-bar form is very flexible. It can be used for any part of a song – verse, chorus, or bridge – and the song doesn't have to be a blues. It is now such a familiar harmonic progression that

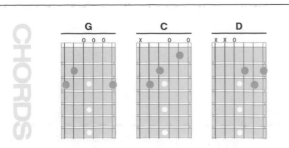

listeners recognize it and sense the changes. This means the 12-bar can contrast with sections that are less formulaic and less predictable for the listener. It also means that the listener's expectation of what will happen can easily be overturned if you use a 12-bar and then alter it in some fashion.

In a traditional 12-bar blues, the first line of a three-line verse is sung over bars 1–4. This line is then repeated over bars 5–8. A second 'answering' lyric line is sung over bars 9–12. Notice that the rate of chord change (how often chords move from one to the next) is slow: chord I occupies the first four bars, and chord V is delayed until bar 9.

This variation shows two popular alternatives. The first is a change to chord IV in bar 2; such 12-bars are called 'quick-change' blues. The second alteration is more chord activity in bars 9-12:

Quick-change 12-bar in G

I				IV				I				I			
G	/	/	/	C	/	/	/	G	/	/	/	G	/	/	/

IV				IV				I				I			
C	/	/	/	C	/	/	/	G	/	/	/	G	/	/	/

V				IV				I				V			
D	/	/	/	C	/	/	/	G	/	/	/	D	/	/	/

These sequences can be given additional harmonic colour if chord types other than plain majors are used. For example, using seventh chords – G7, C7, and D7 – emphasises the blues character, while using Gmaj7, Cmaj7, and D7 has a more romantic flavour, and G6, C6, and D6 a more exotic effect. For now, the focus is on chords I, IV, and V in their simple form and the bars in which they appear. In this variation, the chords in bars 9 and 10 are reversed from the traditional order:

12-bar in G (variation)

I				IV				I				I			
G	/	/	/	C	/	/	/	G	/	/	/	G	/	/	/

IV				IV				I				I			
C	/	/	/	C	/	/	/	G	/	/	/	G	/	/	/

IV				V				I				I			
C	/	/	/	D	/	/	/	G	/	/	/	G	/	/	/

One method for developing the potential of a 12-bar progression is to elongate it, either by repeating part of it or adding extra bars. Here's an elongated 12-bar:

THE THREE-CHORD SONG

(12-bar variation) 14-bar verse

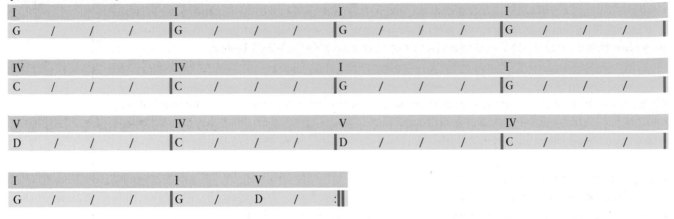

By combining an eight-bar verse with a 12-bar chorus, the blueprint for a complete song structure is generated:

Eight-bar verse and 12-bar chorus in G

Verse

I	IV	V	I
G / / /	C / / /	D / / /	G / / / :‖

Chorus

I	I	I	I
G / / /	G / / /	G / / /	G / / /

IV	IV	I	I
C / / /	C / / /	G / / /	G / / /

V	IV	V	IV
D / / /	C / / /	D / / /	C / / /

There are many examples of songs that use the 12-bar form, but inevitably most of them will come from blues and rock'n' roll. Chuck Berry's 'No Particular Place To Go' goes through the changes exactly as written in the 12-bar in G above, but with a form which alternates one bar of music with a one-bar break. Elvis Presley's 'All Shook Up' has an interesting variation on the 12-bar with eight bars of chord I followed by chords IV, V, and then chord I for two bars. It is in B-flat and looks like this: B♭-B♭-B♭-B♭-B♭-B♭-B♭-B♭-E♭-F-B♭-B♭.

In fact the verses start with six bars of B♭ followed by a two-bar break where, as in the Chuck Berry song, the music stops and the vocals continue and the B♭ chord is only implied. We could

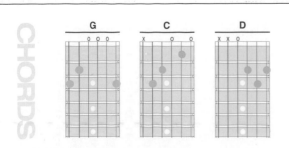

conclude that these breaks are characteristic of rock'n'roll songs, but they can be found in other styles – bear that in mind for your own chord sequences. 'All Shook Up' is also noteworthy among rock'n'roll songs because it has a middle eight. As is often the case, it starts on chord IV, and only uses chords from our three-chord trick. Here's the sequence: Eb-Bb-Eb-Bb-Eb-Bb-Eb-F.

Technique #4: the 16-bar section

Along with the 12-bar, 16 bars is the most popular length for a song section. A 16-bar section can be handled in many ways depending on the amount of repetition there is of the chord changes which make it up. The symmetrical options for structuring the 16 bars are:

• a two-bar phrase played eight times
• a four-bar phrase played four times
• a four-bar phrase played three times with a different phrase for bars 9–12
• a four-bar phrase played three times with a different phrase for bars 13–16
• an eight-bar phrase followed by a four-bar phrase repeated (or vice versa)
• an eight-bar phrase played twice
• a single 16-bar phrase with no repeats.

The second of these is probably the most common in popular songwriting, followed by the next two options. Repeated chord-changes will encourage the repetition of the melodic phrase that goes over those changes. This is less likely in the last option (the least used) as it requires more planning and usually a melody with fewer repeated phrases. In this example, bars 1–4 and 9–12 are the same:

16-bar verse in G

I				IV				I				I			
G	/	/	/	C	/	/	/	G	/	/	/	G	/	/	/

I				IV				V				V			
G	/	/	/	C	/	/	/	D	/	/	/	D	/	/	/

I				IV				I				I			
G	/	/	/	C	/	/	/	G	/	/	/	G	/	/	/

I				IV				I				V			
G	/	/	/	C	/	/	/	G	/	/	/	D	/	/	/

SECTION 1

A 16-bar section without any internal repetition I term 'through-composed'. This lends itself more to reflective songs than uptempo ones, and more to verses than choruses (repetition is important for making a chorus 'hooky'). Here's an example of a through-composed verse:

Through-composed 16-bar verse in G

I				IV				I				I			
G	/	/	/	C	/	/	/	G	/	/	/	G	/	/	/

I				IV				V				V			
G	/	/	/	C	/	/	/	D	/	/	/	D	/	/	/

IV				V				IV				V			
C	/	/	/	D	/	/	/	C	/	/	/	D	/	/	/

I				IV				I				V			
G	/	/	/	C	/	/	/	G	/	/	/	D	/	/	/

In a through-composed verse each four-bar section has a different pattern, although there is usually a similarity between the first and the fourth. This musical similarity can be exploited if the melody and lyric of the first four bars are substantially repeated for the last four. If lyric and melody are shaped in the right way, the feeling of there being any internal four-bar sections is erased.

Another consideration in a three-chord song is that the longer the structure, the more the need is felt for another chord to be introduced. Tempo is another important factor; at a fast tempo, 16 bars go by more quickly than at a slow speed!

As the list of permutations above shows, most 16-bar sections are not actually made up of 16 *different* bars. Some lines may be repeated, as here:

16-bar verse in G

I				IV				V				IV				x3
G	/	/	/	C	/	/	/	D	/	/	/	C	/	/	/	:‖

IV				I				V				V			
C	/	/	/	G	/	/	/	D	/	/	/	D	/	/	/

Although it is 16 bars long, this verse is a four-bar phrase played three times with a final four-bar phrase to 'comment' on the one that's been heard three times.

Here's a popular 16-bar structure in which bars 1–7 and 9–15 are the same but bars 8 and 16 give contrasting endings to the sequences:

THE THREE-CHORD SONG

CHORDS

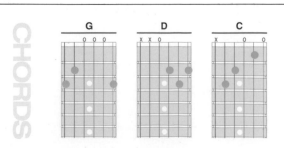

16-bar verse in G

I				IV				I				IV			
G	/	/	/	C	/	/	/	G	/	/	/	C	/	/	/

I				V				I				V			
G	/	/	/	D	/	/	/	G	/	/	/	D	/	/	/

I				IV				I				IV			
G	/	/	/	C	/	/	/	G	/	/	/	C	/	/	/

I				V				I				I			
G	/	/	/	D	/	/	/	G	/	/	/	G	/	/	/

This last 16-bar example, below, is a clever variation on the 12-bar. It takes bars 5–12 of a 12-bar and makes that section bars 9–16. The first four bars are replaced with a different four-bar section to what would be found in a 12-bar, which is repeated:

16-bar verse in G

V				V				I				I			
D	/	/	/	D	/	/	/	G	/	/	/	G	/	/	/ :||

IV				IV				I				I			
C	/	/	/	C	/	/	/	G	/	/	/	G	/	/	/

V				IV				I				I			
D	/	/	/	C	/	/	/	G	/	/	/	G	/	/	/

Songs commonly use 16-bar sections, and often you will find a 16-bar verse followed by an eight-bar chorus. This is the case with 'Brown Eyed Girl', where the aforementioned G-C-G-D four-bar phrase is played four times to make a 16-bar verse and the subsequent chorus is eight bars long. We'll return to this song in Section 2, as the chorus adds a fourth chord. A song like Bob Dylan's 'Shelter From The Storm' has no separate chorus as such - instead, each verse ends with the 'hook' that is the song's title. Various arrangements of four-bar phrases can be repeated to make 16 bars, but this song is rather unusual. In the key of E major, it begins with eight bars of E as an intro. Then there is a 16-bar verse as follows: E-B-A-E-E-B-A-A-E-B-A-A-E-B-A-E. The first four bars are the same as the last four bars; the second four bars are repeated to make the third four bars.

THE THREE-CHORD SONG

SECTION 1

A simple song form

Having met chords I, IV, and V, and looked at four, eight, 12, and 16-bar sections, we're ready to put a whole song structure together. This is the basis on which you write a melody and some lyrics. It will use three chords and have an intro, a verse, a chorus and a bridge:

Song in G

Intro

I				I				I				I			
G	/	/	/	G	/	/	/	G	/	/	/	G	/	/	

Verse

I				I				IV				I			
G	/	/	/	G	/	/	/	C	/	/	/	G	/	/	/

I				I				V				I			
G	/	/	/	G	/	/	/	D	/	/	/	G	/	/	/

Chorus

I				IV				V				I			
G	/	/	/	C	/	/	/	D	/	/	/	G	/	/	/ :‖

Bridge

I				IV				I				IV			
G	/	/	/	C	/	/	/	G	/	/	/	C	/	/	/

I				IV				IV				I			
G	/	/	/	C	/	/	/	C	/	/	/	G	/	/	/

With these sections the song could proceed intro-verse-chorus-verse-chorus-bridge-chorus (the sections are not repeated here to save space). Although it would be possible to write a song using this combination of chords and sections, it is not as interesting as it could be, even within our chosen limits. Many small adjustments could improve it … so let's do some troubleshooting.

Problem 1: the musical progression doesn't have much movement; the harmony feels static. This is because of the positioning of chord I and the number of bars in which it occurs. These four sections have 24 bars in all, and G is found in 16 of them – that's two-thirds. Not only that, but chord I dominates by its position at the start and end of sections. This makes the sequence feel 'fixed'. Only if the subject of the lyric justified this feeling would it be musically appropriate.

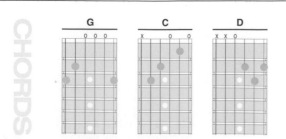

Problem 2: the entire intro is on G. Coupled with the first two bars of the verse, this means the song has six straight bars of G. There could be more going on in the harmony. As written, the intro and verse blur into one another.

Technique #5: spotting the spoilers

You may know the term 'spoiler' from TV-related websites. A spoiler is a posted message that reveals plot details to people who have not yet seen the episode. In this context, we will call the unwanted appearance of a chord ahead of its more effective position a spoiler.

In our three-chord song, the G chords which appear in bars 4, 8, 12, 16, and 24 are all spoilers for the Gs that appear in the bars immediately after. Although the effect of any chord in a key could be weakened in this way, it is most noticeable with chord I and chord V.

How could we reduce the number of spoilers and improve the song progression? One way would be to add another chord, but for the moment there's a limit of three. Instead, play this revised version:

Revised version of song in G

Intro

V				V				V				V			
D	/	/	/	D	/	/	/	D	/	/	/	D	/	/	/

Verse

IV				V				I				IV			
C	/	/	/	D	/	/	/	G	/	/	/	C	/	/	/

IV				V				IV				V			
C	/	/	/	D	/	/	/	C	/	/	/	D	/	/	/

Chorus

I				IV				V				V			
G	/	/	/	C	/	/	/	D	/	/	/	D	/	/	/

Bridge

IV				IV				I				I			
C	/	/	/	C	/	/	/	G	/	/	/	G	/	/	/

IV				IV				I				V			
C	/	/	/	C	/	/	/	G	/	/	/	D	/	/	/

THE THREE-CHORD SONG

Notes:

- The intro is now entirely chord V.
- Chord I is now in only five bars out of 24.
- Chord I arrives in bar 3 and doesn't occur again in the verse. This means that when it does appear, in bar 1 of the chorus, its arrival is more powerful and satisfying.
- The chorus is a four-bar phrase that repeats. The two bars on chord V increase the sense of satisfaction each time the music arrives back at chord I.
- The bridge centers on chord IV for contrast. And chord V at the end of the bridge leads strongly back to either the verse or the chorus.

Technique #6: the dominant crescendo

If the four bars of the revised intro were given rhythmic emphasis and got steadily louder, they would be a dominant crescendo.

The dominant is another name for chord V. Think of The Beatles' version of 'Twist And Shout', where the vocals build up, one by one, on a sustained "Ah———-" before the hook is sung. The same thing occurs, as a conscious allusion in post-modern ironic quotation marks, at the start of David Bowie's 'Let's Dance'. He knew it would remind people of 'Twist And Shout'. Although it was made famous by The Beatles, 'Twist And Shout' was originally written and recorded by the Isley Brothers, a black rhythm and blues band formed by three genuine brothers from Cincinnati, Ohio. The Beatles' version is in the key of D, and is based on a simple 'turnaround' chord sequence of D-G-A-A, moving at the rate of two chords per bar. We will cover turnarounds in more detail later in the book. Occasionally, particularly during the instrumental breaks, this chord sequence becomes D-G-A-G, adding a little interest to the repetitive sequence.

One of the most thrilling and memorable moments of the song is when the music settles on chord V, which in this case is A major. In complete contrast to the rapidly moving two chords per bar of the rest of the song we now have six bars on one chord, while the vocal line ascends through the notes of the chord and the band build to a climax. The fact that this section is six bars rather than a four-bar section adds to the sense of climax – in a way, this section is two bars too long and the listener anticipates the return to chord I two bars before it actually happens.

The dominant crescendo creates the anticipation of changing to chord I. This expectation can be neatly frustrated, as in the revised song above, because the first chord of the verse is chord IV (C) not the expected chord I (G). This is a surprise. The same crescendo could occur on chord IV.

There is no guarantee that a song built on the three-chord sequence of the revised Song in G would be better than one that used the original sequence, all factors considered. But the revision is inherently more interesting and better planned, so it stands a better chance of becoming an impressive song. It is a bit like laying the foundations of a house. What colour you paint the walls, what furniture you put in will enhance the interior – but the foundation must be firm for the house to stand.

Even laying out the sections for a three-chord song, much can be learned about songwriting technique. A songwriter develops a knack for identifying sequences that sound good, fit together well, and have a satisfying ebb and flow of tension, drama, feeling, and balance. Many factors have to be weighed. Some of them come into play only with more complicated progressions and structures. Others, however, can be applied right now to our three-chord song.

To return to a painting analogy, a songwriter using only chords I, IV, and V is like an artist painting with only three bold colours. But a painter can apply these colours with brushes of different types and sizes – a variety of tools. The same is true of songwriting. No matter how simple or how complicated the song, the techniques of good songwriting are always relevant. The remainder of this section covers some of these techniques, including displacement, the 'escalator' effect, varying the rate of chord change, chord inversions, withholding, and the three-chord turnaround.

Technique #7: displacement
DISPLACING CHORD I

Chord I is the most stable, fixed point in a key's harmony. It is the place where things come to rest; symbolically, where questions are answered, where hopes are fulfilled, where characters in songs might find their place. If chord I starts a sequence, the music begins on the point of balance. If it comes at the end, there is a sense of order re-established. If the music both begins and ends on chord I, the progression asserts that everything between is an in-control journey from order to order. Sometimes, therefore, the songwriter needs to prevent chord I from being in either of these positions, at least some of the time, to give the music more instability, change and flow. I call this technique displacement. It means moving an important chord, such as chord I, off the head or tail of a progression, away from the place where it is expected and where it exerts the most influence on the music.

Imagine singing a lyric such as "Don't know where I've been/Don't know where I'm going to" over these chords:

I				IV				V				I			
G	/	/	/	C	/	/	/	D	/	/	/	G	/	/	/

There is a contradiction between the uncertainty expressed in the words and the effect of the chord sequence. You may not know where you're going, but the music certainly does! It knows where it has come from (chord I) and where it's going … chord I! With such words, it would be better to mildly unsettle the progression, as in these two examples:

Variation 1

IV				V				IV				I			
C	/	/	/	D	/	/	/	C	/	/	/	G	/	/	/

continues on next page

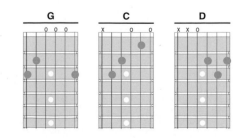

THE THREE-CHORD SONG

THE THREE-CHORD SONG

Variation 2

V				I				V				IV			
D	/	/	/	G	/	/	/	D	/	/	/	C	/	/	/

In both, chord I (G) occurs less often and has been displaced from either the start or both the start and the end of the sequence. The musical result is, relatively, less definite. It is a subtle difference, admittedly – there are only three chords in their simplest forms – but these three chords are the ones that most assert the sense of a stable key. Later on, we will look at ways of making a more drastic change. For good examples of a displaced chord I listen to the main ascending five-chord hook of Fleetwood Mac's 'Silver Springs' (where chord I is the third in the sequence) and Kate Bush's 'Wuthering Heights' (where chord I is the fourth in the chorus sequence.)

DISPLACING CHORD V

After chord I, chord V is the next most likely candidate for displacement. In this example, it means thinking about where D is placed. The aim is to create a progression in which it occurs once and must not be at the beginning or end of the sequence:

IV				I				V				IV			
C	/	/	/	G	/	/	/	D	/	/	/	C	/	/	/

Mostly we seem to expect music to move in two, four and eight bar phrases. Displacing a chord or holding a chord longer than we might expect can introduce something unpredictable and interesting to a chord progression. As mentioned above, 'Twist And Shout' extends the dominant crescendo by two bars, heightening the crescendo by keeping us waiting for the inevitable return to chord I.

A different kind of displacement can be heard in Katie Perry's 'Self-Inflicted'. The intro to this song consists of two bars of D major. This confirms our expectation that the chords will move in two-bar sections and we anticipate the same symmetry that we find in most music. In this song, however, the verse consists of a repeated four-bar phrase containing three bars of D followed by just one of G. The lopsidedness of the four-bar phrase and the delayed arrival on G adds an interesting touch to what could otherwise be a commonplace chord sequence.

Technique #8: the 'escalator' effect

The 'escalator' effect is what happens when you create a sequence of chords in numerical order. Playing I-IV-V creates the feeling of ascending, while V-IV-I does the reverse:

CHORDS

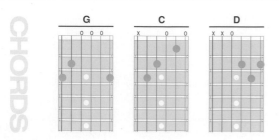

Rising escalator

I				I				IV				V			
G	/	/	/	G	/	/	/	C	/	/	/	D	/	/	/

Descending escalator

V				IV				I				I			
D	/	/	/	C	/	/	/	G	/	/	/	G	/	/	/

The escalator effect is more pronounced when four or five chords are involved, as will be shown later. Then it has a natural affinity with the prechorus, where the effect heightens the expectation of the chorus's imminent arrival. The escalator effect gives a chord progression a powerful feeling of literally that, progression – going towards something, usually chord I or chord V. The effect of repeated rising chords can be heard in Kate Bush's 'Running Up That Hill' and Martha Reeves & The Vandellas' Motown hit 'Heatwave'.

Always be aware of the extent to which the chords in your song are lining up in numerical order, so you can disrupt this if the mood of the song requires it. Emotions such as uncertainty, doubt, sadness, loss or confusion may require a progression in which chords are not moving in numerical order. The fewer chords there are in a song, the harder this is to achieve.

Technique #9: rate of chord change

Another important technique for refining a chord sequence is to consider the rate of chord change. Look at the sequence and ask: how often do the chords change? Does a chord always occupy a whole bar, two bars or half a bar? If almost all the chords in a song last the same number of beats, it might be a good idea to vary them.

Ensuring that the chord-changes exhibit this variety is a shield against monotony. The fewer chords in a song, the more important it is to vary the rate of chord change. This can partly compensate for the lack of harmonic variety in a three-chord song. In a song where the general rate of chord change is one chord to a bar, the most useful alternatives are:

- Two in a bar (chords change on beats 1 and 3)
- Two in a bar (chords change on beats 1 and 4)
- Two in a bar (chords change on beats 1 and 2)
- One in a bar-and-a-half
- One in two bars
- Four in a bar (chords change on each beat)

Here is a sequence where there are two chords in bar 4. This creates extra motion just where it might be handy – at the end of a phrase, as the music turns back to the beginning:

THE THREE-CHORD SONG

Rate of chord change: two to a bar

I				IV				V				IV		V	
G	/	/	/	C	/	/	/	D	/	/	/	C	/	D	/

Notice what happens if the same approach is taken in bar 3:

Rate of chord change: two to a bar

I				IV		V		V		IV		IV		V	
G	/	/	/	C	/	D	/	D	/	C	/	C	/	D	/

Chord I is not desirable at this point because it is better saved for the start of the next time through, so chord IV is added. There are now two bars where the rate of chord change is two chords to a bar. But there's a slight catch: there are now four continuous beats on C. This isn't wrong, but it has a different feel. Remember to check across bar lines to see if an adjustment to the way the chords are changing has this effect.

In the next example, the increased rate of chord change is applied to bars 2–4. This sequence has a stronger sense of movement. Chord I occurs only once, at the start, and activity centres around IV and V:

Rate of chord change: two to a bar

I				IV		V		V		IV		IV		V	
G	/	/	/	C	/	D	/	D	/	C	/	C	/	D	/

So far, the extra chord has appeared on the third beat. Here's an example of how to add a chord on a fourth beat. This is a technique that accentuates the chord change:

Rate of chord change: two to a bar (beats 1+4)

I				IV				V			IV	I		IV	
G	/	/	/	C	/	/	/	D	/	/	C	G	/	C	/

By contrast, the next sequence has a chord V that lasts six beats. This creates a feeling of delay and anticipation of the return to chord I at the start of the next line:

Rate of chord change: one to a bar-and-a-half

I				IV				IV		V		V			
G	/	/	/	C	/	/	/	C	/	D	/	D	/	/	/

Less common is the change of chord on beats 1 and 2. This creates surprise and easily lends itself to accentuation by the rhythm section, especially in upbeat songs. It is often complemented by a

CHORDS

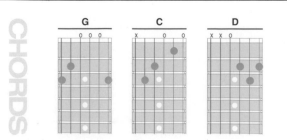

1+4 change, as here in bar 4. If too many of these 1+2 changes are used, they make the music sound 'bumpy' and unsettled, and may cause problems for the melody and lyric because they create a change of note where it might not be wanted. Notice that this also keeps the music on chord V for six beats:

Rate of chord change: two to a bar (beats 1+2)

I				IV				IV	V			V			IV
G	/	/	/	C	/	/	/	C	D	/	/	D	/	/	C

Finally, here's an example of a different chord on each beat, in bar 3. (You can hear this in the verse of the Oasis song 'Wonderwall'.) Used sparingly, this can be dramatic. If it is done too often, the music might bewilder the listener, and this would get worse as the tempo increased. *All rates of chord change that put different chords on adjacent beats are tempo-sensitive.* Only at slower tempi can the listener really hear the differences between the chords (whatever they are). As a technique, four-chords-in-a-bar can add spice to a verse or bridge where the rate of chord change is otherwise one to a bar. It heightens the drama of transitions from one section to another. And it really comes into its own when you have the full range of major and minor chords to combine. Coming at the end of a section, changing chord on each beat can make an effective extra hook, as it does in the chorus of Mott The Hoople's 'All The Young Dudes' and The Cult's 'Soul Asylum'.

Rate of chord change: four to a bar

I				IV				I	V	I	IV	V			
G	/	/	/	C	/	/	/	G	D	G	C	D	/	/	/

In the next example, an alteration to the rate of chord change varies the repetition of a four-bar phrase. Bars 3–4 are 'folded' into bar 7:

Chorus

I				I				I				V			
G	/	/	/	G	/	/	/	C	/	/	/	D	/	/	/

I				I				IV		V		I			
G	/	/	/	G	/	/	/	C	/	D	/	G	/	/	/

Here's a sequence meant to be played at a medium tempo with a rhythmic I-IV change which drives it along. You might find this type of sequence in a 1960s soul song (just imagine the handclaps), and it is similar to the effect of the verse of Graham Parker & The Rumour's 'Heat Treatment':

THE THREE-CHORD SONG

Eight-bar verse in G

I		IV		I		IV		I		IV		I		IV	
G	/	C	/	G	/	C	/	G	/	C	/	G	/	C	/

V		IV		I		IV		I		IV	
D	/	/	/	C	/	/	/	G	/	C	/	G	/	C	/ :||

A few tweaks to the rate of chord change can put new colour into a 12-bar:

12-bar in G with varying chord rate

I				I		IV	I				V
G	/	/	/	G	/	/	C	G	/	/	/	G	/	/	D

IV				IV				I				I			
C	/	/	/	C	/	/	/	G	/	/	/	G	/	/	/

V				IV				I	IV	V	
D	/	/	/	C	/	/	/	G	/	C	/	D	/	/	/

Here is a third version of our full-song example in which a number of chord-rate variations have been inserted:

Song in G, with varying chord rate

Intro

V				V	I	IV	I	V				V	I	IV	I
D	/	/	/	D	G	C	G	D	/	/	/	D	G	C	G

Verse

IV				V				I				I		V	
C	/	/	/	D	/	/	/	G	/	/	/	G	/	D	/

IV				V				IV				V			
C	/	/	/	D	/	/	/	C	/	/	/	D	/	/	/

Chorus

I		V		IV				V		I		V			
G	/	D	/	C	/	/	/	D	/	G	/	C	/	/	/ :|||

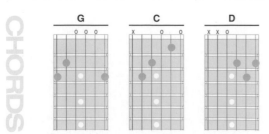

Bridge

IV				IV			V	I				I			
C	/	/	D	C	/	/	D	G	/	/	/	G	/	/	/

IV			V	IV			V	I				V	IV		
C	/	/	D	C	/	/	D	G	/	/	/	D	C	/	/

IV			
C	/	/	/

Notice how it feels right that the bridge should have an extra bar of C after the quick change in bar 8. Bar 9 is a 'breather' bar, a technique that will be explained later.

The effect of frequent change between two chords is to *reduce* their harmonic significance and *increase* their rhythmic significance. Bob Dylan's 'Subterranean Homesick Blues' is a good example of this. The chord changes function more to create a rhythm behind the melody than to interest us with their harmonic colour.

Frequent rate of chord change

I		V		I		V		I		V		I		V	
G	/	D	/	G	/	D	/	G	/	D	/	G	/	D	/

I		V		IV				IV				V			
G	/	D	/	C	/	/	/	C	/	/	/	D	/	/	/

'In the Midnight Hour', the soul classic by Otis Redding, has a verse where each bar contains two chords, E and A. Each chord lasts for two beats, and played eight times this makes an eight-bar section. At the end of the verse the chords change to B and A for four bars, with each chord now lasting a whole bar. The slower rate of chord change seems to add emphasis to the lyric. We then return to four bars of the E and A chords, as before, for the repeated hook line of the song.

R.E.M.'s 'It's The End Of The World As We Know It' has a relatively slow rate of chord change during the verse, with each chord lasting for two bars. This part of the song is mainly based on G and C chords, although B♭ and A chords also make an appearance. In the chorus, however, the chords change twice as fast, with each of the G, C, and Am chords lasting a bar each. This faster rate of change catches the listener's attention for the all-important chorus with a boost in the level of excitement.

Technique #10: inversions

Inversions are another device for getting more mileage out of the major chords in the three-chord trick song. An inversion is a change of the bass note under the chord.

THE THREE-CHORD SONG

There are three notes in any simple major (or minor) chord. G major consists of the notes GBD. The note after which the chord is named is called the root. The middle note is called the third (because it is the third note in the major scale), and the last note is known as the fifth (because it is the fifth note in the major scale). Most of the time, the lowest note in the chord – and the one that is sounded by a bass instrument in the arrangement – will be the root.

However, it is possible to play either of the other notes as the bass; this creates an inversion. If the third is the lowest note, the chord is a first inversion. If the fifth is the lowest note, the chord is a second inversion. Here are the I, IV, and V chords in the key of G in their root and inverted forms, with the names beneath:

D	G	B		G	C	E		A	D	F♯
B	D	G		E	G	C		F♯	A	D
G	B	D		C	E	G		D	F♯	A
Root	**1st**	**2nd**		**Root**	**1st**	**2nd**		**Root**	**1st**	**2nd**
G	**G/B**	**G/D**		**C**	**C/E**	**C/G**		**D**	**D/F♯**	**D/A**

Traditionally, inverted chords are written with a slash (/) followed by the note name of either the third or the fifth. In this book, a lower-case i or ii in front of the Roman numeral is also used to indicate first inversion or second inversion: iV, iiV, etc.

WHY ARE INVERSIONS USEFUL TO SONGWRITERS?

Although G, G/B and G/D are all G chords, each inversion has a subtle character of its own in contrast to the root chord. This means that an additional two shades of that chord's 'colour' can be obtained from each of the three chords in the I-IV-V format. It's not quite that our three chords have suddenly become nine. But if chords I, IV, and V are the primary colours, their inversions offer slightly different but significant shades. Inversions are valuable in three-chord songs because they allow the withholding of a chord until it can make a more effective appearance. You write a verse using G and C and a couple of their inversions, and retain the D chord for a chorus.

'WALKERS' AND 'DREAMERS'

A first inversion has a feeling of movement about it, so I call first-inversion chords 'walkers'. They are like someone moving one leg forward in the act of walking. They imply forward motion, in contrast to the 'standing still' posture of a root chord. The lowest note in a first-inversion chord wants to rise or fall to walk to the next bass note. This makes it excellent for progressions with a descending or ascending bassline.

In slow ballad-type songs a carefully placed first inversion can convey more emotion than a root chord and function almost as a substitute for a minor chord.

Chorus with first inversion

IV				I		iV		IV				I		iV	
C	/	/	/	G	/	D/F#	/	C	/	/	/	G	/	D/F#	/ :‖

Second-inversion chords are harder to describe. I call them 'dreamers'. Not as assertive as the root chord, nor as mobile as the first inversion, they have a dreamy, indefinite feeling that can lend itself to soft-focus effects that suit intros and bridges. In certain musical contexts they serve as a point of stability more flexible than a root chord. Play this eight-bar verse and notice how bars 5–8 sound less focused than 1–4, even though the chords are in the same order:

Verse with second inversion

I				V				IV				IV			
G	/	/	/	D	/	/	/	C	/	/	/	C	/	/	/

I				iiV				iiIV				iiIV			
G	/	/	/	D/A	/	/	/	C/G	/	/	/	C/G	/	/	/ :‖

The classic use of iiI is to delay and then lead to chord V, since it shares the same bass note:

Verse with second inversion

I				IV				iiI				V			
G	/	/	/	C	/	/	/	G/D	/	/	/	D	/	/	/

Inversions can be described as 'instrument sensitive'. They are more common in the music of songwriters who compose on the piano, such as Carole King, Elton John, and Tori Amos (listen to the opening of Elton's 'Someone Saved My Life Tonight' for striking inverted chords). This is because they are easier to play on a keyboard, where only a small adjustment of the left hand is required. Inversions are trickier on the guitar because it is not always easy to find a comfortable chord shape. As a consequence, there are only a small number of inversion shapes that most guitarists use. If the key doesn't permit these easy shapes, a capo can be employed to transpose the song into a more guitar-friendly set of chord shapes where the inversions do occur in those easy forms. For example, try the chord sequence B♭-F/A-E♭/G-F. Without a capo it is not easy, but place a capo at the third fret and it can be played as G-D/F#-C/E-D, which is no problem. There are many examples of this in the songs of Simon & Garfunkel, Bob Dylan, The Beatles, and David Gray.

Practical tip: generating inversions doesn't have to be the responsibility of the guitarist. If a guitarist/singer-songwriter works with a bass player, the guitarist can continue to play root chords and leave it to the bass to generate inversions by playing the third or fifth beneath the chord.

Always be alert to the musical colour imparted by inversions. Inversions are under-used by songwriters who write on the guitar, but they can add movement, drama and a touch of the

THE THREE-CHORD SONG

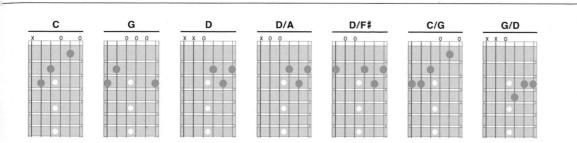

SECTION 1

unexpected to chord progressions. Inversions are one of the factors in the songwriting of Brian Wilson that made The Beach Boys' *Pet Sounds* (1966) such an expressive album. There is also a finely judged first inversion in the chorus of Coldplay's hit 'In My Place' (2002).

In the following example, the second-inversion C has two functions. It saves the root chord IV for a chorus, and it postpones the root chord I to bar 4:

Verse with second inversion

V				V				iiIV				I			
D	/	/	/	D	/	/	/	C/G	/	/	/	G	/	/	/ :‖

If we return to our revised song we can see how inversions might add further interest:

Song in G, with inversions

Intro

iiV				iiV				iiV				V			
D/A	/	/	/	D/A	/	/	/	D/A	/	/	/	D	/	/	/

Verse

IV				V				I				iI			
C	/	/	/	D	/	/	/	G	/	/	/	G/B	/	/	/

IV				V				iIV				iV			
C	/	/	/	D	/	/	/	C/E	/	/	/	D/F♯	/	/	/

Chorus

I				IV				V				V		iiV	
G	/	/	/	C	/	/	/	D	/	/	/	D	/	D/A	/ :‖

Bridge

iiIV				iV				iIV				IV			
C/G	/	/	/	D/F♯	/	/	/	C/E	/	/	/	C	/	/	/

iI				IV				iiI				V			
G/B	/	/	/	C	/	/	/	G/D	/	/	/	D	/	/	/

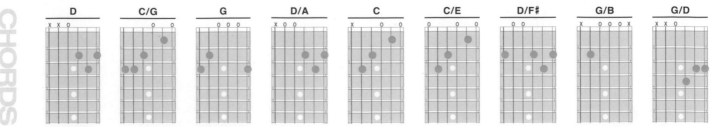

Notes:
- The D/A in the intro makes the first appearance of a root D more of an event.
- The G/B in bar 4 of the verse gives motion to the second of two bars on G. This bass note rises strongly to C, the root of the chord, in bar 5.
- Inversions add interest to the C-D chord change in bars 5–8 of the verse, so bars 7–8 are not an exact repetition of 5–6.
- A rising bassline has been created using the notes C-D-E-F♯. This bassline leads powerfully to the G chord at the start of the chorus.
- In the chorus, a second-inversion D is introduced halfway through bar 4. The bass note A steps down a tone to G as the chorus repeats.
- In the bridge, inversions create the descending bassline G-F♯-E-C under the C and D chords.
- Both G chords in the bridge are inversions. This 'refreshes' the root G for its return in the chorus after the bridge.

Inversions can add a great deal to an otherwise straightforward chord progression. 'Someone Saved My Life Tonight' by Elton John has an intro based on just two chords, A♭ and D♭, each chord lasting for two bars. However, the A♭ chord appears in second inversion, with the fifth, E♭, in the bass. Add a dramatic scale-based piano line and you have a striking and memorable introduction.

The Coldplay song 'In My Place' begins on a chord of A, moving swiftly on to a chord of E in first inversion, with G♯ in the bass. These chords are then followed by C♯m and E in root position. These four chords only occupy two bars of music, and make up the intro and verse of the song. The combination of the first inversion chord with the fast rate of change has an unsettling effect on the music that is well suited to the perplexed nature of the lyrics.

The chorus of this song has an interesting take on the 'three-chord trick' discussed earlier in this chapter. It consists of one bar of D followed by a bar which contains two chords, A and E. In other words, chords IV, I, and V in A major. This two bar phrase is repeated three times, and then followed by a bar of D and a bar of E, making eight bars in total. However, the first three times the E chord appears it is in first inversion, with G♯ in the bass (E/G♯), adding an unexpected colour to this otherwise straightforward chord sequence.

Technique #11: inversions on a stepped bassline

With inversions, it is possible to write a song section with a bassline moving in tones (whole-steps) or semitones (half-steps) harmonized with no more than three chords (I, IV, and V). Later on, we will look at such basslines that include minor chords, but it is important to know how to do this with just I, IV, V, and their inversions. Here is a verse with inversions and a descending bassline going down the notes of a G major scale. The bass notes are indicated on a separate line under the chords:

THE THREE-CHORD SONG

Descending bass

I				iV				iiV				V			
G	/	/	/	D/F♯	/	/	/	C/E	/	/	/	D	/	/	/
g				f♯				e				d			

IV				iI				iiV				iiI		V	
C	/	/	/	G/B	/	/	/	D/A	/	/	/	G/D	/	D	/
c				b				a				d		d	

Here is a similar sequence using the beats 1+4 rate of chord change. This placement accentuates the inversions, and the effect is strengthened further if they are left to the off-beat of the fourth beat of the bar (here they are written on the fourth beat):

Descending bass

I			iV	iIV			V	IV			iI	iiV		IV	
G	/	/	D/F♯	C/E	/	/	D	C	/	/	G/B	D/A	/	C	/
g			f♯	e			d	c			b	a		c	

Inverted chords can create a variation on the escalator effect. In the next example this prechorus has the IV-V change three times in succession; they sound slightly different because the inversions create a rising bassline. The first-inversion G in bar 7 enables the bassline to rise to the root chord IV in bar 8, just in time for the end of the prechorus. If a rising bassline like this has not been used anywhere else in the song it is effective in a prechorus because it heightens the anticipation of reaching the chorus.

Escalator prechorus

IV				V				iIV				iV			
C	/	/	/	D	/	/	/	C/E	/	/	/	D/F♯	/	/	/
c				d				e				f♯			

iiIV				iiV				iI				IV			
C/G	/	/	/	D/A	/	/	/	G/B	/	/	/	C	/	/	/
g				a				b				c			

Bars 1–4 in themselves would make an excellent approach to a chorus. If the rate of chord change were slower, it would further enhance the effect of the rising bassline. This would make a good bridge.

CHORDS

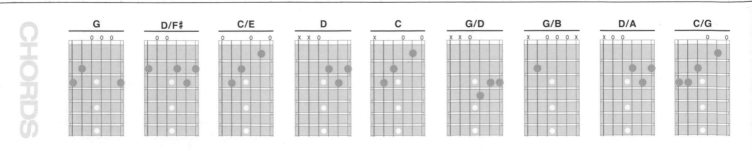

G   D/F♯   C/E   D   C   G/D   G/B   D/A   C/G

Escalator bridge

IV				IV				V				V			
C	/	/	/	C	/	/	/	D	/	/	/	D	/	/	/
c								d							

iIV				iIV				iV				iV			
C/E	/	/	/	C/E	/	/	/	D/F♯	/	/	/	D/F♯	/	/	/
e								f♯							

Summary

Inversions can:

- add interest to a section where a chord is unchanged for two or more bars, provided that the inversion occurs in the last bar before a change and that the bass note preferably rises or falls by a step to the bass note of the next chord.
- harmonize descending and ascending basslines without using chords other than I, IV and V in the key.
- create more of a sense of movement.
- postpone the arrival of a root chord so it has more potency.
- withhold the root chord from an entire section, such as a verse. If root chords appear only in the chorus, the chorus will sound more grounded.
- dilute the strength of chord I or chord V where they reoccur before a full return. In this sense, the inversion displaces the root position of the chord you want to delay.
- express emotions that are not forceful or have less surety.
- add interest to a sequence of IV-V changes.

Technique #12: withholding

There is an old saying: 'Keep your powder dry'. It means that you should retain your ammunition until it's really needed. The same principle applies in a song written with just a few chords.

When writing a three-chord trick, it isn't a good idea to have all three chords in the intro. The obvious chord to hold in reserve is chord I, since delaying its introduction has a potentially stronger effect than delaying one of the other chords. I define 'withholding' as a generalized form of displacement. In my use of the term, a chord is displaced when it is pushed along from the position it is expected to occupy; whereas, it is withheld if it is absent from a section.

This example is a verse which is intended to include the hook of the song in its last couple of bars, instead of having a separate chorus. Bars 1-4 are repeated as 5-8 and 13-16, and they contain only I and V. (This is a variation on the 16-bar verse which has bars 1-4 repeated three times.) Chord IV is withheld and saved for bars 9-12:

16-bar verse, withholding IV

I				V				I				I			
G	/	/	/	D	/	/	/	G	/	/	/	G	/	/	/ :‖

IV				I				IV				I			
C	/	/	/	G	/	/	/	C	/	/	/	G	/	/	/

I				V				I				I			
G	/	/	/	D	/	/	/	G	/	/	/	G	/	/	/

Much of the following verse is constructed on chord IV. Interest is added by the two inversions of IV, so at least the bass note is different. Chord I appears only at the start of the chorus and occupies two bars. Since chord I has not been heard before, the song can afford to stay on it at this point. Note that a chorus that ended on chord IV and went straight back to the verse might be less effective than one that ended on either chord I or chord V, because this verse starts on chord IV. If the chord at the end of a section also starts the next one, the break between sections will be less obvious. This could be done deliberately if you want them to blur into each other.

Withholding chord I

Intro

V				V				V				V			
D	/	/	/	D	/	/	/	D	/	/	/	D			

Verse

IV				IV				iIV				iiIV			
C	/	/	/	C	/	/	/	C/E	/	/	/	C/G	/	/	/

IV				iIV				V				V			
C	/	/	/	C/E	/	/	/	D	/	/	/	D	/	/	/

Chorus

I				I				IV				V			
G	/	/	/	G	/	/	/	C	/	/	/	D	/	/	/ :‖

Lennon and McCartney were such prolific songwriters that we could probably illustrate most of the ideas in this book simply with Beatles songs. 'Love Me Do', their first single, has an intro, verse, and chorus which use just G and C (I and IV in G major). As the verse and chorus are repeated, it is a full 56 seconds before we reach the middle eight and arrive on a D chord with the "someone to love…" lyric. This is as serious a case of withholding a chord (chord V) as you are ever likely to come across.

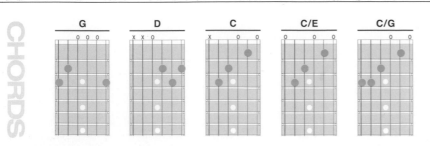

Technique #13: the three-chord turnaround

Important as the previous techniques are, they are eclipsed by the next we will examine when it comes to the art of writing memorable songs. Getting to grips with this technique is like being handed a magic wand that you point at a piece of pewter – shazam! (cough, pause for white smoke to clear) – and turn it into silver. So, cue a small fanfare of trumpets with drum roll for ... the turnaround!

A turnaround is a chord pattern, usually taking two or four bars, fixed by repetition. It is a progression that loops or literally 'turns around'. The guidelines for turnarounds feature in Section 2. In the meantime, it is worth knowing that a four-bar turnaround can be made with only three chords simply by repeating one or more of the chords. As long as the sequence has a certain balance, it works. Turnarounds depend on repetition.

Here are some examples using only chords I, IV, and V. Play them at a medium-to-fast tempo. The rhythmic urgency of a turnaround is weaker at slower tempos. Any of these five examples could be halved so they last for two bars – just play each chord for two beats.

Turnaround chorus (a)

I	I	IV	V
G / / /	G / / /	C / / /	D / / / :||

Turnaround chorus (b)

I	V	IV	V
G / / /	D / / /	C / / /	D / / / :||

Turnaround chorus (c), with 1+4 rate

I	V	IV	V	I	V	IV	V
G / / D			C / / D	G / / D			C / / D :||

Turnaround chorus (d)

I	IV	V	IV
G / / /	C / / /	D / / /	C / / / :||

Turnaround chorus (e)

I	IV	I	V
G / / /	C / / /	G / / /	D / / / :||

Turnarounds can also incorporate inversions and thus benefit from the additional motion imparted to a sequence by first inversion chords.

Turnaround chorus with inversion (a)

I				iI				IV				V			
G	/		/	G/B	/	/	/	C	/	/	/	D	/	/	/ :‖

Turnaround chorus with inversion (b)

I				IV				iIV				V			
G	/		/	C	/	/	/	C/E	/	/	/	D	/	/	/ :‖

Turnaround chorus with inversion (c)

I				iV				iIV				V			
G	/		/	D/F♯	/	/	/	C/E	/	/	/	D	/	/	/ :‖

The following chorus could be developed by halving the number of beats on each of the chords and then adding two bars of chord V to act as a breather after three of the turnarounds. It could also be varied by putting the chords on beats 1+4 instead of 1+3.

Simple turnaround chorus

I				V				I				IV			x4
G	/	/	/	D	/	/	/	G	/	/	/	C	/	/	/ :‖

Revised version

I		V		I		IV		I		V		I		IV	x3
G	/	D	/	G	/	C	/	G	/	D	/	G	/	C	/ :‖

I		V		I		IV		V				V			
G	/	D	/	G	/	C	/	D	/	/	/	D	/	/	/ ‖

Turnaround choruses can be found throughout rock and pop music. Going back to the early days of rock'n'roll there's The Kingsmen's 'Louie Louie', a 'garage band' favourite based on a two-bar pattern of A and D, then E and D. Just to add interest, the asymmetrical chord change comes just after the third beat each time. Other examples are The La's 'There She Goes', which is four bars of G-D-C-C, the Troggs' 'Wild Thing', which is A-D-E-E, or Hanson's 'Mmmbop', which is A-E-D-E. All of these song use chords I, IV, and V in repeated turnaround patterns.

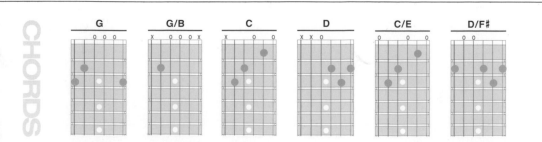
G   G/B   C   D   C/E   D/F♯

SECTION 2
THE FOUR-CHORD SONG

The basic material covered in Section 1 remains relevant no matter how complex your songs become. The techniques we've already introduced can be used to refine and polish your sequences regardless of the number of chords in a song.

At this point, you should feel you can:

- use chords I, IV, and V in a song
- use four, eight, 12, and 16-bar sections to create intros, verses, choruses and bridges
- use ten special techniques to enrich your basic song ideas. These are playing with expectation, spotting a 'spoiler', the dominant crescendo, displacement, the 'escalator' effect, the rate of chord change, inversions, inversions on a step-wise bassline, withholding, and the three-chord turnaround.

Now, having explored the three-chord song, it's time to introduce another chord.

Technique #14: adding a fourth chord

Here are the seven chords of G major, first presented in Section 1, but with the rest of the chord names filled in:

I	II	III	IV	V	VI	VII
G	Am	Bm	C	D	Em	F♯dim

So far, we have used only chords I, IV, and V. The easiest way to write a song with four chords is to choose either II, III, or VI and combine it with the three major chords as you create the progressions of each song section. Notice that these are all minor chords, which in comparison to major chords sound sad. Adding a minor chord provides significant new colour to the palette of harmony. (We'll call chord VII 'Mr Untouchable' and will deal with it later, as it falls into a different harmonic category.)

SECTION 2

Of all the minor chords that we could add to our three-chord trick from Section 1, chord VI is by far the most common. As discussed earlier, Van Morrison's 'Brown Eyed Girl' is built on a turnaround using chords I, IV, and V. Chord VI, Em, is added for the "and you, my brown eyed girl" lyric in the eight-bar chorus. The chords are as follows: C-D-G-Em-C-D-G-D. There is a long wait for the only minor chord in the sequence. which adds to its impact and accentuates its sad quality in the midst of the major chords. This long-delayed minor chord seems to hint at a sense of loss as the lyric recalls times gone by.

The chord sequence I-VI-IV-V can be heard frequently in all styles of music, but it was particularly popular in the rock'n'roll era. The Ben E. King classic 'Stand By Me' is based entirely on these four chords in the key of A major, though in an interesting eight bar structure: A-A-F♯m-F♯m-D-E-A-A. Notice the slight quickening of pace when we come to chords IV and V (D and E), which means that the sequence ends solidly back on the keynote of A. These are just two examples of the large number of songs written using only four chords that we shall examine in greater detail as we bring in new techniques during the course of this chapter.

But before we examine the four-chord song in more depth, let's see how these three minor chords give added potential to the sequences presented in Section 1.

Technique #15: meet the 'sad twin' – simple chord substitution

Every major triad (three-note chord) has a relative minor with which it has a special affinity, because they have two notes in common. Think of these chords as 'twins', with the minor having a melancholy temperament.

The relative minor of G major is E minor. G major is GBD and E minor is EGB – only one note is different. In the same way, A minor (ACE) is the relative minor of C major (CEG) and B minor (BDF♯) is the relative minor of D major (DF♯A). Chords II and IV and chords III and V are twinned in the same way as I and VI. In any major key, this means that:

- chord VI is always the relative minor of chord I
- chord III is always the relative minor of chord V
- chord II is always the relative minor of chord IV.

Consequently, to get certain musical effects, you can substitute a minor for its paired major, and vice versa. The melody will receive a different colour at that moment, but it won't sound wrong.

This is a simple instance of the technique of chord substitution, which has many beneficial applications in songwriting. You could, for instance, substitute an Am for a C or a Bm for a D in any of the examples in Section 1. Try it and see how it sounds.

One song that uses a 'sad twin' substitution is 'Every Breath You Take' by The Police. It uses the same chord sequence as 'Stand by Me', but with one important variation. The song is in A major, and the chords are as follows:

A-A-F♯m-F♯m-D-E-F♯m-F♯m

A-A-F♯m-F♯m-D-E-A-A

Notice that it is a 16-bar chord sequence. The second eight bars follow the 'Stand By Me' sequence exactly. The first eight bars substitute the 'sad twin' F♯ minor chord for the A major chord in the last two bars, a surprising change that adds tension and an element of surprise by delaying the expected return to the keynote.

Technique #16: the secondary three-chord trick

This opens up the possibility of three-chord songs which, instead of using I, IV, and V, use a variety of other combinations. In G major, these include from left to right:

I	II	IV		I	II	V		I	III	IV
G	Am	C		G	Am	D		G	Bm	C

I	III	V		I	II	VI		I	III	VI
G	Bm	D		G	Am	Em		G	Bm	Em

I	VI	IV		I	VI	V		I	II	III
G	Em	C		G	Em	D		G	Am	Bm

And you thought a three-chord song was limited!

I call a song written with any of these three-chord combinations a secondary three-chord trick. Each has its own mood. Those that omit chord V can sound less definite, less securely in the major key (here G major). Of course, chord I remains a fixture, since without it the song would no longer generate its key. However, it is possible to withhold chord I in one section, or, say, in the third of three verses. Such a substitution can be a powerful way to underline a statement or image in the lyric.

Let's say you're writing a love song. Verses 1 and 2 have been optimistic, but verse 3 contemplates that things might go wrong. Just as the lyrics state, "We might not always love as now ...", where there was a G major for the equivalent two bars in the previous verses, chord VI (Em) could be substituted. The sadness of the minor chord provides the right harmonic colour to underline the words. This also works in reverse. In a song primarily made of minor chords (in a minor key; see Section 6), the substitution of a major chord could offer a ray of sunlight breaking in on an otherwise gloomy scene.

THE FOUR-CHORD SONG

In this example, chord II is a substitute for the expected chord IV in bar 6, adding interest:

Four-chord eight-bar verse or chorus in G

I				IV				V				IV			
G	/	/	/	C	/	/	/	D	/	/	/	C	/	/	/

I				II				V				V			
G	/	/	/	Am	/	/	/	D	/	/	/	D	/	/	/

Similarly, here chord III substitutes for chord V in bar 7, instead of having two bars of D to complete the section:

Four-chord eight-bar verse or chorus

I				IV				V				IV			
G	/	/	/	C	/	/	/	D	/	/	/	C	/	/	/

I				IV				III				V			
G	/	/	/	C	/	/	/	Bm	/	/	/	D	/	/	/

Finally, in this example chord VI substitutes for chord I in bar 5, adding interest and delaying the return of chord I until the chorus, thus making its use there more effective:

Four-chord eight-bar verse

I				IV				V				IV			
G	/	/	/	C	/	/	/	D	/	/	/	C	/	/	/

VI				IV				V				V			
Em	/	/	/	C	/	/	/	D	/	/	/	D	/	/	/

From Bob Dylan we can find a good example of a secondary three-chord trick in the song 'Knockin' On Heaven's Door', which uses the chords G, D, and Am. These are chords I, V, and II in G major. If you track down a live version of this song (on YouTube, for example) you may find he is playing it in the higher key of A major, with the chords A, E, and Bm.

Alicia Keys's 'Doesn't Mean Anything' uses a different secondary three-chord trick, based on chords I, VI, and IV. It is in the key of E and has a repeated eight-bar section that is the same for the verse and the chorus: E-E-C#m-C#m-A-A-E-E. Another interesting point about this song is that when chord V finally appears it is in the middle-eight (the "I know I pushed you away" lyric) and appears in first inversion. Note also the faster rate of chord change at this point: each chord lasts for just one bar now. Essentially the repeated sequence is: C#m-B/D#-E-A.

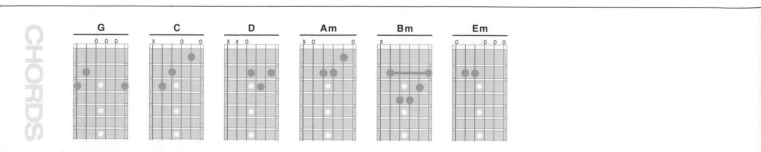

G   C   D   Am   Bm   Em

THE FOUR-CHORD SONG

CHORDS

Technique #17: bar-sharing

A further possibility with chord substitution is bar-sharing, where what was a bar with one major chord becomes a bar with two beats on the major chord and two on its relative minor. This can raise the emotional temperature when a section is repeated (like a later verse), especially if it contrasts with a predominant chord rate of one to a bar. There is an example of this in the last verse of Scott MacKenzie's flower-power anthem 'San Francisco'.

In this 16-bar verse, 1–4 and 9–12 are both repeated but chord substitution adds interest to the repeats. In bar 8, an Em substitutes for the expected G. In bar 14, a Bm substitutes for the second half of a bar of D. In bar 15, an Am substitutes for the expected C. Such substitution is felt stronger proportionally to the expectation about which chord is coming next. The trick is to establish a repeating chord change, like the C-D in bars 9–16, so the listeners are convinced they know what's coming … and then slip in the substituted minor chord for a jolt.

16-bar verse in G

I				V				I				I			
G	/	/	/	D	/	/	/	G	/	/	/	G	/	/	/

I				V				I				VI			
G	/	/	/	D	/	/	/	G	/	/	/	Em	/	/	/

IV				V				IV				V			
C	/	/	/	D	/	/	/	C	/	/	/	D	/	/	/

IV				V		III		II				V			
C	/	/	/	D	/	Bm	/	Am	/	/	/	D	/	/	/

Technique #18: withholding a fourth (minor) chord

Substitution is one way to introduce a fourth chord. But a songwriter is also free to pick one of the minor chords and treat it equally with the three majors. One effective way to use a fourth chord is to withhold it until a significant moment for maximum effect. It could appear once in the middle of a sequence and thereafter reappear at the start or end of another section. Coldplay's hit 'Yellow' has a three-chord trick verse and keeps its single minor chord (VI) till the chorus. Bruce Springsteen's 'The Wrestler' saves its two minor chords for its chorus. Jackson Browne's lengthy classic 'The Pretender' reaches 1:58 before a minor chord appears.

Since the 12-bar structure is so well-known by listeners, you can surprise them by putting in an extra (minor) chord. The Am chord II in bar 10 here substitutes for the expected chord IV, adding a touch of pathos as the 12-bar approaches its end:

THE FOUR-CHORD SONG

SECTION 2

Four-chord 12-bar in G

I				I				I				I			
G	/	/	/	G	/	/	/	G	/	/	/	G	/	/	/

IV				IV				I				I			
C	/	/	/	C	/	/	/	G	/	/	/	G	/	/	/

V				II				I				I			
D	/	/	/	Am	/	/	/	G	/	/	/	G	/	/	/

In this example, the expected change to chord IV in bar 5 is replaced by a change to chord II:

Four-chord 12-bar in G

I				IV				I				I			
G	/	/	/	C	/	/	/	G	/	/	/	G	/	/	/

II				IV				I				I			
Am	/	/	/	C	/	/	/	G	/	/	/	G	/	/	/

V				IV				I				V			
D	/	/	/	C	/	/	/	G	/	/	/	D	/	/	/

In this third example, the expected chord V in bar 9 is replaced by its 'sad twin', chord III. This is expressive in itself and has the added benefit of displacing chord V to bar 12:

Four-chord 12-bar in G

I				IV				I				I			
G	/	/	/	C	/	/	/	G	/	/	/	G	/	/	/

IV				IV				I				I			
C	/	/	/	C	/	/	/	G	/	/	/	G	/	/	/

III				IV				I				V			
Bm	/	/	/	C	/	/	/	G	/	/	/	D	/	/	/

A minor chord might also be included via bar-sharing. This achieves two purposes at once: extra emotional colour from the minor chord and a change in the rate of chord movement.

THE FOUR-CHORD SONG

CHORDS

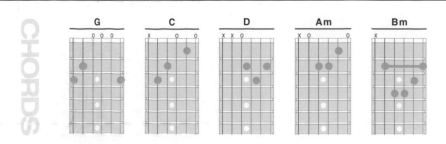

Bar-sharing four-chord 12-bar, bars 9–12

V		III		IV				I				V			
D	/	Bm	/	C	/	/	/	G	/	/	/	D	/	/	/

Bar-sharing four-chord 12-bar, bars 9-12

V				IV				I				II		V	
D	/	/	/	C	/	/	/	G	/	/	/	Am	/	D	/

Four chords in a 16-bar verse

Four chords fit nicely into a 16-bar verse. In this example, chord VI is twice inserted into a 16-bar verse to add variety. In bar 15, it has substituted for chord I. (Chord I could be undesirable here if it is the first chord of the chorus because it would be a spoiler, anticipating its appearance and reducing its effect.) In the same way, notice how in bar 13 the first-inversion G chord replaces a root G that would have been too stable. Remember that an inversion can dilute the strength of chord I or chord V where they are present before a return of the root chord. In this sense, an inversion is a weaker version of displacing either of these chords.

16-bar verse in G with chord VI

I				IV				I				VI			
G	/	/	/	C	/	/	/	G	/	/	/	Em	/	/	/

I				IV				V				V			
G	/	/	/	C	/	/	/	D	/	/	/	D	/	/	/

IV				V				IV				V			
C	/	/	/	D	/	/	/	C	/	/	/	D	/	/	/

iI				IV				VI				V			
G/B	/	/	/	C	/	/	/	Em	/	/	/	D	/	/	/

Em

G/B

SECTION 2

Technique #19: inversions of minor chords

Minor chords also have inversions. There are three notes in a minor triad, and any of the three can be placed in the bass. Em is E G B; Am is A C E; Bm is B D F♯. Just as with a major chord, if the third is the lowest note it makes the minor chord a first inversion, and if the fifth is the lowest note it makes the minor chord a second inversion:

B	E	G		E	A	C		F♯	B	D
G	B	E		C	E	A		D	F♯	B
E	G	B		A	C	E		B	D	F♯
Root	**1st**	**2nd**		**Root**	**1st**	**2nd**		**Root**	**1st**	**2nd**
Em	**Em/G**	**Em/B**		**Am**	**Am/C**	**Am/E**		**Bm**	**Bm/D**	**Bm/F♯**

The musical effect of inverted minor chords is as difficult to describe out of context as their major counterparts. Also, the same challenge of finding playable shapes arises on the guitar. Minor inversions are used much less frequently than major ones, but they can add a beautiful expressiveness to a progression.

The first-inversion minor chord shares something of the mobility of its major equivalent – it too is a 'walker'. But it can also act as an 'intensifier' because the bass note is now the very note of the three that distinguishes the chord from the major. A minor is A C E; A major is A C♯ E – the note that distinguishes the minor is C, the third. So a first-inversion minor chord C E A or C A E (the order of the other two notes doesn't matter) accentuates its minor colour.

The second-inversion minor chord can be a 'dreamer' – but a gloomy one, almost darker and more foreboding than a straight minor, owing to the perfect-fourth interval at the bottom (in an Am chord between E and A, an effect not so noticeable if the notes go E C A). Because E and A are the lowest open strings on a guitar, this is easy to do with an Am.

As we saw in Section 1, bringing in inversions trebled the available chords from three to nine. They do the same for chords II, III, and VI. This means there are nine possible forms of these three minor chords. So a four-chord song can therefore draw on 12 versions of its chords! From just a handful of chords the harmonic possibilities quickly multiply.

The following examples introduce minor inversions of chords II and III. In the first, notice that Am replaces G in bar 5, which makes the second line fresher. Thus G does not appear again until bar 13, where an inversion keeps it from feeling too secure. In bars 11–12, Am appears again, this time changing to a D. In this way it does not repeat the II-IV change in the previous line. Finally, Am appears in first inversion, along with a first-inversion C, to create a rising bassline on the notes B-C-D-E. This would make a strong approach to a chorus that started on a root G.

THE FOUR-CHORD SONG

CHORDS

16-bar verse in G with chord II and inversions

I				IV				I				I			
G	/	/	/	C	/	/	/	G	/	/	/	G	/	/	/

II				IV				V				V			
Am	/	/	/	C	/	/	/	D	/	/	/	D	/	/	/

IV				V				II				V			
C	/	/	/	D	/	/	/	Am	/	/	/	D	/	/	/

iI				iII				V				iIV			
G/B	/	/	/	Am/C	/	/	/	D	/	/	/	C/E	/	/	/
b				c				d				e			

The next 16-bar verse is conceived as self-contained, with the lyric/melodic hook to be placed in the last line, beginning in bar 13. This is a song without a separate chorus, using only a bridge to provide contrast. The first use of III comes in bar 7, where it replaces one of two consecutive Ds. A first-inversion III occurs in bar 10 to take its place in a rising bassline of C-D-E-F♯ that starts in bar 9; inversions of IV and V follow. This bassline moves strongly to the G chord I in bar 13, where the hook line of the lyric would be sung.

As a final twist, the sequence ends with the downbeat ambiguity of a second-inversion minor. The F♯ in the bass will rise to the G in bar 1 when the sequence repeats for verse 2. For a suitable bridge, it would fall to an E, which could be harmonized with either a root chord VI (Em) or a first-inversion chord IV (C/E). This Bm/F♯ is a minor 'echo' of the D/F♯ in bar 12. Compare their sound so you will know which one would suit a given context.

16-bar verse in G, with chord III and inversions

I				IV				I				I			
G	/	/	/	C	/	/	/	G	/	/	/	G	/	/	/

I				IV				III				V			
G	/	/	/	C	/	/	/	Bm	/	/	/	D	/	/	/

IV				iIII				iIV				iV			
C	/	/	/	Bm/D	/	/	/	C/E	/	/	/	D/F♯	/	/	/
c				d				e				f♯			

I				IV				V				iiIII			
G	/	/	/	C	/	/	/	D	/	/	/	Bm/F♯	/	/	/

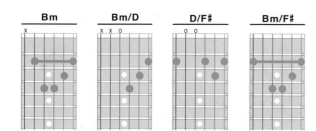

Bm   Bm/D   D/F♯   Bm/F♯

SECTION 2

Chords in inversions are relatively rare in songwriting. As we have seen from the examples in Section 1, songs that use inverted chords tend mostly to use chords in root position, with just the occasional inverted chord for effect or as part of a bassline that moves up or down a scale. Inverted minor chords are even more rare, but that is partly because minor chords themselves are generally less favoured by songwriters than major chords. The main three-chord trick is made up of three major chords, and many songs sound great with just those three chords. Songs with large numbers of minor chords are less common, which means that songs with inverted minor chords are less common still.

Nevertheless, it is possible to come across the occasional song which uses a minor chord in inversion. An example is David Bowie's 'Life On Mars', from the album *Hunky Dory*, a complex song full of chords in inversions over moving basslines. The second chord of this song is G♯m with D♯ bass, which is G♯m in second inversion. The song begins on the chord of E in root position and uses the D♯ in the bass of the G♯ minor chord as part of a descending bassline which then proceeds to D and C♯.

A COMPLETE FOUR-CHORD SONG

Now let's lay out a complete song structure that uses four chords, one of which is minor. The first example uses only verses and bridges – the song form of many early Beatles' songs. For variety, let's have a new (but still guitar-friendly) key: D major. Here are its seven chords:

I	II	III	IV	V	VI	VII
D	Em	F♯m	G	A	Bm	C♯dim

A three-chord song in D would have the chords D, G, and A. To those, let's add one minor – chord III, F♯m.

Verse/bridge four-chord song in D major

Intro

V				V				V				IV			
A	/	/	/	A	/	/	/	A	/	/	/	G	/	/	/

Verse

I				IV				V				I			
D	/	/	/	G	/	/	/	A	/	/	/	D	/	/	/

IV				IV				V				iiV			
G	/	/	/	G	/	/	/	A	/	/	/	A/E	/	/	/

A   G   D   A/E

III	IV	I	V
F♯m / / /	G / / /	D / / /	A / / /

Bridge

IV	IV	IV	V	IV
G / / /	G / / /	G / A /	G / / /	

IV	IV	III	V
G / / /	G / / /	F♯m / / /	A / / /

Notes:

- There's no chord I in the intro.
- The intro has the less common three bars + one bar pattern, instead of four bars on A. The change to G is more of a surprise.
- A second-inversion chord V (A/E) does double service in bar 8 of the verse. It adds more interest than just having two bars on A, and the E bass steps up to the F♯m chord in bar 9. An inversion usually emphasises the stable quality of a root chord approached by step in this way.
- The bridge starts with two-and-a-half bars on chord IV. The rate of chord change contrasts with the verse, where no chord lasted this long.
- It is often a good idea for the bridge to avoid chord I, as it does here. This makes it more of a contrast, which is its function.

Technique #20: the 'breather' bar

In the full-song example above, the F♯m in the verse forms the start of a possible hook which lasts three bars (9–11), with bar 12 on A as an instrumental bar, creating a 'breather' before the next verse or the bridge. Such breather bars do away with the need for a link. If the tempo is quick, it may be desirable to extend it for several bars, because they will go by quickly.

Breather bars within a verse are often used to separate one lyric line from another. Some of the early songs of Bob Dylan use this technique, sometimes in an unpredictable fashion that might create havoc if he were playing with other musicians, since they would not know from one verse to the next how long the gap between lines would be.

A recorded example of breather bars that the band follow accurately is 'Maggie's Farm' on the album *Bringing It All Back Home*. The song is in a fast four-in-a-bar and begins with four bars of G major – the key chord. This is followed by four more bars of G, with singing. Then two more bars - breather bars, with no singing. Next come four more bars with singing, followed by just one breather bar. All highly irregular in terms of phrase length – six bars followed by five bars. The only other chords in the song are Em and D, making this a song built from I, VI, and V, one of our secondary three-chord tricks.

THE FOUR-CHORD SONG

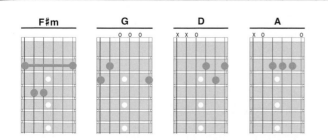

SECTION 2

A more recent use of breather bars can be heard in the Oasis song 'Don't Look Back In Anger'. The song is in C major and uses many chords so it will return for a detailed examination later. Of interest to us now is the moment before the chorus, "So, Sally can wait", when the music settles on chord V (G) for two bars with no vocal line. Up to this point we have had two chords per bar for most of the song, and the extended time on these breather bars delays the expected arrival of the chorus in a similar way to the dominant crescendo discussed in Technique #6.

Here's a second full song, this time using a conventional verse/chorus format:

Verse/chorus four-chord song in D major

Intro

I				IV				VI				V			
D	/	/	/	G	/	/	/	Bm	/	/	/	A	/	/	/

Verse

IV				V				I				I			
G	/	/	/	A	/	/	/	D	/	/	/	D	/	/	/

IV				V				iIV				iV			
G	/	/	/	A	/	/	/	G/B	/	/	/	A/C♯	/	/	/
								b				c♯			

iiIV				V				I				I			
G/D	/	/	/	A	/	/	/	D	/	/	/	D	/	/	/
d															

IV				V				iIV				iV			
G	/	/	/	A	/	/	/	G/B	/	/	/	A/C♯	/	/	/
								b				c♯			

Chorus

I				IV				VI				V			
D	/	/	/	G	/	/	/	Bm	/	/	/	A	/	/	/ :‖

Bridge

VI				VI		V		IV				IV			
Bm	/	/	/	Bm	/	A	/	G	/	/	/	G	/	/	/

VI				VI		V		IV				IV		V	
Bm	/	/	/	Bm	/	A	/	G	/	/	/	G	/	A	/

D · G · Bm · A · G/B · A/C♯

Notes:

- The intro sequence appears again in the chorus, making it familiar when heard a second time.
- In the verse, notice the effect of displacing a I-IV-V sequence in bars 1–4 to IV-V-I.
- Chord VI is deliberately left out of the verse so it has more impact in the chorus.
- For verse 2, it would be appropriate to cut the verse form in half, using only the second eight bars.
- Chord VI (Bm) dominates the bridge, giving it a contrasting minor feel. Notice the alteration to the rate of chord change, with Bm lasting six beats, followed by a quick change from A down to G.
- Notice the quick change in the last bar of the bridge.

Technique #21: the 'false rise' bassline

Looking at the last full-song example, you'll see that bars 7–8 of the verse feature two first inversions that create a rising bassline B-C♯. The C♯ wants to rise to a D; this would normally mean a D chord in bar 9. However, by using the second inversion of chord IV (G/D), this bassline can be completed without prematurely going to chord I. It's a bit like walking up the stairs to a room you thought was painted blue and finding it's been painted red – there's an element of surprise.

    I call this technique the 'false rise'. It is another example of how a chord sequence can play with the listener's expectation. That expectation is eventually satisfied in bars 15–16 of the verse, when the rising bassline B-C♯ leads to a root D in the chorus.

Technique #22: 'walking on stilts' – inversions on an intro

Here is a more sophisticated version of the intro of the previous song, in which all the chords are now first inversions. This creates an intriguing, off-kilter sound. The absence of grounded root chords might be compared to 'walking on stilts': it is an interesting view, but you know you need to get off pretty soon! This is also a good example of the "keep your powder dry" principle. By using an inverted version of this four-bar phrase as an intro, the root-position version in the chorus (D-G -Bm-A) will have more power:

Four-chord song in D, intro with inversions

iI				iIV				iVI				iV			
D/F♯	/	/	/	G/B	/	/	/	Bm/D	/	/	/	A/C♯	/	/	/

Technique #23: the four-chord turnaround

In Section 1, the songwriter's 'magic wand' was introduced – the turnaround. At that point it was produced with only three chords. With the inclusion of a fourth chord the turnaround becomes

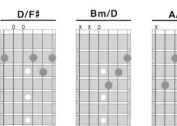

D/F♯   Bm/D   A/C♯

even more powerful. To use the magic analogy again, now it can turn brass into gold. Part of the proof of this will be that many of the progressions in the remaining pages of Section 2 will remind you of famous songs and hits. This is because they have been used many times before, often at the 'hookiest' point in the song.

Four-chord turnarounds gain their extra power not only from the increase of harmonic colour that a fourth (especially minor) chord causes, but because they have an assertive symmetry derived from the number four. Many turnarounds are four chords, four beats each, in a four-bar phrase … that may be repeated four times!

Technique #24: meet the 'Big Three' – the primary turnarounds

Primary turnarounds are those that use the three major chords with one of the three minors: I-II-IV-V, I-III-IV-V, or I-VI-IV-V. I call these the 'Big Three' of turnarounds. Much of the expressive potential of the foundations of harmony is focused into these kinds of progression. Here they are in the two keys we've used so far, G and D:

Primary four-chord turnarounds in G

I				II				IV				V			
G	/	/	/	Am	/	/	/	C	/	/	/	D	/	/	/ :‖

I				III				IV				V			
G	/	/	/	Bm	/	/	/	C	/	/	/	D	/	/	/ :‖

I				VI				IV				V			
G	/	/	/	Em	/	/	/	C	/	/	/	D	/	/	/ :‖

Primary four-chord turnarounds in D

I				II				IV				V			
D	/	/	/	Em	/	/	/	G	/	/		A	/	/	/ :‖

I				III				IV				V			
D	/	/	/	F#m	/	/	/	G	/	/	/	A	/	/	/ :‖

I				VI				IV				V			
D	/	/	/	Bm	/	/	/	G	/	/	/	A	/	/	/ :‖

Many of the techniques already described can be applied to these turnarounds. Let's take one of these, G-Em-C-D, and vary the rate of chord change by increasing it to two chords to a bar:

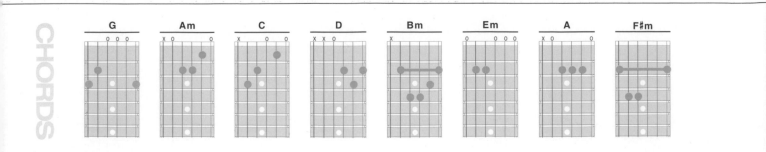

G   Am   C   D   Bm   Em   A   F#m

I		VI		IV		V		I		VI		IV		V	
G	/	Em	/	‖C	/	D	/	‖G	/	Em	/	‖C	/	D	/ :‖

Or making it irregular:

I				VI				VI				IV		V	
G	/	/	/	‖Em	/	/	/	‖Em	/	/	/	‖C	/	D	/ :‖

Slowing the rate of chord change or making it irregular reduces the force of the turnaround's symmetry. It makes it less predictable and 'four-square':

I				VI	IV		IV				V			
G	/	/	/	‖Em	/	C	/	‖C	/	/	/	‖D	/	/	/ :‖

Sam Cooke's 'You Send Me' is based on the most common four-chord turnaround, I-VI-IV-V. It is in the key of G major and the chords are G, Em, C, and D. In this case there are two chords per bar. There are many other examples around: from the early rock'n'roll years we have 'A Teenager In Love' by Dion & The Belmonts, which uses the same sequence in D♭ major: D♭-B♭m-G♭-A♭. Each chord lasts for one bar in this example, while their 'Runaround Sue' is the same sequence in D major with each chord getting two bars. This song also features the often-used IV-I-IV-V chord sequence in the middle eight.

'Dance Away' by Roxy Music also uses the I-VI-IV-V turnaround in F major for the chorus: F-Dm-B♭-C, moving at the rate of one chord per bar. This song also has a verse based on the same chords but this time in E♭ major. We'll return to this song later as the verses have an unusual structure even though they use conventional turnaround-style chord sequences.

'Ask' by British indie band The Smiths is another turnaround-based song, though this time the sequence is I-II-IV-V. It's in the key of G major, making the chords G- Am-C- D. There are two chords per bar in an off-beat rhythm, the second chord in each bar arriving slightly early each time. This song is a good demonstration of how little material is needed in songwriting. Both the verses and choruses are based on this simple two-bar turnaround.

Technique #25: displacement in a turnaround

A turnaround can also be subjected to displacement. This means that the 'logical' order of the turnaround – starting on I and ending on V – is disrupted. Displacement occurs when the order of chords in a turnaround remains the same but the whole thing is shifted a bar or more, with the chord(s) that 'fall off' the end taking up a new position at the beginning. The order no longer lines up with bars 1–4. This has a considerable effect on the sound of the sequence. Displaced turnarounds can also be subject to elongating and changing the rate of chord movement. Here's a turnaround in G subjected to three stages of displacement:

THE FOUR-CHORD SONG

Turnaround in G
Primary form

I				II				IV				V				
G	/	/	/	Am	/	/	/	C	/	/	/	D	/	/	/	:‖

Displaced form 1

II				IV				V				I				
Am	/	/	/	C	/	/	/	D	/	/	/	G	/	/	/	:‖

Displaced form 2

IV				V				I				II				
C	/	/	/	D	/	/	/	G	/	/	/	Am	/	/	/	:‖

Displaced form 3

V				I				II				IV				
D	/	/	/	G	/	/	/	Am	/	/	/	C	/	/	/	:‖

The same four chords – but four different sequences. Notice how moving chord I from either the start or the end of the turnaround makes the progression flow more. Displacement reduces the stability of a turnaround and the feeling that each bar 4 is an end. Of course the three displaced forms can also be considered as non-displaced progressions in their own right. Form 1, for example, in another context might be a chord sequence heard as being in the key of A minor. Looking at these sequences as displaced is just one way of thinking about their effect.

Here is the primary I-III-IV-V turnaround in D major given the same treatment:

Turnaround in D
Primary form

I				III				IV				V				
D	/	/	/	F♯m	/	/	/	G	/	/	/	A	/	/	/	:‖

Displaced form 1

III				IV				V				I				
F♯m	/	/	/	G	/	/	/	A	/	/	/	D	/	/	/	:‖

Displaced form 2

IV				V				I				III				
G	/	/	/	A	/	/	/	D	/	/	/	F♯m	/	/	/	:‖

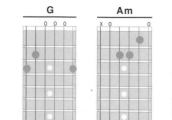

G   Am   C   D   Bm   Em   A   F♯m

Displaced form 3

V				I				III				IV			
A	/	/	/	D	/	/	/	F♯m	/	/	/	G	/	/	/ :‖

Let's look at the primary I-VI-IV-V turnaround in this format, but in a new guitar-friendly key: C major. The chords for C major are:

I	II	III	IV	V	VI	VII
C	Dm	Em	F	G	Am	Bdim

Turnaround in C
Primary form

I				VI				IV				V			
C	/	/	/	Am	/	/	/	F	/	/	/	G	/	/	/ :‖

Displaced form 1

VI				IV				V				I			
Am	/	/	/	F	/	/	/	G	/	/	/	C	/	/	/ :‖

Displaced form 2

IV				V				I				VI			
F	/	/	/	G	/	/	/	C	/	/	/	Am	/	/	/ :‖

Displaced form 3

V				I				VI				IV			
G	/	/	/	C	/	/	/	Am	/	/	/	F	/	/	/ :‖

Displacement can refresh an otherwise clichéd sequence such as I-VI-IV-V. As with the previous examples in G, there can be other ways of interpreting these sequences. Some displaced versions of a turnaround can be tonally ambiguous: the first displaced form of this C example might be heard as being in the key of A minor (minor-key songs are explained in Section 6).

We came across a displaced turnaround when we looked at the chorus of 'Brown Eyed Girl': the chords come in the same order as usual but start on chord IV. This gives us the sequence IV-V-I-VI, which in the key of G major is C-D-G-Em. The Em chord has a very different effect at the end of the four-bar sequence to the usual V chord, D.

The Beatles' 'Let It Be' makes use of several four-chord turnaround sequences in the key of C major. The intro and verses are based on C-G-Am-F or I-V-VI-IV, followed by a three-chord turnaround of C-G-F-C. So we have a four-chord turnaround with a minor chord combined with one of the three-chord turnarounds from Section 1. As there are two chords per bar these two

THE FOUR-CHORD SONG

F

sequences make a repeatable four-bar section. For the choruses the song uses a downward escalator, using the chords Am, G, F, and C. These chords are in reverse numerical order, VI-V-IV-I. There are two chords per bar in this section too, and interestingly the three-chord turnaround that ended the verse sections is used again to end the four-bar chorus sections. The verse and chorus therefore have the same rate of change, and the same four chords. Interest is maintained, however, by reordering the chords for the chorus section.

Technique #26: the 'escalator' turnaround

Another way of handling these four chords is to create a turnaround which, like the primary examples in G and D, uses the escalator effect by keeping the sequence in numerical order: I-IV-V-VI. This order can then be displaced in turn:

Turnaround in C

Primary form

I				IV				V				VI			
C	/	/	/	F	/	/	/	G	/	/	/	Am	/	/	/ :‖

Displaced form 1

IV				V				VI				I			
F	/	/	/	G	/	/	/	Am	/	/	/	C	/	/	/ :‖

Displaced form 2

V				VI				I				IV			
G	/	/	/	Am	/	/	/	C	/	/	/	F	/	/	/ :‖

Displaced form 3

VI				I				IV				V			
Am	/	/	/	C	/	/	/	F	/	/	/	G	/	/	/ :‖

The other two primary turnarounds – I-II-IV-V and I-III-IV-VI – can also have their order changed. Here are two versions of these sequences in C. In both the numerical order is disrupted. In these four examples, the minor chords go third and then fourth:

I-II-IV-V turnaround in C, alternative 1

I				IV				II				V			
C	/	/	/	F	/	/	/	Dm	/	/	/	G	/	/	/ :‖

C	F	G	Am	Dm

I-III-IV-V turnaround in C, alternative 1

I				IV				III				V				
C	/	/	/	F	/	/	/	Em	/	/	/	G	/	/	/	:‖

I-II-IV-V turnaround in C, alternative 2

I				IV				V				II				
C	/	/	/	F	/	/	/	G	/	/	/	Dm	/	/	/	:‖

I-III-IV-V turnaround in C, alternative 2

I				IV				V				III				
C	/	/	/	F	/	/	/	G	/	/	/	Em	/	/	/	:‖

Technique #27: the down escalator – descending turnarounds

In their initial undisplaced form, I-II-IV-V and I-III-IV-V are turnarounds that feature the escalator effect. Because the chords are in numerical order, there is a strong feeling of ascending. The other 'Big Three' turnaround – I-VI-IV-V – does the same if VI is placed last: I-IV-V-VI. By simply reversing the order, a feeling of descent is created, like a trip on a down escalator. Descending turnarounds have a specific use at the end of a song, often with a slowing of the tempo, but they can also introduce contrary movement in any song section.

There are two ways of interpreting this downward movement. Either it is slightly depressing because it isn't rising, or it is comforting because it is sinking down to chord I. Other factors in the song, such as the words and melody, will decide which it is. George Harrison's 'Awaiting On You All' and has a powerful downward pull to its chord sequence, and since the lyric is an assertion of faith this downward trajectory is felt as positive. The same emotion is stirred by the descending opening riff in Blind Faith's 'Presence of the Lord'. A sophisticated songwriter can evoke complex emotions by deliberately mismatching the two. A lyric that speaks of building a new, hopeful future could be sung over a descending sequence that undermines it – or at least implies that maybe things are not going to be straightforward.

Descending turnarounds in D

V				IV				II				I				
A	/	/	/	G	/	/	/	Em	/	/	/	D	/	/	/	:‖

V				IV				III				I				
A	/	/	/	G	/	/	/	F#m	/	/	/	D	/	/	/	:‖

VI				V				IV				I				
Bm	/	/	/	A	/	/	/	G	/	/	/	D	/	/	/	:‖

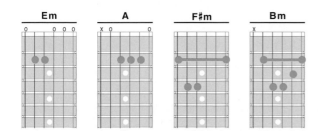

Em   A   F♯m   Bm

THE FOUR-CHORD SONG

SECTION 2

Technique #28: the turnaround with an inversion

Question: what do you get if you cross Techniques #10 and #19 with Techniques #13 and #23? Answer: a turnaround with a major or minor inversion.

It is possible to put a new slant on a turnaround, or 'blunt' its effect if it seems too smooth and predictable, by inverting some of the chords. Invert chord I if you want to keep the turnaround from reaching a point of rest. Invert chords IV or V if you want to give the turnaround extra motion. Invert the minor chord (II, III, or VI) if you want it to have less 'presence', or replace it with the relevant inverted major if you want to withold the minor for another part of the song. The guidelines for this are:

Major inversion substitutes for a root minor chord (examples in G major)
- First inversion of chord I has same bass note as chord III: G/B = Bm
- First inversion of chord IV has same bass note as chord VI: C/E = Em
- Second inversion of chord V has same bass note as chord II: D/A = Am

Minor inversion substitutes for a root major chord (examples in G major)
- First inversion of chord II has same bass note as chord IV: Am/C = C
- First inversion of chord III has same bass note as chord V: Bm/D = D
- First inversion of chord VI has same bass note as chord I: Em/G = G

A turnaround can contain more than one inversion. It can be subject to any of the transforming techniques previously mentioned. Technique #28 has a number of practical uses, as we will shortly see. Remember to take care with the movement of the bass notes when you approach and leave an inverted chord.

TURNAROUNDS WITH A FIRST INVERSION

The first example shows a turnaround in G with a first-inversion Am, which shares a bass note with the next chord. This weakens the sense of four different chords, because iII sounds like a blurred version of IV. Remember this as a general principle: if an inversion's bass note matches the root of one of the other chords, the turnaround will sound less like it has four chords in it.

Turnaround with first inversion

I				iII				IV				V				
G	/	/	/	Am/C	/	/	/	C	/	/	/	D	/	/	/	:‖

The second example has the inversion's bass note already in place in the previous chord:

Turnaround with first inversion

I				iVI				IV				V				
G	/	/	/	Em/G	/	/	/	C	/	/	/	D	/	/	/	:‖

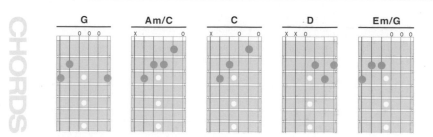

The feeling of the harmony being suspended would increase if chord IV became a second inversion (C/G). The inversion of VI could be exploited to lessen the monotony of repetition, as seen here, where the second time is not the same as the first:

Turnaround with static bass note

I		VI		IV		V		I		iVI		iiIV		V	
G	/	Em	/	|C	/	D	/	|G	/	Em/G	/	|C/G	/	D	/ :||

This example is a good variation on a three-chord I-V-IV-V change, with the iIII adding a touch of pathos to the sequence but without the emphasis of a root III:

Turnaround with first inversion

I				iIII				IV				V			
G	/	/	/	|Bm/D	/	/	/	|C	/	/	/	|D	/	/	/ :||

A powerful escalator effect would result if the other two chords were first inversions, creating a rising bassline of D-E-F♯ to chord I's G:

Turnaround with three first inversions

I				iIII				iIV				iV			
G	/	/	/	|Bm/D	/	/	/	|C/E	/	/	/	|D/F♯	/	/	/ :||
g				d				e				f♯				

Compare this with these two similar sequences:

Four-chord turnaround

I				III				IV				V			
G	/	/	/	|Bm	/	/	/	|C	/	/	/	|D	/	/	/ :||

Three-chord turnaround

I				V				IV				V			
G	/	/	/	|D	/	/	/	|C	/	/	/	|D	/	/	/ :||

Each of the previous three examples has a different emotional strength. A song could employ these in a number of ways to:

• make a 12-bar chorus out of any three, instead of just repeating one three times.
• use any one for the verse and combine the others into a chorus.
• use a different turnaround each for chorus 1, 2, and 3.

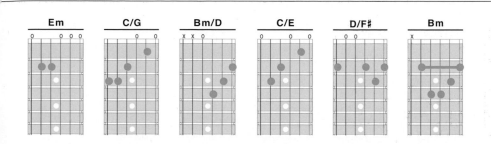

Em   C/G   Bm/D   C/E   D/F♯   Bm

THE FOUR-CHORD SONG

SECTION 2

An inversion can add interest to a turnaround, as here where the inversion occurs only on the fourth repetition:

Turnaround chorus

I		II		IV		V		x3	I		iiI		IV		V	
G	/	Am	/	C	/	D	/ :||		G	/	Am/C	/	C	/	D	/	

TURNAROUNDS WITH A SECOND INVERSION

In this example, the bass note E that we associate with chord VI (Em) turns out to belong to a second-inversion Am:

Turnaround with second inversion

I				iiI				IV				V			
G	/	/	/	Am/E	/	/	/	C	/	/	/	D	/	/	/ :||

This effect is strengthened if the inversion comes after a I-VI-IV-V change, because an expectation has been created that the second chord of bar 3 will be Em:

Chorus turnaround

I		VI		IV		V		I		iiI		IV		V	
G	/	Em	/	C	/	D	/	G	/	Am/E	/	C	/	D	/ :||

The expectation can be further toyed with if the iiI chord is approached by a bass note F♯ under the G chord:

Chorus turnaround variation

I				iiI				IV				V			
G	/	G/F♯	/	Am/E	/	/	/	C	/	/	/	D	/	/	/ :||

The iiIII opens up the opportunity for a descending bassline – all that's needed to complete it is for the C chord to be a first inversion:

Turnaround with second inversion for a descending bassline

I				iiIII				iIV				V			
G	/	/	/	Bm/F♯	/	/	/	C/E	/	/	/	D	/	/	/ :||
g				f♯				e				d			

THE FOUR-CHORD SONG

CHORDS

G   Am   C   D   Am/C   Am/E   Em   G/F♯   Bm/F♯

In the next example, the iiVI replaces either a root III (Bm) or a iI (G/B), either of which would be more likely and are shown for comparison. Use the second inversion of VI if you want the progression to have a sadder feel.

Turnaround with second inversion

I				iiVI				IV				V			
G	/	/	/	Em/B	/	/	/	C	/	/	/	D	/	/	/ :‖

Contrast with root III

I				III				IV				V			
G	/	/	/	Bm	/	/	/	C	/	/	/	D	/	/	/ :‖

Contrast with iI

I				iI				IV				V			
G	/	/	/	G/B	/	/	/	C	/	/	/	D	/	/	/ :‖

Technique #29: walking on stilts revisited – the inversion turnaround

Technique #22 showed how to put an entire intro into major inversions. The same thing can be done to make a turnaround walk on stilts. These two examples show the effect with a mix of first and second inversions of majors and minors:

Inverted turnaround in G

iI				iVI				iIV				iV			
G/B	/	/	/	Em/G	/	/	/	C/E	/	/	/	D/F♯	/	/	/ :‖

Inverted turnaround in D

iI				iiII				iIV				iV			
D/F♯	/	/	/	Em/B	/	/	/	G/B	/	/	/	A/C♯	/	/	/ :‖

Technique #30: the 'trailer' bassline

In the cinema, before the main feature is shown, audiences watch 'trailers' - adverts for coming attractions that are meant to provide enough of the story/characters/action to make you want to see the film. The 'trailer' bassline does the same thing for a chorus turnaround: it provides the exact sequence of bass notes but without the actual chords of the turnaround. Let's say the chorus is going to be this turnaround in D:

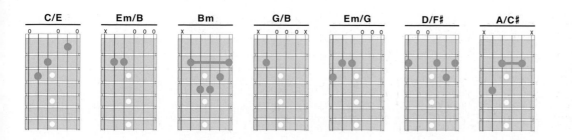

C/E Em/B Bm G/B Em/G D/F♯ A/C♯

THE FOUR-CHORD SONG

Chorus turnaround

I				VI				IV				V			
D	/	/	/	Bm	/	/	/	G	/	/	/	A	/	/	/ :‖

The sequence of bass notes is D-B-G-A. For an intro, we could have either of these trailer basslines using a mix of inversions:

Inversion intro (a)

iVI				iIV				iII				iiI			
Bm/D	/	/	/	G/B	/	/	/	Em/G	/	/	/	D/A	/	/	/ :‖
d				b				g				a				

Inversion intro (b)

iiIV				iiII				iII				iiIII			
G/D	/	/	/	Em/B	/	/	/	Em/G	/	/	/	F♯m/A	/	/	/ :‖
d				b				g				a				

Same bass notes, different chords!

Technique #31: stretching a turnaround

It is possible to 'stretch' a turnaround by multiplying part of it. This is not the same technique as altering the rate of chord change, where the order of chords is kept and no chord is returned to before the turnaround has completed a pass and started again. When a turnaround is stretched, it doubles back to a chord already heard during that pass before advancing again. For stretching to have an impact, the turnaround needs to be heard several times first in its ordinary form.

This example is a I-VI-IV-V in G. On the third time through the chord sequence, the C steps back to Em before continuing forward. This produces a seven-bar phrase instead of the usual eight:

Stretched turnaround, seven bars

I		VI		IV		V		I		VI		IV		V	
G	/	Em	/	C	/	D	/	G	/	Em	/	C	/	D	/

I		VI		IV		VI		IV		V	
G	/	Em	/	C	/	Em	/	C	/	D	/ :‖

If an eight-bar chorus is desired, the stretch could be repeated:

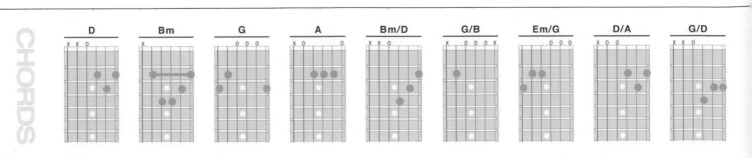

D   Bm   G   A   Bm/D   G/B   Em/G   D/A   G/D

Stretched turnaround, eight bars

I		VI		IV		V		I		VI		IV		V	
G	/	Em	/	C	/	D	/	G	/	Em	/	C	/	D	/

I		VI		IV		VI		IV		VI		IV		V	
G	/	Em	/	C	/	Em	/	C	/	Em	/	C	/	D	/

Stretching is handy whenever there is a lyric or melodic phrase that you want to repeat immediately – perhaps the song's title. For this reason stretching is often heard in final choruses or in the last phrase of a chorus.

The Razorlight song 'Who Needs Love' is a good example of a conventional turnaround that has been stretched by going back over a section which has been heard before. It is based on chords I, VI, IV, and V in the key of A major. The first two bars are A and F♯ minor, but instead of proceeding as normal to D and E major in the next two bars, the opening bars are repeated. Only then do we move on to chords IV and V. This creates an eight bar section as follows: A-F♯m-A-F♯m-D-E-A-F♯m. Notice also the unexpected use of chord VI at the end of the sequence where chord V or chord I might normally be expected.

Earlier, we mentioned the Roxy Music song 'Dance Away' in the context of four-chord turnarounds. The verses of this song stretch the turnaround by going back over chords IV and V. It begins with four bars of solo drums, which are then joined by a descending chord sequence to create an intro. At the point where the vocals enter we have two bars of E♭ followed by two bars of Cm - chords I and VI in E♭ major. Chord IV comes next, as expected, but lasts for just one bar before being followed by chord V. This two-bar pattern of chord IV and V is then played again to create an eight bar sequence as follows: E♭-E♭-Cm-Cm-A♭-B♭-A♭-B♭.

These eight bars are immediately repeated as the second verse, but they are then stretched even further as the last two bars, A♭ and B♭, are played three times, creating an asymmetrical verse which has eight bars in the first section, and ten bars in the second section. This has the effect of delaying the chorus by two bars - building tension - and adds emphasis to the lyric that leads into the chorus: "dressed to kill, and guess who's dying ..."

Technique #32: the truncated 3+4 turnaround

Another way to vary a four-chord turnaround with two chords to a bar is to drop the fourth chord in the second bar, so you end up with the formula 3+4 (it doesn't work so well if the chords are one to a bar). In this example in G, the turnaround is I-IV-II-V but the V is omitted on the first pass. This makes its appearance at the end of the phrase stronger. This is a special application of the withholding technique in which the fourth chord of the turnaround is initially withheld.

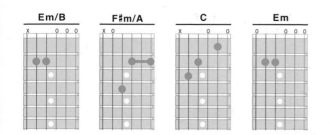

THE FOUR-CHORD SONG

Truncated 3+4 turnaround

I		IV		II				I		IV		II		V		
G	/	C	/	Am	/	/	/	G	/	C	/	Am	/	D	/	:‖

Technique #33: the 'telescoped' turnaround

One well-established songwriting trick is to use the same turnaround twice in a song, but have the chords in the verse change at a slower rate than in the chorus. I call this 'telescoping'. The turnaround could use a rate of one chord every two bars through an eight-bar verse and then change to one chord every bar, or half a bar, during the chorus (the greater the discrepancy, the less likely the listener will feel the two are the same). The arrangement – how many instruments and which ones are playing in each section – can help to hide the similarity.

Turnarounds: a first overview

Let's pause and summarize what has been covered so far about the four-chord turnaround. To do this, we'll start from scratch by creating a turnaround in a new key, A major. This is a popular key for guitar songs because the root notes of its three major chords are the lowest three open strings on the guitar, resulting in resonant chords. Here are its seven chords:

I	II	III	IV	V	VI	VII
A	Bm	C♯m	D	E	F♯m	G♯dim

In the key of A, a three-chord trick song would use A, D, and E. Let's take a I-III-IV-V turnaround and see what happens when it is opened up by applying the techniques described in the previous pages.

Primary

I				III				IV				V				
A	/	/	/	C♯m	/	/	/	D	/	/	/	E	/	/	/	:‖

Displaced

IV				V				I				III				
D	/	/	/	E	/	/	/	A	/	/	/	C♯m	/	/	/	:‖

Descending

V				IV				III				I				
E	/	/	/	D	/	/	/	C♯m	/	/	/	A	/	/	/	:‖

G　　C　　Am　　D　　E　　A　　C♯m

Altered rate of chord change

I				I		III		IV						V		
A	/	/	/	|A	/	C#m	/	|D	/	/	/	|	/	E	/	:||

Varied order

I				IV				III				V				
A	/	/	/	|D	/	/	/	|C#m	/	/	/	|E	/	/	/	:||

Stretched

I		III		IV				III				IV		V		
A	/	C#m	/	|D	/	/	/	|C#m	/	/	/	|D	/	E	/	:||

Partial inversion

I				iiIII				iIV				V				
A	/	/	/	|C#m/G#/	/	/	/	|D/F#	/	/	/	|E	/	/	/	:||

Full inversion

iiI				iIII				iIV				iV				
A/E	/	/	/	|C#m/E	/	/	/	|D/F#	/	/	/	|E/G#	/	/	/	:||

Truncated 3+4

I		IV		III				I		IV		III		V		
A	/	D	/	|C#m	/	/	/	|A	/	D	/	|C#m	/	E	/	:||

As can be seen from these examples, even a single four-chord turnaround has many artistic possibilities. These techniques are always available as options for fine-tuning your chord sequences to make them less predictable, or less emphatic, or more of a hook – whatever is right for the song. And talking of which … let's put this turnaround into a complete song in A, using it in the first instance as a chorus. The overall structure of this song is intro-verse-prechorus-chorus-verse-prechorus-chorus-bridge-chorus-coda. Two other songs follow, in G and D.

Full song in A major, I-IV-V-VI chorus
Intro

I		IV		I		IV		V				iIV			
A	/	D	/	|A	/	D	/	|E	/	/	/	|D/F#	/	/	/	|

Verse

iV				I				IV				IV			
E/G#	/	/	/	|A	/	/	/	|D	/	/	/	|D	/	/	/	:||

continues on next page

D/F#   C#m/E   E/G#   A/E   C#m/G#

THE FOUR-CHORD SONG

Prechorus

V				IV				V				IV			
E	/	/	/	D	/	/	/	E	/	/	/	D	/	/	/

V				V			
E	/	/	/	E	/	/	/

Chorus

I		IV		I		IV		V				VI				
A	/	D	/	A	/	D	/	E	/	/	/	F#m	/	/	/	:||

Bridge

IV				IV				IV				iI			
D	/	/	/	D	/	/	/	D	/	/	/	A/C#	/	/	/

VI				VI				VI				V			
F#m	/	/	/	F#m	/	/	/	F#m	/	/	/	E	/	/	/

Coda

IV				IV				IV				IV			
D	/	/	/	D	/	/	/	D	/	/	/	D	/	/	/

VI				V				IV		I		IV		I	
F#m	/	/	/	E	/	/	/	D	/	A	/	D	/	A	/

Notes:
- The intro has a trailer bassline, with the same chords as the chorus turnaround, except the F#m chord is replaced by a first-inversion D. The intro is similar enough to the chorus to make the chorus sound familiar when reached, but the F#m chord is held in reserve so it has more effect.
- The verse starts on a first-inversion E. The G# in the bass has been prepared by the rising E-F# bass notes of the previous two bars.
- The verse is eight bars, with the first four bars repeated. Notice how the two bars on D balance the faster rate of chord change of bars 1 and 2 in the intro.
- The six-bar prechorus has only IV and V. Chords IV and V are often used in the approach to the chorus, especially in a prechorus. The identity of the prechorus is strengthened if the lyric sung over it is always the same, though the verse lyric may change. The two bars of E are an opportunity for a dominant crescendo.
- The chorus brings in the F#m, withheld until now. It has a 'stretched' form, with the first I-IV change repeated.

CHORDS

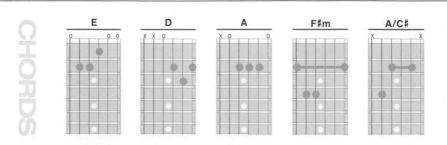

- The bridge starts on D because none of the other sections start on D. Notice the slow rate of chord change (which acts as a breather from the chorus) and the space given to F♯m because it has been not used in the verse, intro or prechorus.
- The coda features a four-bar crescendo on D and then a descending version of the turnaround chorus. Notice that the rhythmic A-D change is now reversed as D-A, which could make an emphatic ending, especially by slowing up through the last four bars.

Full song in G major, I-III-IV-V verse

Intro

III		IV		V				III		IV		V			
Bm	/	C	/	D	/	/	/	Bm	/	C	/	D	/	/	/

Verse

I		III		IV		V		I		III		IV		V	
G	/	Bm	/	C	/	D	/	G	/	Bm	/	C	/	D	/

I		iI		IV		V		I				V			
G	/	G/B	/	C	/	D	/	G	/	/	/	D	/	/	/ :‖

Bridge

IV				IV				V				V			
C	/	/	/	C	/	/	/	D	/	/	/	D	/	/	/

IV				IV				I				V			
C	/	/	/	C	/	/	/	G	/	/	/	D	/	/	/

Coda

I		iI		IV		V		I		iI		IV		V	
G	/	G/B	/	C	/	D	/	G	/	G/B	/	C	/	D	/

I		III		IV		V		I	
G	/	Bm	/	C	/	D	/	G	‖

Notes:

- The overall song structure is intro-verse-verse-bridge-verse-bridge-verse-coda.
- The intro starts on a minor chord yet the song is in a major key. This gives a mild element of surprise.
- The III-IV-V in the intro anticipates the verse turnaround. By omitting chord I, its first appearance at the start of the verse is stronger.

THE FOUR-CHORD SONG

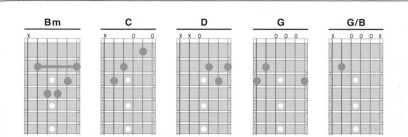

Bm   C   D   G   G/B

SECTION 2

- The third turnaround in the verse creates variety by replacing III with iI. The bass note B is the same.
- After the busy chord-changing of the verse, the bridge offers contrast by staying on the first three chords for two bars each. This rate of chord change 'refreshes' the excitement of the two-beats-to-a-chord turnaround on the verse.
- The coda is modelled on the verse. Notice that the first two turnarounds have G/B as the second chord. This gives chord III more emotional force when it appears in the fifth bar of the coda, in the last turnaround. We want the song to end on a G chord, so the eighth bar of the verse is unnecessary – that is why the coda is only seven bars long.

THE FOUR-CHORD SONG

Full song in D major, I-II-IV-V verse

Intro

I				I			I				iiI				
D	/		/	D/E	/	/	D/G	/	/	/	D/A	/	/	/	:‖

Verse

I				I				II				II			
D	/	/	/	D	/	/	/	Em	/	/	/	Em	/	/	/

IV				IV				V				V			
G	/	/	/	G	/	/	/	A	/	/	/	A	/	/	/

Link

I				I			I				iiI				
D	/		/	D/E	/	/	D/G	/	/	/	D/A	/	/		

Chorus

I		II		IV		V		x3 IV				IV			
D	/	Em	/	G	/	A	/	:‖ G	/	/	/	G	/	/	/

Bridge

II				IV				V				iI			
Em	/	/	/	G	/	/	/	A	/	/	/	D/F♯	/	/	/

II				IV				V				V			
Em	/	/	/	G	/	/	/	A	/	/	/	A	/	/	/

CHORDS

D   D/E   D/G   D/A   Em   G   A   D/F♯

Notes:

- The song structure is intro-verse-link-verse-link-verse-chorus-bridge-chorus-with the link as coda. It takes a different approach because a link splits the verses. This type of structure needs an arrangement which slowly builds in terms of tension, number of instruments, etc, all the while raising expectation as to the eventual arrival of the chorus.
- The intro has a trailer bassline, anticipating the chorus, but the D (chord I) is static.
- The verse runs through the turnaround at a rate of two bars to a chord.
- The anticipated chorus does not appear at the end of verse 1. The verse goes to a link (which is the same as the intro), before proceeding to the next verse.
- The chorus is the same turnaround as the verse, but it has one chord every two beats – a more urgent rate of change.
- The bridge uses a displaced form of the turnaround, starting on the second chord of the sequence, pushing chord I to the fourth bar and even there turning it into a first inversion so it does not eclipse the stability it lends to the chorus, where it is in root position.
- The bridge ends with two bars of chord V as a buildup to the return to the chorus or (more interesting) as a transition to a quiet reprise of the intro as link, with repeat, and then the chorus.

Varying the order of the chords in the four-chord turnaround is a technique that rewards both study and experimentation. We have already seen this in the song 'Let It Be'. This particular re-ordering of the I, IV, V, and VI chords has proven to be very resilient in the hands of songwriters, being used again and again. The chord sequence in question is I-V-VI-IV, and here are a few of the large number of songs in which it features.

Jason Mraz recorded the song 'I'm Yours' in the key of B major. The chords are B, F♯, G♯m, and E, and the majority of the song uses this eight-bar chord sequence, each chord being played for two bars.

The Train song 'Hey, Soul Sister' is another example of this I-V-VI-IV four-chord turnaround, this time in the key of E major. Once again each chord lasts for two bars, and both verses and choruses are built on the same chord sequence: E-E-B-B-C♯m-C♯m-A-A.

Chipmunk had a hit record with 'Look for Me' using the same chord sequence but this time in C major, with each chord lasting for only one bar. The faster rate of change seems well suited to the repetitive dance-based music of Chipmunk, whereas the slower rate of change used in the other two examples seems better suited to the more song like approach of Jason Mraz and Train. Finally, from the world of stadium rock, and demonstrating how versatile this four-chord sequence can be, there is U2's 'With Or Without You', which has one chord per bar in D major: D-A-Bm-G: four chords, four bars, one entire song.

OTHER TURNAROUNDS

You might be thinking that all the songwriting possibilities of turnarounds must be exhausted by now … but it isn't so. Even after all the stretching, reversing, inverting and other techniques, there is still more to be done with turnarounds.

THE FOUR-CHORD SONG

SECTION 2

Technique #34: secondary turnarounds

So far, all the examples have worked with the three primary turnarounds: I-II-IV-V, I-III-IV-V, and I-VI-IV-V. These combine the key's three major chords (I, IV, and V) with one of the minor chords (II, III, or VI). However, there are many other possible turnarounds, even when just drawing on chords I to VI. Any turnaround that omits chord IV or V, for example, can be categorized as a secondary turnaround. If only chords I through VI are available, this means the inclusion of two minor chords instead of one. Here are some examples in G:

Turnaround with no chord IV

I				II				III				V			
G	/	/	/	Am	/	/	/	Bm	/	/	/	D	/	/	/ :‖

I				III				V				VI			
G	/	/	/	Bm	/	/	/	D	/	/	/	Em	/	/	/ :‖

I				II				V				VI			
G	/	/	/	Am	/	/	/	D	/	/	/	Em	/	/	/ :‖

Turnaround with no chord V

I				II				III				IV			
G	/	/	/	Am	/	/	/	Bm	/	/	/	C	/	/	/ :‖

I				III				IV				VI			
G	/	/	/	Bm	/	/	/	C	/	/	/	Em	/	/	/ :‖

I				II				IV				VI			
G	/	/	/	Am	/	/	/	C	/	/	/	Em	/	/	/ :‖

More radical is a turnaround which omits chord I. This can still be in the same key, creating an expectation that can be fulfilled in another section where chord I finally appears. This example is a powerful instance of the escalator effect – except, since it repeats, it won't immediately lead you to chord I.

Turnaround with no chord I, in G major

II				III				IV				V			
Am	/	/	/	Bm	/	/	/	C	/	/	/	D	/	/	/ :‖

If you want the sense of the key to be more secure, even though chord I is missing, turn chord V into a seventh:

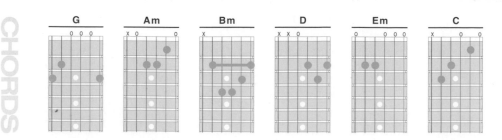

VI				III				IV				V			
Em	/	/	/	Bm	/	/	/	C	/	/	/	D7	/	/	/ :||

IV				II				VI				V			
C	/	/	/	Am	/	/	/	Em	/	/	/	D7	/	/	/ :||

V				VI				III				IV			
D7	/	/	/	Em	/	/	/	Bm	/	/	/	C	/	/	/ :||

Technique #35: the turnaround as link

Turnarounds can also be used as links at the end of a verse, leading into another verse, or at the end of a chorus, going to the next verse. Repeat each two-bar phrase to get a four-bar link. These are especially good if there are no turnarounds anywhere else in the song, as they will then provide an urgent feeling of movement. For this purpose, a three-chord turnaround is sufficient, but you can draw on any of the six chords and their inversions. If the section the link follows has minor chords, it is better to take them out of the link; if there are none, the minor chord in the link will be expressive – so choose accordingly.

Three-chord turnaround links

I				IV		V	
D	/	/	/	G	/	A	/ :||

I				II		V	
D	/	/	/	Em	/	A	/ :||

I				VI		V	
D	/	/	/	Bm	/	A	/ :||

I				II		IV	
D	/	/	/	Em	/	G	/ :||

I				IV		VI	
D	/	/	/	G	/	Bm	/ :||

Turnarounds can also be 'floated' over a pedal note, usually the first or fifth note of the scale. This technique, which suits intros and links, is described more fully in Section 9.

THE FOUR-CHORD SONG

D7

SECTION 2

SUMMARY OF TURNAROUNDS

- Turnarounds make powerful hooks. They especially suit choruses.
- An instrumental version of a turnaround chorus makes a great intro.
- Turnarounds are more effective at medium-to-quick tempos.
- Played with sufficient rhythmic accent, a turnaround can become a riff.
- A displaced turnaround which neither begins nor ends on chord I or V is a good way of refreshing a predictable sequence such as I-VI-IV-V.
- A single turnaround can be refreshed by repeating it in a different key. This is called transposition and is described in Section 8.

CAUTIONARY POINTS

Handy as turnarounds are, they nevertheless should come, like cigarettes, with a health warning that reads: "Turnarounds are addictive and can seriously damage your songwriting." Turnarounds too easily become a quick fix. They can make a songwriter musically lazy. So remember:

- The power of a turnaround declines according to the number used in a song. One turnaround in a song grabs the attention if used properly. If verse, chorus and bridge are all turnarounds, each will sound weaker. This is especially true if all are primary turnarounds in escalator form, starting on I and ending on V, or starting on I and moving in numerical order through four of the key's primary six chords.

- If a song has more than one turnaround, only one should take the escalator form. Use whatever technique you can to make them sound less similar. For example, change the chord rate in one of them from 1+3 to 1+4. Use displacement, inversions, stretching, reversing, etc. Change the balance of the number of minors to majors in the turnaround. Use only three chords in one of them.

- Too much reliance on turnarounds makes your songs sound the same as each other (and a lot of other people's).

- The indiscriminate use of turnarounds has done more damage to popular songwriting than almost anything else. This goes for the listener as well as the songwriter. Exposure to their careless use is the musical equivalent of passive smoking.

SECTION 3
SONGS WITH FIVE AND SIX CHORDS

In Section 2, three minor chords were added to the three majors introduced in Section 1. We then used this pool of six chords (and their inversions) to construct four-chord turnarounds. But songwriters regularly employ any combination of these six chords, and it is possible to write a song with four, five, or six chords and no turnaround. With more chords (18, counting the inversions), there are more creative possibilities and some techniques get easier.

Adding a fifth chord opens up many possibilities for writing chord sequences. Retaining chords I, IV, and V and adding two of the three minor chords is a common approach. For example, the chorus of 'Self Inflicted' by Katie Perry adds chords VI and III, Bm, and F♯m. It also has an interesting structure, as it has a six bar-section followed by an eight-bar section. The six-bar section is as follows, one chord per bar: D-A-Bm-F♯m-G-A. The melodic line then goes back to the beginning of the chorus but this time the last two bars are repeated: D-A-Bm-F♯m-G-A-G-A. This creates an eight-bar section. The two missing bars in the first half of the chorus have a disconcerting effect, and also focus attention on the hook line, "these wounds are self inflicted". Ending with an eight-bar section re-balances the chorus, giving a satisfactory conclusion which leads back to the restated intro and subsequent verse.

The same set of chords is used in the verse of 'Don't Look Back in Anger' by Oasis. This song is in C major and adds Am and Em (chords VI and III) to the usual I, IV, and V. First, we have an intro which alternates between chords I and IV (C and F). The chord sequence for the verse is as follows: C-G-Am-Em-F-G-C-G. Notice the similarity between this sequence and the Katie Perry song above. Only the final two bars are different with the change I-V instead of IV-V. Also we have a slower tempo and each chord only lasts for two beats, creating a four-bar phrase.

Here are some general opportunities when using all six chords of a major key:

- Sections can be entirely minor or major, for contrasts of mood.
- It is easier to have one section as a turnaround and the others not.
- Displacement of either chord I or chord V is easier to achieve.

SECTION 3

- Sequences do not have to be so repetitive.
- The three minor chords can be distributed into separate sections —for example, II in the verse, III in the chorus, VI in the bridge.

Here are two six-chord song examples, in the keys of A and C:

Full song in A, six chords

Intro

III	III	II	II
C♯m / / /	C♯m / / /	Bm / / /	Bm / / /

Verse

V	I	IV	I	IV	V
E / / /	A / / /	D / A /	D / E /		

IV	V	III	IV	V
D / / /	E / / /	C♯m / / /	D / E / :‖	

Chorus

I	V	VI	IV
A / / /	E / / /	F♯m / / /	D / / / :‖

Bridge

II	II	II	IV
Bm / / /	Bm / / /	Bm / / /	D / / /

II	II	II	IV	V	IV
Bm / / /	Bm / / /	Bm / D /	E / D /		

Notes:
- Notice the placing of the minor chords: the intro is wholly minor, the verse mostly major, the chorus mixed, and the bridge mostly minor.
- Chord II is used only in the intro and bridge; chord III is used only in the intro and verse; chord VI appears only in the chorus.
- There are different rates of chord change.
- There are no inversions. Inverting chords II and III in the intro would add a different colour.
- The bridge contrasts with the chorus by staying on a single chord for three bars.
- The chorus has the popular I-V-VI-IV turnaround – but it is the only turnaround in the song.

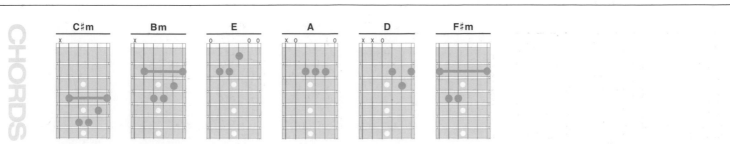

C♯m Bm E A D F♯m

Full song in C, six chords

Intro

I				V				I				V			
C	/	/	/	G	/	/	/	C	/	/	/	G	/	/	/

Verse

IV				II				V			VI	V			
F	/	/	/	Dm	/	/	/	G	/	/	Am	G	/	/	/ :||

IV				IV				iI				II		V	
F	/	/	/	F	/	/	/	C/E	/	/	/	Dm	/	G	/

Chorus

I				IV				V				VI			
C	/	/	/	F	/	/	/	G	/	/	/	Am	/	/	/

I				IV				V				IV			
C	/	/	/	F	/	/	/	G	/	/	/	F	/	/	/

Bridge

II		III	IV	V				II		III	IV	VI			
Dm	/	Em	F	G	/	/	/	Dm	/	Em	F	Am	/	/	/

II		III	IV	V				V				III		II	
Dm	/	Em	F	G	/	/	/	G	/	/	/	Em	/	D	/

Notes:

* The intro creates an expectation that the verse will start on chord I, but it actually starts on chord IV.
* The verse withholds chord I in root position, with only a brief use of the first inversion, C/E.
* A brief Am chord breaks up the steady rate of chord change in the verse.
* Chord III is held in reserve until the bridge, as part of a II-III-IV-V escalator turnaround. The second time through this turnaround, it has a different fourth chord (Am instead of G).

SONGS WITH FIVE AND SIX CHORDS

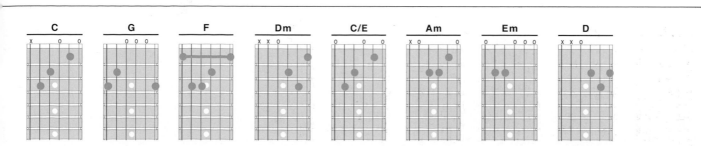

SECTION 3

Technique #36: the through-composed verse

A through-composed verse is one in which nothing repeats. Instead of being built by repetitions of smaller sections, such as four four-bar phrases, a through-composed verse is shaped as a single form. While not as common as verses with repeated sections, they are a fascinating form to try – and writing them is certainly facilitated by having more chords to work with. Writing verses of this type can have a stimulating effect on how you phrase the melody, encouraging the melody to avoid the repetition of a few short phrases and instead take a longer arch.

If the lyric hook-line is incorporated into such a verse, either at the beginning or end (or both, if you want to make it cyclic), then a couple of through-composed verses make an attractive form for a complete song. This is suited to slow ballads and 'miniature' songs that clock in under two minutes. If the lyric hook is in the last four bars, those could be repeated to make the end of the song.

In this example, imagine that the melody stops in bar 15, leaving bar 16 as a breather:

Through-composed 16-bar verse in D

IV				V				II				II		iI	
G	/	/	/	A	/	/	/	Em	/	/	/	Em	/	D/F♯	/

IV				iIV				V				VI		V	
G	/	/	/	G/B	/	/	/	A	/	/	/	Bm	/	/	A

VI				V				IV				iiVI			
Bm	/	/	/	A	/	/	/	G	/	/	/	Bm/F♯	/	/	/

II				III				I				V			
Em	/	/	/	F♯m	/	/	/	D	/	/	/	A	/	/	/

Notes:

• There are no repeating patterns of change, no turnarounds.

• The rate of chord change varies.

• Three inversions are used. The D/F♯ means the first root D chord will not be heard until bar 15. That is the climax of the verse, the point towards which the melody and lyric are working. The G/B enables a two-bar stay on G and an approach to A from above by step. The Bm/F♯ in bar 12 continues the descending bass line of bars 9–12 without using chord III (F♯m), which is saved for bar 14.

• Bar 16 would probably be unsung, to create a breathing space before the verse circles back to the beginning.

A   D/F♯   G/B   Bm   Bm/F♯   F♯m

Technique #37: reharmonizing

Having all six chords – the three majors and their relative minors – means you can now write songs that use the technique of reharmonizing. This takes two forms. The first is chord substitution, where the melody remains the same as in a previous verse but the chords change from major to relative minor (or vice versa). In D major, the substitutable pairs are D/Bm, G/Em, and A/F♯m. This will often suggest itself for the last verse. Substitution can be used as a way of adding new emotional colour to a third and final verse, to give it more impact than the first two. Imagine a verse that goes:

Verse 1 & 2 in D major

II				IV				I				V			
Em	/	/	/	G	/	/	/	D	/	/	/	A	/	/	/ :‖

To make this verse more interesting the third time through, use chord substitution:

Verse 3 with reharmonized bars 3–4

II				IV				VI				III			
Em	/	/	/	G	/	/	/	Bm	/	/	/	F♯m	/	/	/

II				IV				I				V			
Em	/	/	/	G	/	/	/	D	/	/	/	A	/	/	/

It is probably better to leave the second line as it was, but the effect could be repeated. One way of enhancing the effect is to link reharmonization to bar-sharing, where several chords share a bar:

Verse 3 with reharmonized bars 2–3

II				IV		II		I		VI		V			
Em	/	/	/	G	/	Em	/	D	/	Bm	/	A	/	/	/

II				IV				I				V			
Em	/	/	/	G	/	/	/	D	/	/	/	A	/	/	/

In this case, the relative minors are played for only two beats each.

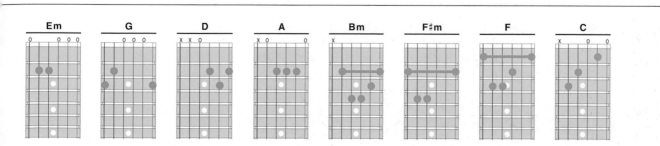

SECTION 3

REHARMONIZING A LAST CHORUS

The second type of reharmonizing involves changing chords that are not part of a relative pair. This technique has a classic pop use on the final chorus of a song, where the hook-line is reharmonized and repeated. For this example, we will use C major, whose six chords pair up C/Am, F/Dm, and G/Em. Let's assume the chorus originally looked like this:

Chorus 1 & 2 in C major

IV				V				I				V			
F	/	/	/	G	/	/	/	C	/	/	/	G	/	/	/

IV				V				I				I			
F	/	/	/	G	/	/	/	C	/	/	/	C	/	/	/

A well-known technique, heard on some early Beatles hits and the last chorus of Elvis Costello's 'This Year's Model', is to repeat the hook (which in this instance is the second line of the chorus) and reharmonize it. Here Am replaces G in bar 4, a change repeated in the next line but with the additional alteration of C to Em in bar 7:

Last chorus

IV				V				I				VI			
F	/	/	/	G	/	/	/	C	/	/	/	Am	/	/	/

IV				V				III				VI			
F	/	/	/	G	/	/	/	Em	/	/	/	Am	/	/	/

IV				V				I			
F	/	/	/	G	/	/	/	C		

A further refinement would be to substitute Dm (chord II) for F (chord IV) on its final appearance in bar 9.

Am

Dm

Technique #38: chord substitution in a turnaround

The same technique can be used to substitute a whole turnaround. Every turnaround can be transformed by reversing the polarity of the chords from major to minor. The major and minor forms could be used in many ways. The minor form might be played in an intro or bridge, with the major form is the chorus. The minor form might be used for the second of three choruses, to add interest. The minor form might be reserved for an instrumental break. All the usual techniques such as inversions, displacement, rate of chord change, stretching, telescoping, etc, can be used for these sequences. If the melody and/or lyric remain the same when this type of chord change is made it will be heard as a substitution. If the melody and lyric are different then the minor form of the turnaround will be more likely heard as a replacement. Remember also that these minor turnarounds have their own identity as sequences. They are substitutes for these major turnarounds only in a context where the latter is established in the song first.

Here are three popular turnarounds in C and their minor forms:

Turnaround 1, major form

I				II				IV				V			
C	/	/	/	Dm	/	/	/	F	/	/	/	G	/	/	/ :‖

Turnaround 1, minor form

VI				IV				II				III			
Am	/	/	/	F	/	/	/	Dm	/	/	/	Em	/	/	/ :‖

Turnaround 2, major form

I				III				IV				V			
C	/	/	/	Em	/	/	/	F	/	/	/	G	/	/	/ :‖

Turnaround 2, minor form

VI				V				II				III			
Am	/	/	/	G	/	/	/	Dm	/	/	/	Em	/	/	/ :‖

Turnaround 3, major form

I				VI				IV				V			
C	/	/	/	Am	/	/	/	F	/	/	/	G	/	/	/ :‖

Turnaround 3, minor form

VI				I				II				III			
Am	/	/	/	C	/	/	/	Dm	/	/	/	Em	/	/	/ :‖

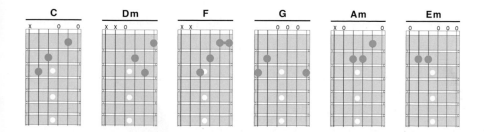

ADDING FLAT DEGREE CHORDS

SECTION 3

The chord sequence Ab-Bb-Eb-Cm may well now appear familiar. It is chords IV, V, I, and VI in Eb major and is a turnaround sequence that has been displaced so that it starts on chord IV. In the Toploader song 'Dancing In The Moonlight' this chord sequence is modified in two ways to create a four-bar turnaround that is used for every section of the song; intro, verses, choruses and instrumental.

Firstly, the Ab chord at the beginning of the sequence is replaced by its relative minor, Fm, which in this context is chord II. The musical effect of this is subtle, but the sequence II-V-I, with its roots rising a perfect fourth each time is in some ways more powerful than IV-V-I. It seems to point more strongly towards chord I. Secondly, a passing chord is added between the Eb chord and the following Cm. Instead of there being a whole bar of Eb, we have two beats of Eb followed by two beats of Bb/D; that is to say, Bb major with D in the bass. This is Bb major in first inversion, and creates a descending bassline which goes Eb, D, C. Again the musical effect is subtle, but the descending bassline seems to add movement to the sequence, moving the music swiftly on from its arrival point at chord I. The effect of these two changes is to give a new lease of life to an otherwise traditional and commonplace turnaround.

Substituting chord II for chord IV is not unusual in turnaround chord sequences. In this way, the often-used I-VI-IV-V turnaround can be played I-VI-II-V. An example is the Neil Sedaka song 'Oh! Carol', which uses this sequence in the key of B, with each chord lasting for two bars: B-B-G♯m-G♯m-C♯m-C♯m-F♯-F♯.

So far, the song examples have been confined to chords I through VI and their inversions, making 18 chords – using our painting metaphor, six colours with three shades of each. The remaining sections in the book reveal how this can be increased, giving you even more colours to 'paint' your music.

SECTION 4
ADDING FLAT DEGREE CHORDS

Chords I–VI are all derived from the major scale. But if some of the notes of the scale are reduced by a semitone (half-step), as often happens in blues and blues-influenced music, then new chords will be formed. Three in particular are part of almost every songwriter's palette and are crucial to rock music. Learning about the first means that we must discover why one of the original seven was put aside, namely chord VII – 'Mr Untouchable'.

Solving the mystery of chord VII

Here are the seven chords of C, G, D and A major, the keys used so far:

I	II	III	IV	V	VI	VII
C	Dm	Em	F	G	Am	Bdim

I	II	III	IV	V	VI	VII
G	Am	Bm	C	D	Em	F#dim

I	II	III	IV	V	VI	VII
D	Em	F#m	G	A	Bm	C#dim

I	II	III	IV	V	VI	VII
A	Bm	C#m	D	E	F#m	G#dim

WHY HAS CHORD VII BEEN LEFT UNUSED?

Chord VII was omitted because it is neither major nor minor. It falls into a third category, the diminished chord. The theoretical reason for this is not important for our purposes. Suffice to say that the diminished chord is almost never used in popular songs. It is unsettling, discordant and hard to sing over. We will meet it again, in its extended form as a diminished seventh, in two techniques described later: key changing (Section 8) and chromatic chord sequences (Section 9).

Technique #39: woke up this morning with an extra chord – the ♭VII

There is a way to alter chord VII that makes it much more handy for songwriting. Follow this formula: take the seventh degree of a major scale, lower (flatten) it by a semitone (half-step), and treat that note as the root of a major chord. This chord is numbered ♭VII, the '♭' indicating that it is built on a lowered degree of the scale. If this is done in the keys above, here is the result:

		I	VII	=	♭VII
Key of	C	Bdim	=	B♭

		I	VII	=	♭VII
Key of	G	F♯dim	=	F

		I	VII	=	♭VII
Key of	D	C♯dim	=	C

		I	VII	=	♭VII
Key of	A	G♯dim	=	G

The ♭VII chord is everywhere in the harmony of popular music, regardless of genre. It is typical of blues-influenced rock'n'roll and rock, as well as soul and European folk music. The ♭VII chord:

- brings a sense of the unexpected.
- can 'toughen up' a chord sequence.
- can be used in a three-chord trick or a three-chord turnaround.
- can be used in a four-chord turnaround.
- in first inversion has the same bass note as chord II (so a first-inversion ♭VII could replace II).
- in second inversion has the same bass note as chord IV (so a second-inversion ♭VII could replace IV).

The ♭VII chord can be approached comfortably from chord I, II, IV, or VI; less so from III and V. Here are some examples in G major, beginning with one that moves from chord I to ♭VII:

I-♭VII

I				♭VII				V				I			
G	/	/	/	F	/	/	/	D	/	/	/	G	/	/	/ :‖

For a variation on a 12-bar verse using the ♭VII chord, take a six-bar sequence like this and repeat it.

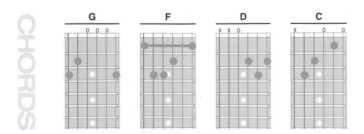

12-bar verse (6x2)

I				IV		V		I				bVII		IV	
G	/	/	/	C	/	D	/	G	/	/	/	F	/	C	/

II				V		IV			
Am	/	/	/	D	/	C	/	:‖	

Eight-bar verse or chorus

I				IV				V				IV			
G	/	/	/	C	/	/	/	D	/	/	/	C	/	/	/

bVII				IV				V				V			
F	/	/	/	C	/	/	/	D	/	/	/	D	/	/	/

The next example is one of the classic 1960s uses of the bVII chord as an approach chord to V when V goes to I. (The V-I change at the end of a section or phrase is called a perfect cadence.) Listen for the touch of surprise that bVII brings, and an equal – and sometimes touching – surprise when it finds its way to chord V. To bring out the emotional potential of the bVII-V change, save it for the end of a section and don't repeat it very much. Repetition will undo this particular magic:

bVII-V

I				IV				bVII				V			
G	/	/	/	C	/	/	/	F	/	/	/	D	/	/	/

What makes this sequence additionally satisfying is that the bassline can rise F-F#-G if V is a first inversion:

bVII-V, rising bassline

I		IV		bVII				iV				I			
G	/	C	/	F	/	/	/	D/F#	/	/	/	G	/	/	/
				f				f#				g			

The bassline can start rising even earlier if the previous chords are inversions as well:

bVII-V, rising bassline

iiI				iIV				bVII				iV			
G/D	/	/	/	C/E	/	/	/	F	/	/	/	D/F#	/	/	/
d				e				f				f#			

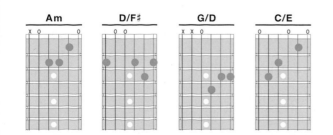

Am   D/F#   G/D   C/E

Here is the same sequence in the key of C. The ♭VII is emphasised because it is the only root chord:

♭VII-V, rising bassline

iiI				iIV				♭VII				iV			
C/G	/	/	/	F/A	/	/	/	B♭	/	/	/	G/B	/	/	/
g				a				b♭				b			

A more exotic version of the same bassline could end with a second inversion of III:

♭VII-III, rising bassline

iiI				iIV				♭VII				iiIII			
C/G	/	/	/	F/A	/	/	/	B♭	/	/	/	Em/B	/	/	/
g				a				b♭				b			

The ♭VII is naturally at home in any blues or blues-influenced context:

12-bar in G, with ♭VII (a)

I				I		♭VII		I				I		♭VII	
G	/	/	/	G	/	F	/	G	/	/	/	G	/	F	/

IV				IV				I				I		♭VII	
C	/	/	/	C	/	/	/	G	/	/	/	G	/	F	/

V				V		♭VII		I				I		♭VII	
D	/	/	/	D	/	F	/	G	/	/	/	G	/	F	/	:‖

12-bar in G, with ♭VII (b)

I		IV		I				♭VII		IV		I			
G	/	C	/	G	/	/	/	F	/	C	/	G	/	/	/

I		IV		I				♭VII		IV		I			
G	/	C	/	G	/	/	/	F	/	C	/	G	/	/	/

IV				IV		V		I		IV		I		♭VII	
C	/	/	/	C	/	D	/	G	/	C	/	G	/	F	/	:‖

The Beatles' 'Help' uses the ♭VII prominently with a verse which begins on an A chord for two bars, followed by two bars of C♯m and F♯m. These are chords I, III, and VI in A major. The next bar of this eight-bar phrase is a split bar which has two beats of D and two beats of G, chords IV and ♭VII.

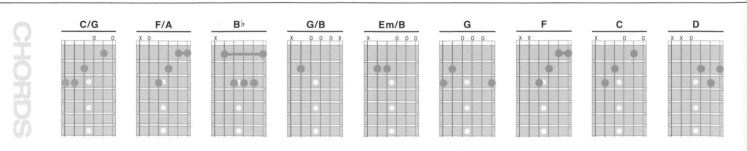

C/G   F/A   B♭   G/B   Em/B   G   F   C   D

Finally we arrive home on a bar of the home chord, A. The bVII chord only lasts for two beats but add a surprise element at the end of the phrase, given that the other chords have been very much 'in the key'.

In the song 'Get Back', which is also in the key of A, The Beatles again slot in a brief bVII and IV chord, although this time the positions are reversed, with the G chord coming before the D chord and then resolving to the key chord A.

Another Beatles' song, 'We Can Work It Out', begins with a bar split between D and G, chords I and IV. This bar is then repeated and followed by another split bar of C and D, creating a three-bar phrase with prominent use of the bVII chord.

'Tender' by Blur takes a similar approach in A major by building verses on a two-bar phrase involving chord I and chord bVII (G). The two-bar phrase is played four times in a normal verse and consists of one bar of A followed by a bar which is split between G and A.

'I'm A Believer' was a 1960s hit for The Monkees but was composed by Neil Diamond, a noted songwriter and performer. The song is almost entirely built on chords I, IV, and V. The eight-bar verse is constructed from a four-bar section played twice, using chords I and V (G and D): G-D-G-G. This is followed by an eight-bar pre-chorus or link, using mostly I and IV (G and C): C-G-C-G-C-G-D-D. Then comes the "Then I saw her face" chorus, and the use of the bVII chord. The rate of change increases with a one bar pattern split between G and C and repeated for eight bars: G-C-G-C-G-C etc. The tag at the end of the chorus is a stroke of genius. The rate of change slows to one chord per bar, and we have I, IV, I, and the bVII used as an approach to chord V: G-C-G-F-D-D. This is a six-bar phrase with a surprising route to chord V that emphasises the joyous stating of the song's hook.

A similar occurrence of the use of chord bVII occurs in the Katie Perry song 'Self-Inflicted'. This time, we are looking at the linking passage that joins the verse to the chorus, with the lyric "every bone's been broken, but my heart is still wide open". This time, the link passage is only four bars in length, and with the song in D major the target is chord V (A). The sequence is VI-IV-bVII-V or Bm-G-C-A. Once again the bVII is the surprise chord that pushes strongly towards chord V, launching the song into the chorus.

Technique #40: bVII turnarounds

The bVII chord can be used in three-chord turnarounds like those laid out at the end of Section 1. There is no problem with I-bVII-V replacing I-IV-V, but there is a risk that the key can be obscured with I-IV-bVII.

CAUTION: HARMONIC AMBIGUITY AHEAD!

When a song has chords drawn only from I to VI, there is usually little doubt about its key. As the range of harmonic colour increases because of additional chords, there is a chance of harmonic ambiguity. The bVII chord brings with it this risk. This is for two reasons: the omission of chord V makes I-IV-bVII sound as if it could be in a different key, and bVII itself is constructed on a scale degree which is not in the major scale. Compare these two examples of a three-chord sequence that is a favourite of rock bands ('Sweet Home Alabama' and 'More Than A Feeling', to name but two examples):

Turnaround in D

I				I				♭VII				IV			
D	/	/	/	D	/	/	/	C	/	/	/	G	/	/	/ :‖

Turnaround in G

V				V				IV				I			
D	/	/	/	D	/	/	/	C	/	/	/	G	/	/	/ :‖

The chords are the same and in the same order, but their tonal roles (shown by the Roman numerals) are different, hence the harmonic ambiguity of the sequence – is it in D major or G major? Tables 1–4 in the Appendix show how a single chord can play many harmonic roles, like someone going to six fancy dress parties as six different characters.

Look at table 5 in the Appendix, and you will see that G major is the key one step down on the table from D major. The ambiguity of the ♭VII chord always relates to the key one step down on the table from the key you are in; the chord change I-♭VII can be mistaken for V-IV in the key that's lower on the table.

Sometimes the order of a sequence, if repeated, will override the ambiguity, especially if chord I is in a leading position. Nevertheless, it is prudent to be aware of this issue. Many a songwriter in this situation has been puzzled to discover that, after starting a song with what he or she thought was a I-♭VII-IV turnaround in D, they have felt strangely compelled to write a bridge with an Am in it (chord II in G but not in D) instead of F♯m (chord III in D but not in G), because their ears were saying it was 'right'.

Here are two ways of removing the ambiguity from this progression. In the first example, a Dmaj7 in bar 2 emphasises that the key is D, because this type of seventh chord does not occur on D in the key of G major:

Three-chord turnaround with ♭VII

I				I^7				♭VII				IV			
D	/	/	/	Dmaj7	/	/	/	C	/	/	/	G	/	/	/ :‖

In this example, a fourth chord, A7, is played in bar 4. If the key were G major, this chord would more likely be Am7:

Four-chord turnaround with ♭VII

I				I				♭VII				IV		V7	
D	/	/	/	D	/	/	/	C	/	/	/	G	/	A7	/ :‖

D C G Dmaj7 A7

Harmonic ambiguity is not in itself bad, and it can be creatively exploited. In songwriting it is a matter of whether this ambiguity is effective or appropriate for the song you're writing, or whether it becomes a distraction. It might be used to illustrate the uncertainty of a situation described in a lyric – if the person you're singing about doesn't know where he stands, maybe the chords shouldn't either! It is often a question of the correct amount of ambiguity, and extreme feelings might be portrayed with a harmony that is even more disturbed. (There will be more on this when we encounter the 'dark outriders' in Section 9). But most popular songs tend to be harmonically unambiguous.

Keeping the issue of harmonic ambiguity in mind, here are some turnarounds in G using the bVII chord:

Three-chord turnaround with bVII (a)

I				V				bVII				V			
G	/	/	/	D	/	/	/	F	/	/	/	D	/	/	/ :‖

Three-chord turnaround with bVII (b)

I				IV				bVII				IV			
G	/	/	/	C	/	/	/	F	/	/	/	C	/	/	/ :‖

Three-chord turnaround with bVII (c)

I				bVII				IV				bVII			
G	/	/	/	F	/	/	/	C	/	/	/	F	/	/	/ :‖

Four-chord turnaround with bVII (a)

I		V		bVII		IV		bVII				V			
G	/	D	/	F	/	C	/	F	/	/	/	D	/	/	/ :‖

Four-chord turnaround with bVII (b)

I				IV				V				bVII			
G	/	/	/	C	/	/	/	D	/	/	/	F	/	/	/ :‖

Four-chord turnaround with bVII (c)

I				III				bVII				IV			
G	/	/	/	Bm	/	/	/	F	/	/	/	C	/	/	/ :‖

Four-chord turnaround with bVII (d)

I				bVII				VI				V			
G	/	/	/	F	/	/	/	Em	/	/	/	D	/	/	/ :‖

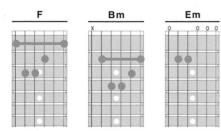

F   Bm   Em

ADDING FLAT DEGREE CHORDS

SECTION 4

These examples are in D major:

Four-chord turnaround with ♭VII (a)

I				II				♭VII				V				
D	/	/	/	Em	/	/	/	C	/	/	/	A	/	/	/	:‖

Four-chord turnaround with ♭VII (b)

I				♭VII				IV				V				
D	/	/	/	C	/	/	/	G	/	/	/	A	/	/	/	:‖

Four-chord turnaround with ♭VII (c)

I				♭VII				VI				V				
D	/	/	/	C	/	/	/	Bm	/	/	/	A	/	/	/	:‖

Four-chord turnaround with ♭VII (d)

I				III				ii♭VII				IV				
D	/	/	/	F♯m	/	/	/	C/G	/	/	/	G	/	/	/	:‖

Three-chord turnarounds involving the ♭VII chord are popular with rock bands because the ♭VII imparts a bluesy quality to chord sequences involving I, IV, and V. 'Sweet Home Alabama', for example, is in the key of D major and is built on a turnaround using the chords D and C in one bar and G in the second bar. In other words chords I, ♭VII, and IV. Such is the power of this sequence and the guitar riff associated with it that the entire song can be built on this two bar pattern.

'Sweet Child O' Mine' by Guns N' Roses uses a similar chord sequence in the key of D♭ major. This time the chords return to chord I at the end of the phrase, and each chord lasts for two bars, making an eight-bar section: D♭–D♭–C♭–C♭–G♭–G♭–D♭–D♭. This sequence is used for the intro and for the verses. Since the guitars are detuned by a semitone the playing shapes are those for D major: D-D-C-C-G-G-D-D.

Another example of chord ♭VII in a rock context is the song 'Back In Black' by Australian band AC/DC. This song is in the key of E major and its opening guitar riff and hook use the same chords as the above examples, remaining on chord IV in a similar way to 'Sweet Home Alabama': E-D-A. Once again, the chords are compressed into just a two-bar phrase: two beats of E and D followed by a bar of A.

Technique #41: introducing the ♭III and ♭VI

Here are the chords of G major with ♭VII replacing VII:

I	II	III	IV	V	VI	♭VII
G	Am	Bm	C	D	Em	F

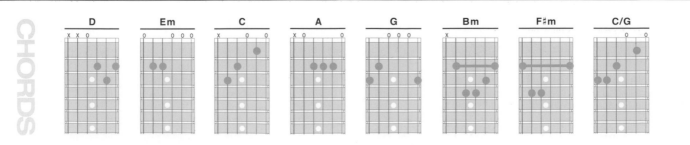

There are two other chords that can be made by lowering degrees of the scale and treating the flattened note as the root of a major chord: ♭III and ♭VI. In G major, these chords are B♭ and E♭.

I	II	♭III	III	IV	V	♭VI	VI	♭VII
G	Am	B♭	Bm	C	D	E♭	Em	F

The ♭III and ♭VI:

- bring a sense of the unexpected and add spice to a sequence.
- are often found in blues, R&B and hard-rock songs.
- can 'toughen up' a chord sequence, especially when they replace the minor chords III and VI.
- can be used in a three-chord trick or a three-chord turnaround.
- can be used in a four-chord turnaround.
- can make a powerful contribution to an intro or bridge, or contrast a verse with a chorus.

Here are some examples of the ♭III and ♭VI in action:

Verse with ♭III in C

I	♭III	IV	♭III
C / / /	E♭ / / /	F / / /	E♭ / / / :||

Verse with ♭III in G

I	IV	♭III	IV
G / / /	C / / /	B♭ / / /	C / / / :||

Verse with ♭III in D

I	V	♭III	IV
D / / /	A / / /	F / / /	G / / / :||

Verse with ♭III in A

I	♭VII	IV	♭III
A / / /	G / / /	D / / /	C / / / :||

Verse with ♭VI in C

I	VI	♭VI	V
C / / /	Am / / /	A♭ / / /	G / / / :||

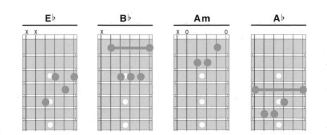

E♭   B♭   Am   A♭

ADDING FLAT DEGREE CHORDS

ADDING FLAT DEGREE CHORDS

Verse with ♭VI in G

I				♭VI				IV				V				
G	/	/	/	E♭	/	/	/	C	/	/	/	D	/	/	/	:‖

Verse with ♭VI in D

I				V				♭VI				VI				
D	/	/	/	A	/	/	/	B♭	/	/	/	Bm	/	/	/	:‖

Verse with ♭VI in A

I				♭VII				♭VI				V				
A	/	/	/	G	/	/	/	F	/	/	/	E	/	/	/	:‖

Now let's introduce another popular guitar key, essential for blues and rock: E major. Here are the conventional seven chords:

I	II	III	IV	V	VI	VII
E	F#m	G#m	A	B	C#m	D#dim

The three flattened chords in this key are:

♭III	♭VI	♭VII
G	C	D

Since these are easy guitar-chord shapes, it is not hard to understand the popularity of E major for writing songs with these extra chords.

Verse with ♭III in E

I				♭III				V				IV				
E	/	/	/	G	/	/	/	B	/	/	/	A	/	/	/	:‖

Verse with ♭III in E (classic blues)

I				IV		♭III		V				♭III		IV		
E	/	/	/	A	/	G	/	E	/	/	/	G	/	A	/	:‖

It is perfectly acceptable to combine chord III or VI with its flattened version, as here:

Verse with III and ♭III in E

I				III				V		IV		♭III				
E	/	/	/	G#m	/	/	/	B	/	A	/	G	/	/	/	:‖

CHORDS

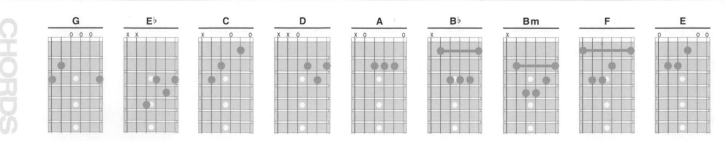

G   E♭   C   D   A   B♭   Bm   F   E

USING ♭III AND ♭VII FOR THREE-CHORD SONGS

Here are the three-chord patterns from the beginning of Section 2. Chord III and/or VI are now replaced with their flattened equivalents:

I	♭III	IV
G	B♭	C

I	♭III	V
G	B♭	D

I	II	♭VI
G	Am	E♭

I	♭III	♭VI
G	B♭	E♭

I	♭VI	IV
G	E♭	C

I	♭VI	V
G	E♭	D

I	II	♭III
G	Am	B♭

We mentioned 'Tender' by Blur in the context of songs which use the ♭VII chord. The use of flat degree chords continues in this song in the chorus; that is, the "come on, come on, come on, get through it" section. Beginning on the key chord of A major for one bar, the second bar uses the chords D and C (IV and ♭III). We then return to A major, and this is followed by a bar of E and D (V and I), making a repeated four bar phrase.

Use of the ♭III chord can also be heard in the middle-eight of the Righteous Brothers song 'Unchained Melody'. Most of this song is based on a conventional I-VI-IV-V turnaround in the key of C using the chords C, Am, F, and G. Each chord lasts for one bar, and one chord per bar continues for the "I need your love" section which uses this harmonically more interesting eight bars: C-G/B-Am-G-F-G-C-C. Notice the descending bassline provided by chord V in first inversion, G/B.

The middle eight does what so many middle eights do: it goes to chord IV. But the rate of change is faster here, with two chords in each bar: F-G-F-E♭-F-G-C. This four-bar phrase is played twice. In the context of a song which contains so much material completely within the key of C major the E♭ chord (♭III) is something of a surprise.

ADDING FLAT DEGREE CHORDS

B   G#m

The Beatles' 'It Won't Be Long' is a rare example of a song with a verse which uses a simple alternation of chords I and ♭VI, which in this case are E and C. This is in the "Every night, when everybody has fun..." section. The chords are: E-C-E-E-C-E-E. The interrupted first phrase leads to a distinctive seven-bar section. This is a highly unusual song which begins with a chorus and also has a middle-eight, both of which involve some rarely encountered chords that we will return to later in the book.

Technique #42: inversions of ♭III and ♭VI

As with any other chords, ♭III and ♭VI have first and second inversions. These inversions have the same bass note as other chords that may occur in the song and therefore can make exotic substitutes for them. In G major:

- The first inversion of ♭III has the same root note as V (B♭/D and D).
- The first inversion of ♭VI has the same root note as I (E♭/G and G).
- The second inversion of ♭III has the same root note as ♭VII (B♭/F and F).
- The second inversion of ♭VI has the same root note as ♭III (E♭/B♭ and B♭).

In this example, the bassline E-G-A-G has a different chord on the two Gs because ♭VI is inverted:

Partial inversion intro

I				ii♭VI				IV				♭III			
E	/	/	/	C/G	/	/	/	A	/	/	/	G	/	/	/
e				g				a				g			

In the following six-bar verse, a chromatic descending bassline of E-D♯-D-C♯-C-B links the chords. The term chromatic (literally, 'of colour') describes notes or chords not found in a particular key. The E major scale does not include the notes D and C, so a descending bassline that is purely in E would use the notes E-D♯-C♯-B. The notes D and C are, in this context, chromatic. Both the ♭VI and ♭III chords are inverted to make this chromatic bass line possible. Notice the mild shock as the unexpected ♭III and ♭VI chords appear:

Verse with chromatic bassline

I				iV				ii♭III				VI			
E	/	/	/	B/D♯	/	/	/	G/D	/	/	/	C♯m	/	/	/
e				d♯				d				c♯			

E   C/G   A   G   B/D♯   G/D   C♯m

♭VI		i♭III		IV		V	
C	/	G/B	/	A	/	B	
c		b		a		b	

Technique #43: the ♭VI-♭VII-I approach

There is a way of linking the ♭VI chord to the ♭VII for a smooth, ascending progression toward chord I, creating an alternative to the usual IV-V-I approaches and finishes. This sequence is popular because the move to ♭VI (often from V) is unexpected, and the bass ascends in tones (whole-steps) with a triumphant effect:

♭VI-♭VII chorus in D

I				II				IV				I			
D	/	/	/	Em	/	/	/	G	/	/	/	D	/	/	/

V				♭VI				♭VII				I			
A	/	/	/	B♭	/	/	/	C	/	/	/	D	/	/	/

16-bar ♭VI-♭VII-I in E

I				iI				IV				V			
E	/	/	/	E/G♯	/	/	/	A	/	/	/	B	/	/	/ :‖

I				iI				IV				♭VI		V	
E	/	/	/	E/G♯	/	/	/	A	/	/	/	C	/	B	/

♭VI		♭VII		I				♭VI		♭VII		I			
C	/	D	/	E	/	/	/	C	/	D	/	E	/	/	/

Here are two four-chord song structures in which ♭III or ♭VI mix with I, IV, and V:

Verse/chorus song with ♭III in G major
Intro

I				♭III				IV				V			
G	/	/	/	B♭	/	/	/	C	/	/	/	D	/	/	/

Verse

I		IV		I		IV		I		IV		V			
G	/	C	/	G	/	C	/	G	/	C	/	D	/	/	/ :‖

continues on next page

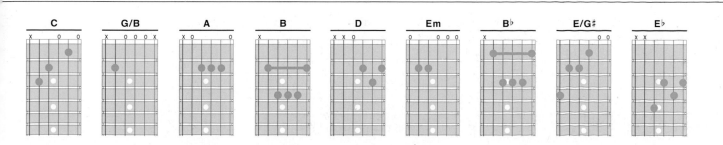

C   G/B   A   B   D   Em   B♭   E/G♯   E♭

(vertical right margin) ADDING FLAT DEGREE CHORDS

ADDING FLAT DEGREE CHORDS

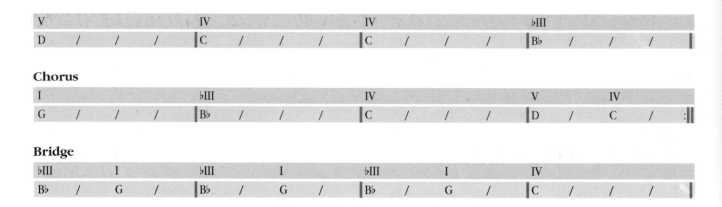

V				IV				IV				bIII			
D	/	/	/	C	/	/	/	C	/	/	/	Bb	/	/	/

Chorus

I				bIII				IV				V		IV	
G	/	/	/	Bb	/	/	/	C	/	/	/	D	/	C	/ :||

Bridge

bIII		I		bIII		I		bIII		I		IV			
Bb	/	G	/	Bb	/	G	/	Bb	/	G	/	C	/	/	/

Notes:
- The intro puts the bIII in context by making it part of an escalator sequence. This means that although it is not 'in key', some of the rough edges are smoothed off for the listener.
- The intro is re-used for the chorus, with the addition of a C chord on the last two beats of the turnaround.
- The verse alters the rate of chord change.
- The four-bar lead-in to the chorus goes downward. This is important because it makes an effective contrast with the rising chorus.
- The bridge echoes the rate of chord change on the verse's opening but makes central use of the bIII chord.
- Chord V is rested during the bridge.

Verse/bridge song with bVI in G major

Intro

IV				IV				bVI				V			
C	/	/	/	C	/	/	/	Eb	/	/	/	D	/	/	/

Verse

I				IV				V				I			
G	/	/	/	C	/	/	/	D	/	/	/	G	/	/	/

IV				V				IV				V			
C	/	/	/	D	/	/	/	C	/	/	/	D	/	/	/

Bridge

bVI				bVI				I				I			
Eb	/	/	/	Eb	/	/	/	G	/	/	/	G	/	/	/

CHORDS

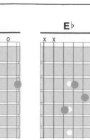

D C Bb G Eb

♭VI				♭VI				I				V			
E♭	/	/	/	E♭	/	/	/	G	/	/	/	D	/	/	/

Notes:
- Chord I is delayed until the start of the verse.
- The ♭VI chord is used in the intro and with more emphasis in the bridge, to give it additional interest.
- Chord IV is rested during the bridge.

Now let's use the ♭III and ♭VI chords in turnarounds and subject them to the variation techniques mentioned in earlier sections. Here is a I-♭III-IV-V turnaround in D major:

Turnaround with ♭III in D major

Primary

I				♭III				IV				V			
D	/	/	/	F	/	/	/	G	/	/	/	A	/	/	/ :‖

Displaced

♭III				IV				V				I			
F	/	/	/	G	/	/	/	A	/	/	/	D	/	/	/ :‖

Descending

V				IV				♭III				I			
A	/	/	/	G	/	/	/	F	/	/	/	D	/	/	/ :‖

Altered rate of chord change

I		♭III	IV		V					V				
D	/	/	F	G	/	/	/	A	/	/	/	A	/	/	/ :‖

Varied order

I				IV				♭III				V			
D	/	/	/	G	/	/	/	F	/	/	/	A	/	/	/ :‖

Stretched

I		♭III		IV				♭III				IV		V	
D	/	F	/	G	/	/	/	F	/	/	/	G	/	A	/ :‖

continues on next page

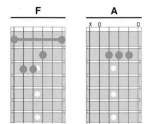

ADDING FLAT DEGREE CHORDS

Partial inversion

I				iibIII				iIV				V			
D	/	/	/	F/C	/	/	/	G/B	/	/	/	A	/	/	/ :‖
d				c				b				a			

Full inversion

iiI				ibIII				iIV				iV			
D/A	/	/	/	F/A	/	/	/	G/B	/	/	/	A/C♯	/	/	/ :‖
a				a				b				c♯			

Truncated 3+4 formula

I		bIII		IV				I		bIII		IV		V	
D	/	F	/	G	/	/	/	D	/	F	/	G	/	A	/ :‖

Now let's look at a I-IV-V-bVI turnaround in E major:

TURNAROUND WITH bVI IN E MAJOR

Primary

I				IV				V				bVI			
E	/	/	/	A	/	/	/	B	/	/	/	C	/	/	/ :‖

Displaced

V				bVI				I				IV			
B	/	/	/	C	/	/	/	E	/	/	/	A	/	/	/ :‖

Descending

bVI				V				IV				I			
C	/	/	/	B	/	/	/	A	/	/	/	E	/	/	/ :‖

Altered rate of chord change

I				IV				V				V		bVI	
E	/	/	/	A	/	/	/	B	/	/	/	B	/	C	/ :‖

Varied order

I				IV				bVI				V			
E	/	/	/	A	/	/	/	C	/	/	/	B	/	/	/ :‖

CHORDS

D · F/C · G/B · A · D/A · F/A · A/C♯ · E · B

Stretched

I		IV		I				IV		V		♭VI			
E	/	A	/	E	/	/	/	A	/	B	/	C	/	/	/ :||

Partial inversion

I				iIV				iV				♭VI			
E	/	/	/	A/C♯	/	/	/	B/D♯	/	/	/	C	/	/	/ :||
e				c♯				d♯				c			

Full inversion

iiI				iIV				iiV				ii♭VI			
E/B	/	/	/	A/C♯	/	/	/	B/F♯	/	/	/	C/G	/	/	/ :||
b				c♯				f♯				g			

Truncated 3+4 formula

I		IV		V				I		IV		V		♭VI	
E	/	A	/	B	/	/	/	E	/	A	/	B	/	C	/ :||

The ♭VII chord can be useful as a way of climbing back to chord I from chord V. An example of this is the chorus of 'Sweet Child Of Mine', whose verse we looked at earlier in the context of three-chord 'rock' turnarounds. The chorus goes from A♭, which is chord V, to chord ♭VII, which in this context should be called C♭. The music then progresses to the tonic chord, D♭. This means that this song is effectively made up of two three-chord turnarounds, which is unusual, but perhaps more likely to be encountered in a rock situation.

The Police's 'Every Breath You Take' makes use of a rising ♭VI to ♭VII chord sequence in its middle-eight, but with an interesting twist. The song is in the key of A, and is based on conventional turnaround chords, I, VI, IV, and V. In the middle-eight, with the lyric "Since you've gone I'm lost without a trace" the chords take an abrupt dive to chord ♭VI, which is F, then rise a whole step to chord ♭VII, G. Each chord lasts for two bars, creating a four-bar phrase which is then repeated. The ninth bar of the middle-eight returns again to the F chord, but just when you expect to hear the same phrase again, with the rise to the G chord, the song abruptly returns to chord I (A). This surprising middle sequence provides a boost that is the making of the song, which otherwise uses completely diatonic material.

Technique #44: reharmonizing with ♭VII, ♭III, and ♭VI

Like the three minor chords (II, III, and VI), the three lowered chords (♭VII, ♭III, and ♭VI) can be used to reharmonize a melody. However, because ♭III and ♭VI contain two notes each which are not in

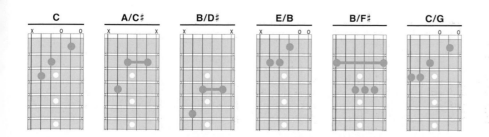

ADDING FLAT DEGREE CHORDS

the major scale, care must be taken to ensure that the note sung does not clash with the chord. If such a clash occurs simply adjust the offending melody note so that it fits with the altered chord. The general effect of reharmonizing an established progression with these chords will be to toughen it up. Let's demonstrate this using the full song in A example from Section 3. In A major, ♭III is C, ♭VI is F, and ♭VII is G. Each section is shown here in its original form with possible reharmonizing chords in brackets. Not every one would be used, and even those that are would probably not be used every time a section was played. The reharmonized chord might occur in verse 3, chorus 3, if the intro were repeated as a link or coda, or if the bridge were played twice.

Full song in A, with reharmonizing options

Intro

III				III [♭III]				II				II [♭VII]			
C♯m	/	/	/	C♯m [C]/	/	/	/	Bm	/	/	/	Bm [G] /	/	/	/

Verse

V				I				IV		I [♭III]		IV		V	
E	/	/	/	A	/	/	/	D	/	A [C]	/	D	/	E	/

IV				V				III				IV		V	
D	/	/	/	E	/	/	/	C♯m	/	/	/	D	/	E	/ :‖

Chorus

I				V				VI [♭VI]				IV			
A	/	/	/	E	/	/	/	F♯m [F] /	/	/	/	D	/	/	/ :‖

Bridge

II				II				II				IV	[♭VI]		
Bm	/	/	/	Bm	/	/	/	Bm	/	/	/	D	[F]	/	/

II				II				II			IV	V		IV	
Bm	/	/	/	Bm	/	/	/	Bm	/	D	/	E	/	D	/

Technique #45: hard-rock songs

There is a well-established formula for writing hard-rock songs with a Stones/Bad Company/Black Crowes/White Stripes feel which involves using the ♭III and ♭VI chords.

CHORDS

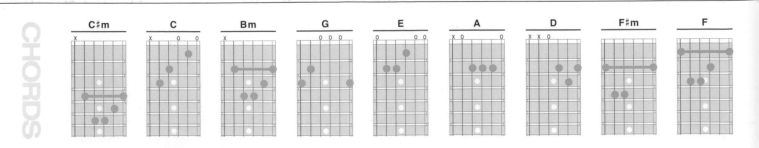

C♯m   C   Bm   G   E   A   D   F♯m   F

Step 1. Choose a key – let's take A major. Here are the seven chords:

I	II	III	IV	V	VI	VII
A	Bm	C♯m	D	E	F♯m	G♯dim

Step 2. Use the ♭VII to replace the diminished VII:

I	II	III	IV	V	VI	♭VII
A	Bm	C♯m	D	E	F♯m	G

Step 3. Replace the three minor chords – II, III, and VI – with ♭III and ♭VI.

I	♭III	IV	V	♭VI	♭VII
A	C	D	E	F	G

We now have six chords, all major. These can be put together in the usual ways to get a rock progression. The normal rules apply about not using them all at once, creating turnarounds, etc. The emphasis will still fall on chords I, IV, and V, so think of ♭VII, ♭III, and ♭VI as secondary choices. Song sequences that use these six chords lend themselves to guitar solos on the pentatonic minor and blues scales. These chords are effective if played as fifths: A5, C5, D5, E5, F5, and G5 (see Section 7 for information about chord types). In the key of E, also commonly used for rock songs, this set of chords would be E, G, A, B, C, and D – almost the same, but with B instead of F.

Hard-rock song in A major

Intro

I				I		♭VII		I				I		♭VII	
A	/	/	/	A	/	G	/	A	/	/	/	A	/	G	/

Verse

I		♭III		♭VII		♭III		I		♭III		♭VII		I	
A	/	C	/	G	/	C	/	A	/	C	/	G	/	A	/ :||

♭VI				♭VI				IV				IV			
F	/	/	/	F	/	/	/	D	/	/	/	D	/	/	/

♭VI				♭VI				V				V		♭VII	
F	/	/	/	F	/	/	/	E	/	/	/	E	/	G	/

Chorus

I				♭VII		IV	x3	♭VII				V			
A	/	/	/	G	/	D	/ :||	G	/	/	/	E	/	/	/

continues on next page

ADDING FLAT DEGREE CHORDS

Bridge

♭VI		♭III		♭VII		I		IV				IV			
F	/	C	/	G	/	A	/	D	/	/	/	D	/	/	/

♭VI		♭III		♭VII		I		♭VI				V			
F	/	C	/	G	/	A	/	F	/	/	/	E	/	/	/

Notice the varying rate of chord change, and that the intro uses only two chords. The verse has two parts: the first half is a riff-type figure where bar 2 and 4 are alternate endings; the second half brings in the ♭VI chord. Notice how the ♭VII in bar 16 makes a harder-sounding approach to chord I in the chorus than going from chord V. The chorus uses the popular rock turnaround I-♭VII-IV.

The Rolling Stones' 'Brown Sugar' repeats a section of the intro after the chorus, and uses the same four bars of music played four times for the 16-bar saxophone solo. The song is in the key of C major, but the chords jump to E♭ and then back to C for this section, each chord lasting one bar. The next bar is two beats of A♭ and two beats of B♭, and we return again to C via chord IV (F) in the final bar. This song therefore uses all of the flat degree major chords that can replace the standard minor or diminished chords in the key: E♭ major instead of E minor, A♭ major instead of A minor, and B♭ major instead of B diminished. These chords give the song a rocking, bluesy quality that would not be found if the regular minor chords were used.

For an example based upon the 12-bar chord sequence we can examine 'Sunshine Of Your Love' by Cream, which is in D major and begins with a chordal riff based on D and C. After four times through the riff the chords move to G and F (IV and ♭III), and then return to the opening riff played twice. The ending consists of a bar of A followed by a bar split between C and G (♭VII and IV). Each time through the riff takes two bars, so we end up with a 24-bar sequence based mostly on chords I, IV, and V, but with ♭III and ♭VII adding the blues/rock flavour.

F   C   G   A   D   E

SECTION 5
REVERSE POLARITY
PLAYING WITH MAJORS AND MINORS

As you have played through Sections 1–4, the range of chords has gradually increased. First there were the three major chords I, IV, and V. To these were added the three minors of the key, II, III, and VI, making six. You learned about a flattened chord, ♭VII, and then two more lowered-degree chords, ♭III and ♭VI. This provides a resource of nine chords in a single major key. If the first and second inversions of these chords are added, it makes a total of 27.

This section of *The Songwriting Sourcebook* will increase the number of available root chords from nine to 13 with a technique I call reverse polarity. Polarity in this context means whether a chord is major or minor; *reverse polarity* means changing a chord from major to minor, or minor to major. It describes what happens when a chord is reversed from what it would normally be in the key. Reverse polarity can apply to chords II, III, VI, and IV: chords II, III, and VI turn from minor to major; chord IV turns from major to minor. Here are the changes in the keys already used for examples:

I	II	III	IV	V	VI	VII
C	Dm	Em	F	G	Am	Bdim
	D	**E**	**Fm**		**A**	

I	II	III	IV	V	VI	VII
G	Am	Bm	C	D	Em	F♯dim
	A	**B**	**Cm**		**E**	

I	II	III	IV	V	VI	VII
D	Em	F♯m	G	A	Bm	C♯dim
	E	**F♯**	**Gm**		**B**	

SECTION 5

I	II	III	IV	V	VI	VII
A	Bm	C#m	D	E	F#m	G#dim
	B	**C#**	**Dm**		**F#**	

I	II	III	IV	V	VI	VII
E	F#m	G#m	A	B	C#m	D#dim
	F#	**G#**	**Am**		**C#**	

The musical effect of putting one of these chords into a song is surprise – a reverse-polarity chord creates the impression that the music is about to change key, but then it doesn't. They are like doors opened halfway so you can glance into a room, then quickly closed before you can enter. The function of reverse-polarity chords as doors to different keys is covered in Section 8.

We are so accustomed to hearing music in major keys that our ear expects chords II, III and VI to be minor and chord IV to be major. When this is altered, we register the fact even if we do not know music theory. Songwriters experimenting intuitively with chords feel this surprise when they put one of these chords into a progression. They may like the effect and write a song featuring it.

USE CAUTION WITH REVERSE-POLARITY CHORDS.

Even more than ♭III and the ♭VI, these four chords must not be thought of as having the same level of importance as chords I to VI. They should be used sparingly, usually no more than two in a single section of a song. Because they contain one note foreign to the major scale of the key, they can trip up soloists if used in an instrumental passage, disrupt the sense of key and create exotic changes in the melody line. They are, however, handy for contrasting one section of a song with another. A common weakness of songs is that the bridge is often less interesting than either the verse or chorus. A reverse-polarity chord can really give the bridge a lift.

CAN REVERSE POLARITY BE APPLIED TO CHORDS I, V, OR VII?

Not really – it would severely disrupt the stability of the home key. Reversing chord I is tantamount to a key change from tonic major to tonic minor. If chord V is changed to minor, it will imply a key change down one step on the table of keys (see table 5 in the Appendix). It might also suggest a 'mixolydian song', in which the chords are created from a type of scale in which the seventh note of a major scale is flattened (this is described in more detail in *How To Write Songs On Guitar*.) An example of a mixolydian sequence is the E-Bm-Asus4-A turnaround that drives The Verve's 'Bitter Sweet Symphony' for its entire duration of 5:58! (In E major, chord V should be a B, not a Bm.)

Chord VII cannot be subjected to reverse polarity because it is diminished; the effect of changing it to a major or minor chord is dealt with under the heading of chromatic chords in Section 9.

CAN REVERSE POLARITY CHORDS COMBINE WITH LOWERED DEGREE CHORDS?

The answer to this is yes, but you have to be careful that two in close proximity don't make the song progression sound as though it has lost its way from the home key. Marshall Crenshaw's 'What Do You Dream Of?' is a fine example of incorporating D as the ♭VII of E, and G as the ♭III, into the verse, and then using II^ (F♯) as the door into a key-change of B major for the chorus (F♯ is chord V of B major). This chorus ends with a A-B (♭VII-I) change in B. The Police's 'Every Breath You Take' enlivens its basic I-VI-IV-V turnaround with a ♭III and a II^, and its bridge gives the listener a break from the home key by moving from a ♭VI to ♭VII (F to G).

When you consider the rock/indie nature of most of his compositions, Paul Weller turns out to use surprisingly sophisticated chord sequences, which may be one reason for his longevity as an artist. One of his early songs from the days of The Jam is 'Eton Rifles'. This song begins in A minor with vigorously played chords on guitar over a bass riff. The song turns out, however, to be in C major, and at the end of the intro there is a bar divided between two beats of F and two beats of G (chords IV and V), which leads into the start of the verse and the home chord of C major. The whole of the verse is built on a bar of C (chord I) followed by a bar of D (chord II^). Normally, we would expect chord II to be minor, but in this case its polarity has been reversed. (In this book, the sign ^ following a Roman numeral indicates a reverse-polarity chord.)

Technique #46: the reverse-polarity turnaround

The quickest way to get a feeling for what a major/minor shift can do is to take the primary turnarounds in Section 2 and subject them to reverse polarity, creating the sequences I-II^-IV-V, I-III^-IV-V and I-VI^-IV-V.

Here are reverse-polarity turnarounds in the keys of C, G, D, A, and E major. These turnarounds can be subjected to the usual variations – displaced, variant order, partial and full inversion, reversed order, stretching, etc. Notice that these sequences are entirely major. To some extent, they all have something of a breezy optimism and freedom reminiscent of 1960s pop.

Reverse-polarity turnarounds in C major

I				II^				IV				V			
C	/	/	/	D	/	/	/	F	/	/	/	G	/	/	/ :‖

I				III^				IV				V			
C	/	/	/	E	/	/	/	F	/	/	/	G	/	/	/ :‖

I				VI^				IV				V			
C	/	/	/	A	/	/	/	F	/	/	/	G	/	/	/ :‖

Reverse-polarity turnarounds in G major

I				II^				IV				V			
G	/	/	/	A	/	/	/	C	/	/	/	D	/	/	/ :‖

continues on next page

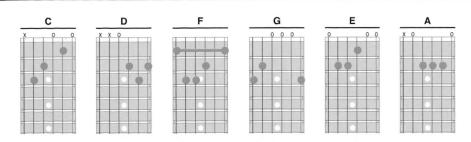

I				III^				IV				V			
G	/	/	/	B	/	/	/	C	/	/	/	D	/	/	/ :||

I				VI^				IV				V			
G	/	/	/	E	/	/	/	C	/	/	/	D	/	/	/ :||

Reverse-polarity turnarounds in D major

I				II^				IV				V			
D	/	/	/	E	/	/	/	G	/	/	/	A	/	/	/ :||

I				III^				IV				V			
D	/	/	/	F♯	/	/	/	G	/	/	/	A	/	/	/ :||

I				VI^				IV				V			
D	/	/	/	B	/	/	/	G	/	/	/	A	/	/	/ :||

Reverse-polarity turnarounds in A major

I				II^				IV				V			
A	/	/	/	B	/	/	/	D	/	/	/	E	/	/	/ :||

I				III^				IV				V			
A	/	/	/	C♯	/	/	/	D	/	/	/	E	/	/	/ :||

I				VI^				IV				V			
A	/	/	/	F♯	/	/	/	D	/	/	/	E	/	/	/ :||

Reverse-polarity turnarounds in E major

I				II^				IV				V			
E	/	/	/	F♯	/	/	/	A	/	/	/	B	/	/	/ :||

I				III^				IV				V			
E	/	/	/	G♯	/	/	/	A	/	/	/	B	/	/	/ :||

I				VI^				IV				V			
E	/	/	/	C♯	/	/	/	A	/	/	/	B	/	/	/ :||

The traditional use of the second-inversion chord I (iiI) is to delay, then lead to, chord V, since it shares the same bass note. It works even better when it comes after reverse-polarity chord II (II^), because that creates the expectation of a key change to what would have been the same root note. Compare:

REVERSE POLARITY

CHORDS

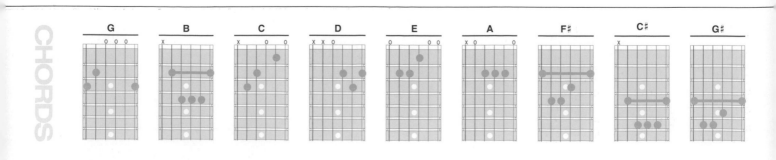

Verse with II^ (key change)

I				VI				II^ [V]				I			
A	/	/	/	F♯m	/	/	/	B	/	/	/	E	/	/	/

Verse with II^ and iiI

I				VI				II^ [V]				iiI			
A	/	/	/	F♯m	/	/	/	B	/	/	/	A/E	/	/	/

V			
E	/	/	/

The Oasis song 'She's Electric' begins with a four-chord turnaround of chords I, III^, VI, and IV. Each chord lasts for two beats creating a two-bar section as follows: E-G♯-C♯m-A. This is an example of a reverse polarity turnaround, as the G♯ chord is major, but in this key we would expect it normally to be minor.

Reverse polarity turnarounds are also possible with just three chords. The Rolling Stones' 'Sweet Virginia' from the *Exiles On Main Street* album is based entirely on the chords D, B, and A major, played as a four-bar turnaround: D-B-A-A. These are chords I, VI^, and V in D major, as in this key we would normally expect chord VI to be B minor.

Technique #47: the 'slush-maker'

The turnarounds above omit one reverse polarity chord: IV as a minor. I call this chord the 'slush-maker'. Try playing a I-IV (C-F) change, then this sequence — and you'll hear why:

The slush-maker

I				IVm				I				IVm			
C	/	/	/	Fm	/	/	/	C	/	/	/	Fm	/	/	/ :||

The IVm chord has an instantly recognisable tragic-but-sweet gloom about it that has made it popular in romantic ballads and weepy MOR songwriting. If you wish to darken the emotion of a song in an appealing way, reach for IVm. It is pure melodrama. In the right context – such as a James Bond theme song (think of 'You Only Live Twice') – it can be simultaneously erotic, grandiose, and forlorn. Imagine that it is the darkest hour, just before dawn, and the prisoner's last meal turns out to be a huge slice of cheesecake. That's the IVm for you. Radiohead have put this chord to some memorable uses in some of their songs (such as 'No Surprises') and for a tougher use of the IVm seek out Robert Plant's hit 'Heaven Knows'. Amy Winehouse's 'Love Is A Losing Game' uses the IVm as part of its hook (and a ♭VI in the verse).

REVERSE POLARITY

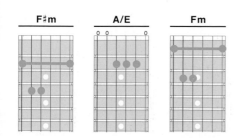

Here is IVm substituting for IV in the final bar of an eight-bar sequence:

IVm verse in C

I				I				VI				VI			
C	/	/	/	C	/	/	/	Am	/	/	/	Am	/	/	/ :‖

IV				IV				II				IVm		V	
Fmaj7	/	/	/	Fmaj7	/	/	/	Dm	/	/	/	Fm	/	G	/ :‖

In this example there is an unexpected return to IVm after a two-beat appearance:

IVm verse in C

IV				IV		V		I				IVm			
F	/	/	/	Fm	/	G	/	C	/	/	/	Fm	/	/	/ :‖

The art of using IVm often lies in the choice of approach chord. The smoothest approach is from chord IV, and the strongest progression is to chord I. The IVm-I change is so emotionally powerful that it has become a favourite way of ending a song (see Section 9 for more about endings).

IVm can also put a new slant on a link. Compare these two links in D major:

IV link

I				IV		V	
D	/	/	/	G	/	A	/

IVm link

I				IVm		V	
D	/	/	/	Gm7	/	A	/

In this intro in C major, IVm is approached from chord II. The combination of the two minor chords sets up a strongly tragic atmosphere:

Intro

II				IVm				I				I			
Dm	/	/	/	Fm	/	/	/	C	/	/	/	C7	/	/	/

IVm often follows a straight IV and then resolves to I. Notice in this bridge how chord I occurs first as an inversion. The second time, IVm unexpectedly moves to II^, which is V of the dominant key, E. E major is momentarily established before a return to A in the next section (Section 8 will explain key-changing in depth).

REVERSE POLARITY

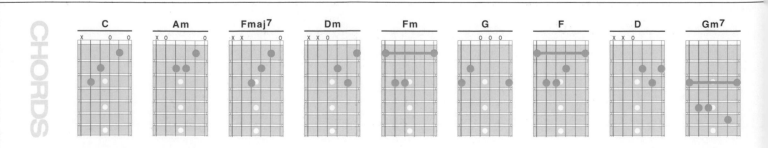

CHORDS

IVm bridge in A

IV				IVm				iI				I			
D	/	/	/	Dm	/	/	/	A/C#	/	/	/	A7	/	/	/

IV				IVm				II^ [V]				I		I [V]	
D	/	/	/	Dm	/	/	/	B7	/	/	/	E	/	E7	/

Any of the four-bar sections of this verse could rearranged and recycled as a four-bar turnaround:

IVm 16-bar verse in C

I				IV				IVm				V			
C	/	/	/	F	/	/	/	Fm	/	/	/	G	/	/	/

I				VI				IVm				III			
C	/	/	/	Am	/	/	/	Fm	/	/	/	Em	/	/	/

I				IV				V				IVm			
C	/	/	/	F	/	/	/	G	/	/	/	Fm	/	/	/

I				II				IVm				I			
C	/	/	/	Dm	/	/	/	Fm	/	/	/	C	/	/	/

As a rule of thumb, two reverse-polarity chords in close proximity are less effective than one and create key instability. To hear how disconcerting it can be to have two reverse-polarity chords together, try these three sequences (they could also have either chord IV or chord V in the last bar):

II ^ and IVm in C major

I				II^				IVm				I			
C	/	/	/	D	/	/	/	Fm	/	/	/	C	/	/	/ :‖

III ^ and IVm in C major

I				III^				IVm				I			
C	/	/	/	E	/	/	/	Fm	/	/	/	C	/	/	/ :‖

VI ^ and IVm in C major

I				VI^				IVm				I			
C	/	/	/	A	/	/	/	Fm	/	/	/	C	/	/	/ :‖

REVERSE POLARITY

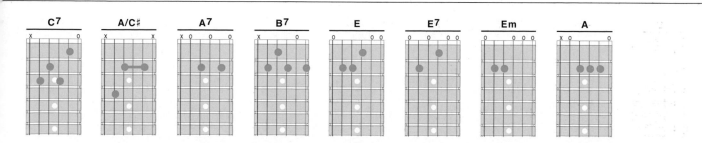

It would it be wise to do this only if the emotion or theme of the song requires an unsettling effect. It is certainly not easy to imagine the chorus of a commercial hit song using one of these ideas!

The verse of the Oasis song 'Don't Look Back in Anger' was analysed back at the start of Section 3. It is followed by a linking section joining the verse to the chorus, with the lyric "so I start a revolution from my bed". Initially, this section of the song is based on a two-bar phrase played three times. The first bar of this phrase consists of chord IV followed by IVm (F and Fm), each lasting for two beats. The second bar is the tonic chord, C major.

The chords which complete this section are G-A♭-Am-G-F-G-G. All these chords occupy one bar each, except the Am to G change, which is telescoped into one bar. Notice the breather bars discussed in Section 2 (two bars of G) at the end of this sequence.

Another song that makes prominent use of the IV-IVm chord change is the Everly Brothers' 'The Air That I Breathe', also a hit for British band The Hollies. The verses of this song are based on an eight-bar chord sequence that includes a reverse polarity chord III: A-A-C♯-C♯-D-Dm-A-A. The C♯ chords would normally be minor in the key of A major, in which key D and Dm are chords IV and IVm.

Interestingly, the Radiohead song ' Creep' uses exactly the same sequence, although this time in the key of G. The entire song is based on just this eight-bar chord sequence: G-G-B-B-C-Cm-G-G. The change from C to Cm is the tragic-sounding IV to IVm chord sequence.

Technique #48: IVm and the lowered-degree chords

The IVm chord can be combined with the three lowered-degree chords from Section 4 – ♭VII, ♭III, and ♭VI – but there is a risk of harmonic instability. In practical terms, harmonic instability means that an audience may not be able to relate to the emotion of the song. These are also unusual-sounding progressions:

IVm and ♭III in G major

I				♭III				IVm				V				
G	/	/	/	B♭	/	/	/	Cm7	/	/	/	D	/	/	/	:‖

IVm and ♭VI in G major

I				♭VI				IVm				V				
G	/	/	/	E♭	/	/	/	Cm7	/	/	/	D	/	/	/	:‖

IVm and ♭VII in G major

I				♭VII				IVm				V				
G	/	/	/	F	/	/	/	Cm7	/	/	/	D	/	/	/	:‖

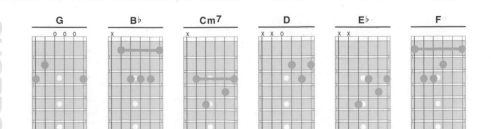

Technique #49: common tones

One of the ways unrelated chords can be made to sit more comfortably with each other is if they have a note in common – a common tone. This is especially effective if the common tone is featured in the melody or played solo by one of the instruments in the recording.

IVm and ♭III do not have a common tone. In C major, IVm contains the notes F A♭ C and ♭III is E♭ G B♭. If chords do not have a common tone as simple majors and minors, one can sometimes be found by turning one or both into seventh chords (see Section 7). To jump ahead a little bit, here is an example: if IVm becomes a minor seventh chord (Fm7 = F A♭ C E♭), there is now a common tone, E♭:

IVm and ♭III in C major

I				♭III				IVm7				V				
C	/	/	/	E♭	/	/	/	Fm7	/	/	/	G	/	/	/	:‖
				e♭				e♭								

Here are the other combinations of IVm with ♭VI and ♭VII. In both there is a common tone, so the use of sevenths creates two common tones:

IVm and ♭VI in C major

I				♭VI				IVm7				V				
C	/	/	/	A♭	/	/	/	Fm7	/	/	/	G	/	/	/	:‖
c				c+e♭				c+e♭								

IVm and ♭VII in C major

I				II^7				IVm				V				
C	/	/	/	B♭7	/	/	/	Fm	/	/	/	G	/	/	/	:‖
				f+a♭				f+a♭								

This sequence shows IVm coming after II and eventually moving to VI:

IVm after II in C major

I		III		II		IVm		VI				V				
C	/	Em7	/	Dm	/	Fm	/	:‖ Am	/	/	/	G	/	/	/	:‖
		d		d+f		f+c		c								

Here is a full song using reverse-polarity chords:

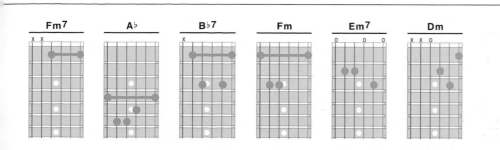

Verse/chorus song in E, with reverse polarity

Intro

V				V		IV		V				V		IV	
B	/	/	/	B	/	A	/	B	/	/	/	B	/	A	/

Verse

IVm				IVm				I				iI			
Am	/	/	/	Am	/	/	/	E	/	/	/	E/G♯	/	/	/

IVm				♭VI	IVm			I				iI			
Am	/	/	/	C	Am	/	/	E	/	/	/	E/G♯	/	/	/

Chorus

VI				VI^				II				V			
C♯m	/	/	/	C♯	/	/	/	F♯m	/	/	/	B	/	/	/

Bridge

II^				III^		IV		I				♭VI			
F♯	/	/	/	G♯	/	A	/	E	/	/	/	C	/	/	/

II^				III^		IV		III			
F♯	/	/	/	G♯	/	A	/	G♯m	/	/	/

Notes:
- The intro uses chords V and IV only.
- The verse starts unexpectedly on IVm and then returns to IVm in bar 5, via a iI chord.
- Bar 6 of the verse uses chord substitution to add interest – ♭VI is the relative major of IVm.
- The chorus moves from VI to VI^ and avoids chord I.
- The bridge brings in II^, III^, ♭VI, and III.

Technique #50: inversions of reverse-polarity chords

The first inversion of these chords is difficult to use, as the bass note is not on the scale of the key. Compare the following first inversion chords with the scale of G major and notice that the lowest notes C♯, D♯, A♭, and G♯ are all foreign to the key:

Chord		iII^	iIII^	iIVm		iVI^	
Scale:	G	A	B	C	D	E	F♯
		E	F♯	G		B	
		C♯	**D♯**	**E♭**		**G♯**	

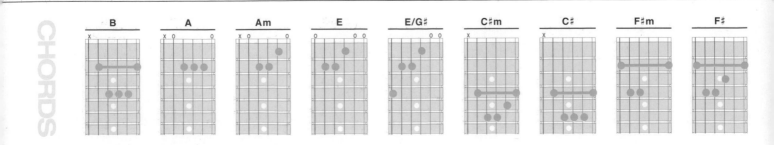

B   A   Am   E   E/G♯   C♯m   C♯   F♯m   F♯

These inversions can fit if they are used in a chromatic bassline (see Section 9).

II^, III^, IVm, and VI^ can all be used in second inversion. Using a second inversion can sometimes make the chord fit in more smoothly because the resulting bass notes are in the major scale and can therefore be part of a descending or ascending bassline. Whatever the key, the rules are:

- The second inversion of II^ has the same root note as chord VI.
- The second inversion of III^ has the same root note as chord VII.
- The second inversion of IVm has the same root note as chord I.
- The second inversion of VI^ has the same root note as chord III.

Reverse-polarity second inversion in G

I				iiII^				IV				V			
G	/	/	/	A/E	/	/	/	C	/	/	/	D	/	/	/

In this example, iiIII^ offers an exotic variation to the expected iV chord (D/F♯) that would usually harmonize such a descending bassline:

Reverse-polarity second inversion in G

I				iiIII^				VI				V			
G	/	/	/	B/F♯	/	/	/	Em	/	/	/	D	/	/	/

In this third example, the bass note is unchanged in bars 1–2 and 3–4. The harmony floats over it:

Reverse-polarity second inversion in G

I				iiIVm				iV				iiIII			
G	/	/	/	Cm/G	/	/	/	D/F♯	/	/	/	Bm/F♯	/	/	/

In this final example, the progression is harmonizing a rising G-B-C-D bassline. The first four bars have the conventional I-III-IV-V sequence, but the next four have the unusual harmony derived from the reverse-polarity VI^. The bassline remains the same:

Reverse-polarity second inversion in G

I				III				IV				V			
G	/	/	/	Bm	/	/	/	C	/	/	/	D	/	/	/
g				b				c				d			

I				iiVI^				IV				V			
G	/	/	/	E/B	/	/	/	C	/	/	/	D	/	/	/
g				b				c				d			

REVERSE POLARITY

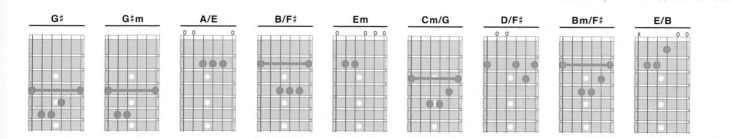

G♯   G♯m   A/E   B/F♯   Em   Cm/G   D/F♯   Bm/F♯   E/B

SECTION 6
SONGS IN MINOR KEYS

So far we've restricted ourselves to writing in a major key, with chords created from the major scale. However, there is such a thing as a minor key, in which chord I is a minor chord. A songwriter might choose to compose in a minor key if a song has a theme of loss or sadness. It is also possible for a major-key song to change to a minor key for one section – like a bridge – to express what the lyrics are saying at that point. Changing from major to minor within a song is covered in Section 8.

WHAT IS THE DIFFERENCE BETWEEN A MAJOR KEY AND A MINOR KEY?

Minor keys are slightly more complicated than major keys. There is only one major-scale pattern from which the harmony of a major key is derived, but there are several variations on the minor scale. Each variation results in alternative chord options. We don't need to concern ourselves with all the scales here; instead, we will go straight to a list of songwriting chords for the minor key.

Every major key has a relative minor which shares the same chords. Compare the chords for C major with that of its relative minor, A minor:

I	II	III	IV	V	VI	VII
C	Dm	Em	F	G	Am	Bdim

I	II	III	IV	V	VI	VII
Am	Bdim	C	Dm	Em	F	G

We have the same set of chords – they are merely in a different order. More precisely, they have changed their harmonic function. It is important to remember the difference between harmonic function and pitch identity: the chord G in the key of C major has the same pitch identity as the chord G in the key of A minor – they are the same chord. But when G is chord V in C major, it has a different harmonic function from chord VII in A minor.

For convenience, we will call this version of A minor 'modal' A minor. There are seven scales called modes which pre-date the modern system of keys. One of them, the Ionian mode, became the major scale. Another, the Aeolian mode, is also known as the 'natural minor' scale. The chords above are derived from this scale, which has the same notes as the major scale (but starts on a different note).

THAT OLD DIMINISHED PROBLEM

Because A minor and C major share the same chords, we still have that problematic B-diminished chord. In the minor key, instead of being chord VII it is chord II – which in some ways is more awkward. So, just as with chord VII in the major key, the diminished chord II of the minor key tends not to be used. Instead, the B is often harmonized with a first inversion of chord VII (G/B) or a second inversion of chord V (Em/B). This is the same procedure as the one used for handling chord VII in a major key when the seventh note of the scale is required in a bassline. When this is done, the harmonic function of the chord has changed.

If a root chord is needed on B, the best bet would be to flatten it and turn it into a major chord (B♭) – like the ♭VII chord, except here it is a ♭II, a semitone (half-step) above the root. Here is a strange chord sequence in E minor that has the ♭II:

Minor verse with ♭II

♭II				I				VII		III		I				
F	/	/	/	‖Em	/	/	/	‖D	/	G	/	‖Em	/	/	/	:‖

Here are the keys of G, D, and A major and their relative minors of E minor, B minor, and F♯ minor, with the 'modal' minor chords:

	I	II	III	IV	V	VI	VII
Major	G	Am	Bm	C	D	Em	F♯dim

	I	II	III	IV	V	VI	VII
Modal minor	Em	F♯dim	G	Am	Bm	C	D

	I	II	III	IV	V	VI	VII
Major	D	Em	F♯m	G	A	Bm	C♯dim

	I	II	III	IV	V	VI	VII
Modal minor	Bm	C♯dim	D	Em	F♯m	G	A

	I	II	III	IV	V	VI	VII
Major	A	Bm	C♯m	D	E	F♯m	G♯dim

	I	II	III	IV	V	VI	VII
Modal minor	F♯m	G♯dim	A	Bm	C♯m	D	E

SONGS IN MINOR KEYS

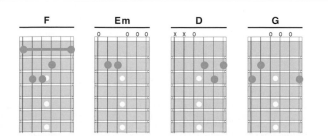
F   Em   D   G

SECTION 6

If the major key and its relative minor share the same chords why don't they sound the same? The answer is harmonic function – it is that, not pitch identity, which shapes how a chord sounds in a musical context. Played on its own, pitch identity will determine the effect of a chord; for example, this is a minor chord and its pitch is A. In a song the context is not always clear, and there can be an ambiguity which is sometimes resolved only by other factors. Consider this, one of the most popular minor-chord sequences:

I-VII-VI in A minor

I				VII				VI				VI		VII		
Am	/	/	/	G	/	/	/	F	/	/	/	F	/	G	/	:‖

Compare it with this in C major:

VI-V-IV in C major

VI				V				IV				IV		V		
Am	/	/	/	G	/	/	/	F	/	/	/	F	/	G	/	:‖

Played as isolated sequences, they sound identical. Thought of in terms of their respective keys, they have a different harmonic function. In a song it may not be clear which is which – although it should be if the overall structure of the song is considered.

Major keys are more common than minor keys and there are relatively few songs that are entirely in a minor key. Many songs which have prominent minor sections turn out to be in a major key, or at least are sufficiently ambiguous that they have a prominent major-key section. An example is The Beatles 'And I Love Her', which has a two-chord intro of C#m and F#m for one bar each with a guitar lick linking the two chords. These chords continue under the verse for six bars and convincingly establish the minor tonality. However, this eight-bar section ends with a bar of A and B majors and the arrival, after so many minor chords, on the happy sound of E major, which coincides suitably with the words "and I love her". These chords are probably better described as VI, II, IV, V, and I in E major than I, IV, VI, VII, and III in C# minor.

The middle eight ("a love like ours...") begins on C#m like the verse and, whilst it goes to B major at first it then alternates between C#m and G#m, again reinforcing the minor tonality of the song. At the end of this section the B major chord returns, this time as a seventh (B7) and once more the E major tonality seems more prominent.

Contrast with this the Nirvana song 'Come As You Are', which begins with a guitar riff that outlines the chords of E minor and D major and is used as both an intro and a 16-bar verse. There then follows an eight-bar chorus of sorts, using the chords E minor and G major. So far, the song has been built on chords I, VIIm, and III in E minor. The only other section of the song, with the "no I don't have a gun" lyric, uses the chords A and C major, but this major-flavored eight bars is not enough to disturb the minor tonality of the song, which is convincingly in E minor throughout.

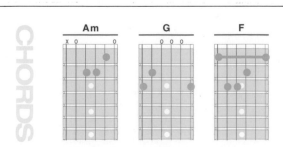

Am   G   F

Technique #51: the 'classical' minor key

There is a variation of the minor scale which does make the minor key distinguishable from its relative major. In fact, in strict theory terms this is the only 'correct' minor key and what we have labelled the modal minor isn't a key at all, because modes and keys are different systems of organizing music. However, for popular songwriting, we can allow the modal minor to be termed a key.

This second type of minor key was used in much Classical and Romantic composition. It requires one simple change: chord V becomes a major chord and the major-seventh note (G♯ in A minor) is available to the singer or soloist, especially over this chord. You can hear the effect of this major chord V in the minor key in songs like The Pretenders' 'Talk Of The Town', Paul McCartney's 'Another Day', and Elvis Costello's 'I Want You'. K T Tunstall's 'Black Horse And The Cherry Tree' has verses entirely based on a two-bar riff alternating between E minor and B major, chords I and V.

Another song which simply alternates between chord I and chord V in a minor key is Carlos Santana's 'Smooth', whose verses alternate between A minor and E major in a two-bar pattern. In this Latin-American flavoured song some interest is added to the chord sequence in the form of bass notes which create 'slash' (/) chords. The note F occurs under the A minor chord as an approach note to the E major chord which also arrives slightly early. In many of the E major bars the bass note B is added as an approach note returning to the A minor chord. Leaving out the syncopation, the sequence appears as follows: Am-Am/F-E-E/B.

The verses of the Amy Winehouse song 'You Know I'm No Good' from her *Back To Black* album are based on a three chord sequence of Dm, Gm, and A – chords I, IV, and V. The Dm chord returns at the end to complete a repeatable four-bar section. This chord sequence, with its 'classical' chord V, helps to place the song solidly in a minor key.

Here are the 'classical' minor chords (ignoring that problematic II) for A minor and E minor:

I	III	IV	**V**	VI	VII
Am	C	Dm	**E**	F	G

I	III	IV	**V**	VI	VII
Em	G	Am	**B**	C	D

In this book, chord V in a minor key is assumed to be a major chord in keeping with the classical minor key. The modal minor chord V will be shown with an 'm' after it to indicate reverse polarity, like IVm in the major key. VII is always assumed to be a major chord a tone (whole-step) below the keynote.

Every time a chord sequence uses the change V-I (E-Am or B-Em), the classical minor key's identity is underlined. There is no confusion with the relative major, as there can be with the chord change Em-Am or Bm-Em, where Vm-I in the minor can be confused with III-VI in the relative major. It is possible to use both forms of chord V in the same minor-key song, but better if they appear in separate sections.

There is one further harmonic option for the songwriter, and that is to reverse the polarity of chord IV from minor to major:

I	III	IV^	V	(Vm)	VI	VII
Am	C	**D**	E	(Em)	F	G

I	III	IV^	V	(Vm)	VI	VII
Em	G	**A**	B	(Bm)	C	D

The chord change Am to D (I-IV^ in a minor key) is often heard in Latin music as well as rock, being a favourite chord change for Santana and Pink Floyd (it is heavily featured on *Dark Side Of The Moon*). There is no risk of confusion with the relative major, because this chord change will not occur in that key (in C major, chord II is Dm, not D), but there is possible harmonic ambiguity with the major key one tone below the minor. Compare these:

I	III	IV^	V	(Vm)	VI	VII
Am	C	**D**	E	(Em)	F	G

I	II	III	IV	V	VI	♭VII
G	**Am**	Bm	C	**D**	Em	F

I-IV^ in this version of A minor is the same as II-V in G major. The ambiguity can be minimised by using the major form of chord V (here, E) as this chord is minor (Em) in the major key.

If all these options for the modal and classical versions of the minor key are combined, we get this composite minor:

SONGWRITER'S COMPOSITE MINOR KEY

I	III	IV	(IV^)	V	(Vm)	VI	VII
Am	C	Dm	(D)	E	(Em)	F	G

This gives you eight chords to choose from for a minor-key song – and don't forget that all eight chords can be played in first and second inversions (8 x 3 = 24). Now let's see how these eight chords work in practice.

Technique #52: the minor three-chord trick

As we saw in Section 1, a three-chord trick song uses only I, IV, and V. Its minor-key equivalent could use any of these combinations in A minor:

Minor three-chord trick

I				IV				V				I			
Am	/	/	/	Dm	/	/	/	E	/	/	/	Am	/	/	/

I				IV				Vm				I			
Am	/	/	/	Dm	/	/	/	Em	/	/	/	Am	/	/	/

I				IV^				V				I			
Am	/	/	/	D	/	/	/	E	/	/	/	Am	/	/	/

I				IV^				Vm				I			
Am	/	/	/	D	/	/	/	Em	/	/	/	Am	/	/	/

Technique #53: the secondary minor three-chord trick

A secondary minor three-chord trick might use any of the following sequences. In some cases, these three chords also occur in a major key, so there is a chance of harmonic ambiguity (additional chord types are given as a means to reduce this). The only way to substantially differentiate the minor from its relative major is to bring in V as a major chord. The sequences which include V are underlined, because they have the strongest minor identity.

I	III	IV	
Am	C	Dm	(use Cmaj7 to reduce F major)

I	III	IV^	
Am	C	D	(use C7 to reduce G major)

I	III	Vm	
Am	C	Em	(use Csus4 to reduce G major)

I	III	V	
Am	C	E	

I	III	VI	
Am	C	F	(use Cmaj7 to reduce F major)

I	IV	VI	
Am	Dm	F	(use Am9 or Dm6 to reduce F major)

SONGS IN MINOR KEYS

SECTION 6

I	IV^	VI
Am	D	F

I	IV	VII
Am	Dm	G

I	IV^	VII
Am	D	G

(use G7 to reduce strong G major feel)

I	VI	Vm
Am	F	Em

I	VI	V
Am	F	E

I	Vm	VII
Am	Em	G

I	V	VII
Am	E	G

Technique #54 : the four-chord minor song

To write a four-chord minor song, add one of chords III, VI, and VII to I, IV (or IV^), and V (or Vm). A four-chord song in a minor key can omit chord V, but this may weaken the impression of the minor key.

   The principle of keeping your powder dry now applies in reverse. It's the major chords that are held in reserve. For the strongest minor feel, use minor forms of I, IV, and V (Am, Dm, and Em) and then choose one of III, VI, or VII (C, F, or G), but hold it back until a point in the song where you want the music to lift away from the sad effect of the minor chords. That way, the major chord acts as a ray of sunshine cutting through the gloom. The usual rules of chord substitution apply – the chords remain paired as before, and each minor chord has its relative major.

Eight-bar verse or chorus in A minor

I				IV				Vm				IV			
Am	/	/	/	Dm	/	/	/	Em	/	/	/	Dm	/	/	/

I				VI				Vm				V			
Am	/	/	/	F	/	/	/	Em	/	/	/	E	/	/	/

Am   Dm   Em   F   E

Bars 1–4 could have been repeated to make an eight-bar verse, but chord VI acts as a substitute for chord IV in bar 6, adding interest. The change from Em to E in bars 7–8 is a typical minor-key trick. It can be heightened if the E is turned into a first inversion (E/G♯), so that when chord V changes from minor to major the bass goes up two tones (whole-steps). The bass note then rises to an A for the next chord I. If this has already happened several times in the song because this is a chorus, then the A could be treated as a first-inversion F (F/A) or even a second-inversion Dm (Dm/A) to create surprise (the 'false rise', Technique #21) in a bridge:

Chorus

I				VI				Vm				iV			
Am	/	/	/	F	/	/	/	Em	/	/	/	E/G♯	/	/	/

Bridge (a)

iVI				VII				VI				VI			
F/A	/	/	/	G	/	/	/	F	/	/	/	F	/	/	/

Bridge (b)

iiIV				VI				III				VII			
Dm/A	/	/	/	F	/	/	/	C	/	/	/	G	/	/	/

Although shown here as alternatives, both could be used in a song that has two bridges.

The intro of Dido's 'Thank You' from the *No Angel* album begins on a G♯m chord, but in the second half of the bar the bass note (from the bass guitar) moves to the note E. G♯m/E is the same as a chord of E major 7, and this adds that uniquely dreamy major-seventh quality to the song's opening. However, the presence of this major chord does not disturb the essential minor tonality of the song.

The verses are based on chords I, VI, VII, and III. Here is the four-bar sequence, one chord per bar except for the last, which has two: G♯m-E-F♯-B-F♯/A♯. Nevertheless, the melody and a strong placing of G♯m at the beginning of the sequence emphasise the minor tonality of this section. Notice the clever use of the F♯ major chord in first inversion to provide a link in the bass between B and G♯m.

Technique #55: minor-key blues

The 12-bar structure can be used for a minor-key blues. In this example, the change from Vm to V is introduced in bar 10 not only to achieve harmonic variety but also to change the rate of chord movement:

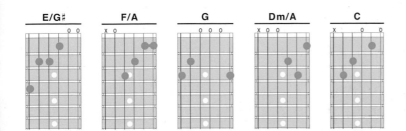

SONGS IN MINOR KEYS

12-bar in A minor

I	I	I	I
Am / / /	Am / / /	Am / / /	Am / / /

IV	IV	I	I
Dm / / /	Dm / / /	Am / / /	Am / / /

Vm	Vm V	I	I V
Em / / /	Em / E /	Am / / /	Am / E / :||

12-bar variation in E minor

I	IV	I	I
Em / / /	Am / / /	Em / / /	Em / / /

IV	IV	I	I
Am / / /	Am / / /	Em / / /	Em / / /

V	IV	I III	IV V
B / / /	Am / / /	Em / G /	Am / B / :||

Remember that a 12-bar structure can be part of a song that is not in itself a pure 12-bar blues.

12-bar variation in B minor

I	I	I	I
Bm / / /	Bm / / /	Bm / / /	Bm / / /

IV	IV	I	I
Em / / /	Em / / /	Bm / / /	Bm / / /

Vm	VI IV	VII IV	III bII
F#m / / /	G / Em /	A / Em /	D / C / :||

In this 12-bar, the last three bars have a different rate of chord change and bring in the other chords of B minor to add more interest. Notice the contrast between the relatively static feel of the first eight bars and the activity in the last four, and in bar 12 the use of the major chord on the lowered (flattened) second of the scale (C instead of C♯), the minor-key equivalent of the ♭VII chord. To make this minor progression less gloomy change the minor chords into minor sevenths.

CHORDS

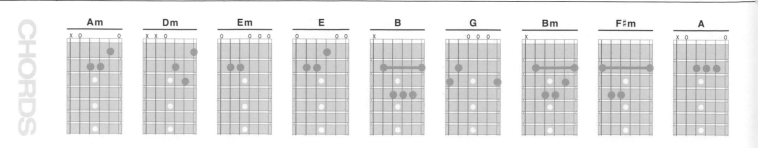

Am   Dm   Em   E   B   G   Bm   F♯m   A

Technique #56: the 16-bar minor section

In this example the harmony is static, with the change from I to V in the first, second and fourth lines of the verse. Bars 9–12 provide contrast by bringing in four chords not used in the other three lines before bars 13–16 return to the original sequence. But there is a twist in the tail, which is that after so many Em (Vm) chords the very last one is an E (V).

16-bar verse in A minor

I		Vm		I				I		Vm		I				
Am	/	Em	/	Am	/	/	/	Am	/	Em	/	Am	/	/	/	:‖

III				IV				VII				VI				
C	/	/	/	Dm	/	/	/	G	/	/	/	F	/	/	/

I		Vm		I				I		V		I				
Am	/	Em	/	Am	/	/	/	Am	/	E	/	Am	/	/	/

Here is a through-composed verse in A minor. Unlike the previous example, there are no sections that repeat within it.

16-bar verse in A minor, through-composed

I				III				IV				VI				
Am	/	/	/	C	/	/	/	Dm	/	/	/	F	/	/	/

V				V				IV				VII				
E	/	/	/	E	/	/	/	Dm	/	/	/	G	/	/	/

VI				iIII				IV				iI				
F	/	/	/	C/E	/	/	/	Dm	/	/	/	Am/C	/	/	/

iVII		Vm		VII		Vm		I				V				
G/B	/	Em	/	G	/	Em	/	Am	/	/	/	E	/	/	/

SONGS IN MINOR KEYS

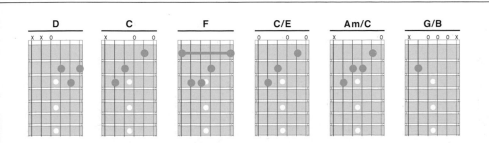

Notes:

• The climbing bassline A-C-D-F in the first line is contrasted with a descending one, F-E-D-C (and then B), in the third line.

• The descending bassline in line three is created with inversions.

• The rate of chord change encompasses one chord to two bars, one chord to one bar and two chords to a bar.

• Notice how after bar 1 the root-position chord I is withheld until bar 15, so the sense of 'reaching home' is stronger.

• Both versions of chord V (major and minor) are used.

Bruce Springsteen's 'Cover Me' is a great example of a minor-key blues in the rock idiom. The intro of the song is based on one repeated bar of music which begins with a Bm chord but then moves swiftly to D and A majors. In other words it is using chords I, III, and VII in B minor to create a three-chord turnaround which, unusually, happens within the space of one bar. In spite of the presence of two major chords, the tonality of this intro is unmistakably minor.

When the vocals begin, this pattern is played four times, giving us the four bars of chord I that we expect in a 12-bar sequence. We then have two bars of E minor, and two more bars of the B minor turnaround. These are chord IV and chord I as we would expect in the middle four bars of the 12-bar. The final four bars take a less predictable route back to B minor, with a bar of G (chord VI) followed by a bar of A major (chord VII), ending with another two bars of the B minor turnaround.

Common minor-key progressions

Here is a selection of common minor-key progressions. The majority of these are descending sequences, because there's something about descending chords which chimes with the sadness evoked by minor-key songs. Notice how most move from chord I down to chord V, and that chords IV and V occur in both major and minor forms.

These progressions can be combined with each other or repeated as turnarounds. The bassline can move stepwise by the use of inversions until eventually it is moving by semitones (half-steps). The progressions are shown in A minor, D minor, and E minor, the three most popular minor keys on guitar. Often, when a guitarist-songwriter wants to write in another minor key, a capo is used so these chord shapes are available. For example, if you wanted the first of the A minor progressions in the key of C minor, put a capo at the third fret and play the shapes written; if you wanted the first of the D minor progressions in the key of F minor put a capo at the third fret and play the shapes written; if you wanted the first of the E minor progressions in the key of G minor put a capo at the third fret and play the shapes written. Good examples of this type of minor progression would be The Lovin' Spoonful's 'Summer In The City', Fleet Foxes' 'Mykonos', or the verse of Neil Young's 'Like A Hurricane'.

Am	G	F	E	Em	Em/G	Dm/F	D/F#	E/G#

Chord progressions in A minor

I				VII				VI				VII			
Am	/	/	/	G	/	/	/	F	/	/	/	G	/	/	/

I				VII				VI				V			
Am	/	/	/	G	/	/	/	F	/	/	/	E	/	/	/

I				VII				VI				Vm			
Am	/	/	/	G	/	/	/	F	/	/	/	Em	/	/	/

I				iVm				VI				Vm			
Am	/	/	/	Em/G	/	/	/	F	/	/	/	Em	/	/	/

I				iVm				iIV				Vm			
Am	/	/	/	Em/G	/	/	/	Dm/F	/	/	/	Em	/	/	/

I				VII				iIV^				V			
Am	/	/	/	G	/	/	/	D/F♯	/	/	/	E	/	/	/

I				VII				iIV^				Vm			
Am	/	/	/	G	/	/	/	D/F♯	/	/	/	Em	/	/	/

I				VII				iIV^				IV			
Am	/	/	/	G	/	/	/	D/F♯	/	/	/	F	/	/	/

I				VII				iIV^				VI		V	
Am	/	/	/	G	/	/	/	D/F♯	/	/	/	F	/	E	/

I				iV				VII				iIV^			
Am	/	/	/	E/G♯	/	/	/	G	/	/	/	D/F♯	/	/	/

I				iV				VII				iIV^			
Am	/	/	/	E/G♯	/	/	/	G	/	/	/	D/F♯	/	/	/

VI				V			
F	/	/	/	E	/	/	/

I				iiIII				iIV^				iIV		V	
Am	/	/	/	C/G	/	/	/	D/F♯	/	/	/	Dm/F	/	E	/

C/G

SONGS IN MINOR KEYS

Chord progressions in D minor

I				VII				VI				VII			
Dm	/	/	/	C	/	/	/	B♭	/	/	/	C	/	/	/

I				VII				VI				V			
Dm	/	/	/	C	/	/	/	B♭	/	/	/	A	/	/	/

I				VII				VI				Vm			
Dm	/	/	/	C	/	/	/	B♭	/	/	/	Am	/	/	/

I				iVm				VI				Vm			
Dm	/	/	/	Am/C	/	/	/	B♭	/	/	/	Am	/	/	/

I				iVm				iIV				Vm			
Dm	/	/	/	Am/C	/	/	/	Gm/B♭	/	/	/	Am	/	/	/

I				VII				iIV^				V			
Dm	/	/	/	C	/	/	/	G/B	/	/	/	A	/	/	/

I				VII				iIV^				Vm			
Dm	/	/	/	C	/	/	/	G/B	/	/	/	Am	/	/	/

I				VII				iIV^				IV			
Dm	/	/	/	C	/	/	/	G/B	/	/	/	Gm	/	/	/

I				VII				iIV^				VI		V	
Dm	/	/	/	C	/	/	/	G/B	/	/	/	B♭	/	A	/

I				iV				VII				iIV^			
Dm	/	/	/	A/C♯	/	/	/	C	/	/	/	G/B	/	/	/

I				iV				VII				iIV^			
Dm	/	/	/	A/C♯	/	/	/	C	/	/	/	G/B	/	/	/

VI				V			
Bb	/	/	/	A	/	/	/

I				iiIII				iIV^				iIV		V	
Dm	/	/	/	F/C	/	/	/	G/B	/	/	/	Gm/Bb	/	A	/

CHORDS

Dm   C   B♭   Am/C   Gm/B♭   G/B   Gm   A/C♯   F/C

Chord progressions in E minor

I	VII	VI	VII
Em / / /	D / / /	C / / /	D / / /

I	VII	VI	V
Em / / /	D / / /	C / / /	B / / /

I	VII	VI	Vm
Em / / /	D / / /	C / / /	Bm / / /

I	iVm	VI	Vm
Em / / /	Bm/D / / /	C / / /	Bm / / /

I	iVm	iiIV	Vm
Em / / /	Bm/D / / /	Am/E / / /	Bm / / /

I	VII	iIV^	V
Em / / /	D / / /	A/C♯ / / /	B / / /

I	VII	iIV^	Vm
Em / / /	D / / /	A/C♯ / / /	Bm / / /

I	VII	iIV^	IV
Em / / /	D / / /	A/C♯ / / /	Am / / /

I	VII	iIV^	VI	V
Em / / /	D / / /	A/C♯ / / /	C /	B /

I	iV	VII	iIV^
Em / / /	B/D♯ / / /	D / / /	A/C♯ / / /

I	iV	VII	iIV^
Em / / /	B/D♯ / / /	D / / /	A/C♯ / / /

VI	V
C / / /	B / / /

I	iiIII	iIV^	iIV	V
Em / / /	G/D / / /	A/C♯ / / /	Am/C /	B /

Em   D   B   Bm/D   Am/E   Bm   B/D♯   G/D   Am/C

SECTION 6

Full minor song

Here's a complete song that uses the eight chords of the minor key.

Verse/chorus song in E minor

Intro

VI		VI		V		V	
C / / /		C / / /		B / / /		B / / /	

B / / /			

Verse

IV		IV		iI		iI	
Am / / /		Am / / /		Em/G / / /		Em/G / / /	

VI		VI		iI		VII	
C / / /		C / / /		Em/G / / /		D / / /	

IV		IV		iIII	VI	VII	
Am / / /		Am / / /		G/B /	C /	D / / /	

Chorus

I		VI		VII		V	
Em / / /		C / / /		D / / /		B / / /	:‖

Bridge

Vm		Vm	IV	III		III	VII
Bm / / /		Bm /	Am /	G / / /		G /	D /

Vm		Vm	IV	III		III	IV
Bm / / /		Bm /	Am /	G / / /		G /	Am /

Notes:

- The five-bar intro gives a suspenseful build-up to the verse, withholding chord I.
- Chord I appears in the verse only as a first inversion (Em/G).
- Chords Vm and V are avoided in the verse.
- The VII-I chord change is used to move into the chorus turnaround.
- The first appearance of Vm is in the bridge.
- In the bridge, Am (IV) is less harmonically ambiguous than A (IV^) would be, because Bm-A-G would sound more like a progression in D major or B minor.

C   B   Am   Em/G   D   Bm   G   Em

One of the most famous songs in a minor key is The Animals' 1960s hit 'House Of The Rising Sun'. In the key of A minor it uses chords I, III, IV^, VI, and V to create a dramatic steadily rising sequence full of sadness and tragedy. Notice that the tonic chord is the only minor chord in the sequence because of the reversed polarity of chord IV, but the sequence is still unmistakably minor. Although essentially a 16-bar sequence, a clever arrangement sees the eight-bar intro played between the verses. Here is the intro: Am-C-D-F-Am-E-Am-E. A full 16-bar verse would be as follows, the last eight bars being the same as the intro: Am-C-D-F-Am-C-E-E-Am-C-D-F-Am-E-Am-E. However, at bar 15 the Am chord is treated as the first bar of the eight-bar introduction that is played between the verses. In fact we never hear the full 16-bar verse; the early arrival of the intro continually truncates the verse to 14 bars.

'Stairway To Heaven' by Led Zeppelin is also in A minor and is widely considered to be one of the greatest rock songs of all time. Its four-bar introduction and verse sequence uses inverted chords to create a chromatic bassline (moving in semitones), with chord IV as a reverse polarity D major (in first inversion) instead of D minor. Part of the song's musical journey is to a more archaic version of A minor in which G♯ and F♯ (and chords in which they occur) are no longer heard.

Technique #57: the minor turnaround

Many of the progressions shown above can be played as turnarounds. The primary turnarounds in a minor key are I-III-IV-V, I-VI-IV-V, and I-VII-IV-V, along with their 'modal' equivalents in which V is a minor chord. Here they are in the key of E minor:

Primary turnarounds in E minor

I	III	IV	V
Em / / /	G / / /	Am / / /	B / / / :‖

| I | VI | IV | V |
| Em / / / | C / / / | Am / / / | B / / / :‖ |

| I | VII | IV | V |
| Em / / / | D / / / | Am / / / | B / / / :‖ |

Modal minor

I	III	IV	Vm
Em / / /	G / / /	Am / / /	Bm / / / :‖

| I | VI | IV | Vm |
| Em / / / | C / / / | Am / / / | Bm / / / :‖ |

| I | VII | IV | Vm |
| Em / / / | D / / / | Am / / / | Bm / / / :‖ |

SONGS IN MINOR KEYS

SECTION 6

Note that all three modal-minor turnarounds also suggest the key of G major. These turnarounds can be subjected to all the techniques described in Section 2.

The Amy Winehouse song 'Back To Black' is unusual. Firstly, it uses two different minor turnarounds. Secondly, there is no variation in the harmonic rhythm; each chord lasts for two bars. The intro, verses, and choruses are based on Dm, Gm, B♭, and A. Notice that on this occasion chord IV is in its correct minor polarity and chord five, being major, comes from the 'correct' classical rather than natural minor scale. The only other chord sequence in the song appears in the slower tempo section to accompany the lyric "black ...". Once again we have chords I, IV, and V, but the chord of F major (chord III) replaces the earlier B♭ chord.

Another song that uses minor turnarounds is Agnes's 'Release Me'. This song has its ambiguous moments, as it begins with the chorus, which starts with a B♭ major chord. However, there is no mistaking the overall minor tonality of the song; the chorus turnaround is B♭-Dm-C-Gm; these are chords VI, I, VII, and IV in D minor. The verses then confirm the minor tonality by beginning in D minor but with the polarity of chord IV inverted: Dm-B♭-G-G.

The only other chord sequence in the song is the four-bar link between the verse and chorus; two bars of F major and two bars of A major. A major is chord V to D minor's chord I, and thus points very strongly towards D minor, so our ears expect D minor to be the first chord of the chorus. Cleverly, the songwriter has added interest to the chord sequence by reversing the order of the first two chords of the turnaround.

SECTION 7
WORKING WITH CHORD TYPES

So far, The Songwriting Sourcebook has focused on simple major and minor chords (triads). Experienced guitarists and keyboard players know that any major or minor chord can be turned into sus2, sus4, sixth, seventh, 9th, 11th, 13th, and other chord types. (Guitarists can find the shapes for these in a chord dictionary such as my Chord Master).

The exact effect of these can only be properly gauged in a song when all other musical factors are taken into account, including the lyric and the manner and style of performance and recording. So in the pages that follow, the suggested effect can be no more than a generalization subject to influence from location within an actual song. These do not have any direct relevance to the rules that govern the hierarchy of chords a songwriter draws on, as set out in the previous six sections, but let's take a look at some of the common chord types and see what a songwriter can do with them.

Technique #58: the dominant 7

After straight majors and minors, the most common chord type is the dominant 7, written A7, D7, E7, etc. This type of seventh chord is a major chord with one note added; the added note is a tone (whole-step) below the root note. In traditional harmony there is only one of these chords in a key and it is on the fifth note (the dominant) of the major or minor scale – thus the name dominant 7. However, because some popular music is based on blues harmony the dominant 7 chord can also appear built on chords I and IV.

The main uses of the dominant 7 are:

• as a decoration of chord V to reinforce the identity of the key
• to strengthen V-I changes where it is desired that these emphasise the home key (as at the end of a song)
• to add a harder edge to a chord sequence or song section

SECTION 7

- to make the progression sound less settled
- to enhance a song intended to be in a blues or rock style
- to modulate to a new key by changing the harmonic function of a chord
- to strengthen a dominant crescendo.

As with all the chords in this section, the dominant 7 can be used to add interest if the music stays on a single chord for a number of bars. Going to the dominant 7 form of the chord for the final bar (or bars) suggests activity. This works especially well if the next chord is IV or II (C or Am in G), because in both instances the seventh will fall a semitone to a note in the succeeding chord.

Dominant 7 addition (a)

I				I				I				I			
G	/	/	/	G	/	/	/	G	/	/	/	G7	/	/	/

Dominant 7 addition (b)

I				I				IV				I			
G	/	/	/	G7	/	/	/	C	/	/	/	G	/	/	/

In this example, the C7 and D7 create a tough contrast with the minor chords that have been centre-stage in the bridge to that point; the D7 would probably lead to chord I in the next section:

Bridge of a song in G

III				VI				III				III			
Bm	/	/	/	Em	/	/	/	Bm	/	/	/	Bm	/	/	/

VI				VI				IV				V			
G	/	/	/	Em	/	/	/	C7	/	/	/	D7	/	/	/

These examples demonstrate how a sequence of dominant 7s makes for a tougher-sounding progression than if these chords were straightforward G, C, and D:

Dominant 7 intro or link in G

V				IV				I		IV		I		IV		
D7	/	/	/	C7	/	/	/	G7	/	C7	/	G7	/	C7	/	:||

Verse of a song in G

I				IV				V				V			
G7	/	/	/	C7	/	/	/	D7	/	/	/	C7	/	/	/

G   G7   C   Bm   Em   C7   D7

I				IV				V				V		IV	
G7	/	/	/	C7	/	/	/	D7	/	/	/	D7	/	C7	/

The classic use of the dominant 7 in rock is in a 12-bar:

12-bar in E

I				IV				I				I			
E	/	/	/	A	/	/	/	E	/	/	/	E7	/	/	/

IV				IV				I				I			
A	/	/	/	A7	/	/	/	E	/	/	/	E7	/	/	/

V				IV				I		I		V			
B7	/	/	/	A7	/	/	/	E	/	E7	/	B7	/	/	/ :||

Dominant 7 chords can also be linked into sequences that create harmonic ambiguity. This sequence never really settles:

Chained dominant 7s

V				I [V]				I [V]				I [V]			
A7	/	/	/	D7	/	/	/	G7	/	/	/	C7	/	/	/

I [V]				I [V]				I [V]				I [V]			
F7	/	/	/	B♭7	/	/	/	E♭7	/	/	/	A♭7	/	/	/

We took a look at The Beatles' 'Hey Jude' in Section 1 and found an eight-bar section using chords I, IV, and V in F major. A closer examination reveals that the the third chord in the sequence is in fact a dominant seventh, C7. Sticking to chords I, IV, and V, and then using V as a dominant seventh chord explains the bluesy, gospel quality of the song. The exact chord sequence should be written as follows: F-C-C7-F-B♭-F-C-F.

Technique # 59: the major 7

There is a second type of seventh chord that can be made from a major chord. In this one, the added note is a semitone (half-step) below the root note. It is written Amaj7, Dmaj7, Emaj7, etc. In traditional harmony, the major 7 occurs on chords I and IV in the major key. The emotive nature of the major 7 lends itself to medium-to-slow tempos and more reflective songs.

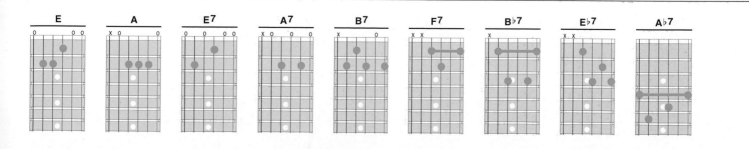

The main uses of the major 7 are:

- as chord I, to reinforce the home major key.
- to strengthen V-I changes where it is desired that these emphasise the home key.
- to soften a chord sequence or song section.
- to make a progression sound dreamier and more romantic.
- to enhance a song intended to be in a ballad style.
- to emphasise a new key once it has been reached.
- to provide a soft final chord.

Sometimes the major seventh can inject a mournful feeling that might be usually done by a minor chord if minor chords are being withheld from a particular song section. Coldplay's 'Yellow' is an example of this, there being a major seventh form of IV in the verse along with I and V. An unexpected major seventh can also make an arresting hook. The intro of Elton John's 'Bennie & The Jets' starts with a Gmaj7 which is chord I, which changes to a major seventh on the bVII of G, Fmaj7.

Many a gentle ballad has sailed tearfully into the sunset or lazed in the sunshine with this famous change between chord I and IV in their major 7 forms:

Major 7 verse of a song in G

I				IV				I				IV			
Gmaj7 /	/	/		Cmaj7 /	/	/		Gmaj7 /	/	/		Cmaj7 /	/	/	:‖

The major 7 chord makes a natural transition to its relative minor. Compare these two chord sequences:

Verse (a)

I		iV		VI				IV		iI		II			
G	/	D/F♯	/	Em	/	/	/	C	/	G/B	/	Am	/	/	/	:‖

Verse (b) with major 7s

I		I		VI				IV		IV		II			
G	/	Gmaj7	/	Em	/	/	/	C	/	Cmaj7	/	Am	/	/	/	:‖

In Verse (a), inversions put a passing note in the bass. In Verse (b), this passing note is transferred to the top of the chord and all the chords are in root position. Both are effective.

Here's another time-honoured way of using a major 7 to add interest to a basic change. The underlying movement is I-IV. By using the 7ths like this, it is as if two chords have been made to sound like four:

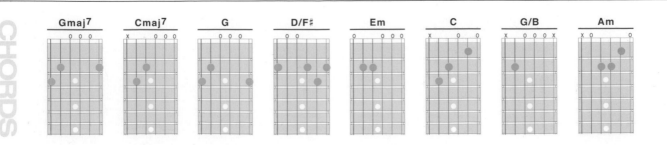

Gmaj7 Cmaj7 G D/F♯ Em C G/B Am

Verse with major 7s

I				I				IV				IV			
G	/	/	/	Gmaj7 /		/	/	C	/	/	/	Cmaj7 /		/	/ :‖

By using the major 7 and the dominant 7 one after the other, a sense of movement is created within the same chord. The root stays the same, but a single note changes within the chord, descending in semitone steps. If chord I is the first chord initiating this type of progression the likeliest chord to follow is chord IV, but either chord II or VI would work – they both have the note which is next in the semitone descent:

Verse with major 7

I				I				I				IV			
G	/	/	/	Gmaj7 /		/	/	G7	/	/	/	C	/	/	/ :‖
g				f♯				f				e			

And there's no reason why the dominant 7 chord shouldn't return to the major 7, like this:

Verse with major 7

I				I				I				I			
G	/	/	/	Gmaj7 /		/	/	G7	/	/	/	Gmaj7 /		/	/ :‖
g				f♯				f				f♯			

If the same descending idea is applied to chord IV, this progression results:

Verse with major 7

I				I				I				IV			
G	/	/	/	Gmaj7 /		/	/	G7	/	/	/	C	/	/	/
g				f♯				f				e			

IV				IV				IV				II		V	
C	/	/	/	Cmaj7 /		/	/	C7	/	/	/	Am	/	D7	/ :‖
c				b				b♭				a			

If the two bars on C are not interesting enough, Em could be substituted in bar 4. Having two chords in bar 8 creates interest by altering the rate of chord change. If D7 took the place of Am, it would cancel the hint from the C7 that the music was about to change key.

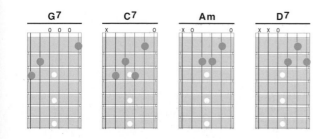

IS IT POSSIBLE TO HAVE ANY OTHER MAJOR 7 CHORDS IN A MAJOR KEY?

If a major 7 is used for chord V, the sense of key is weakened. This is because the extra note in this chord will always imply the scale of the major key a fifth above the one you are in (the next step up on the key table; see the Appendix). For example, a Dmaj7 chord in the key of G implies D major. Bars 1–4 of the next example show how this sounds, with bars 5–8 providing the fully 'in key' version where D7 prevents any ambiguity:

Verse with major 7

I				IV				V				IV			
G	/	/	/	Cmaj7 /		/	/	Dmaj7	/	/	/	Cmaj7 /		/	/

I				IV				V				IV			
G	/	/	/	Cmaj7 /		/	/	D7	/	/	/	Cmaj7 /		/	/

What about ♭III, ♭VI, and ♭VII? All three could be turned into major 7s, and in no case will the added note violate the scale of the key you are in. However, they will generate more harmonic ambiguity by suggesting keys lower on the table:

♭VII as major 7 in C

I				VI				III				♭VII			
C	/	/	/	Am	/	/	/	Em	/	/	/	B♭maj7 /		/	/ :‖

Here is the effect of a chain of major 7 chords:

Chained major 7s

I				IV				I				IV			
Amaj7 /		/	/	Dmaj7 /		/	/	Gmaj7	/	/	/	Cmaj7 /		/	/

I				IV				I				IV			
Fmaj7 /		/	/	B♭maj7 /		/	/	E♭maj7	/	/	/	A♭maj7 /		/	/

We discussed the brief use of a major seventh chord, created by altering a bass note, in the Dido song 'Thank You' in Section 6. Major 7 chords are not common in rock and pop music, but nevertheless there are some very distinct occasions when they can be heard.

The middle section of the Oasis song 'She's Electric' (with the lyric "and I want you to know...") is built on a repeated eight-bar section which begins with a simple alternation of A major and A major 7: A-Amaj7-A-Amaj7-A-C♯m-E-E. The C♯m chord is very similar to Amaj7, but just different enough to add interest at this point. The song is in E major, but the long period of time on A, together with the Amaj7 chords, seems to suggest a key change to A major. This means some

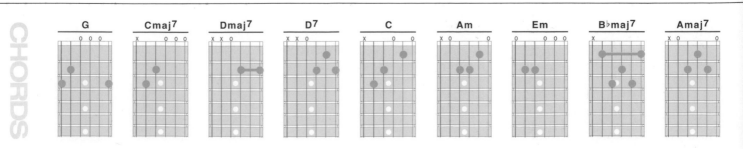

cleverness is required to negotiate the way smoothly back to the home key. First we have four bars of E, which is chord I, but in this context seems to sound more like chord V. These bars are followed by two bars of F#m and two bars of B (chords II and V in E major), and the modulation back to the home key is achieved as the B chord points unequivocally back towards E major.

Major sevenths are frequently encountered as passing chords between I and I7. One example of this is The Beatles' 'Something', with verses that begin on C major, and then progress to Cmaj7, C7 and subsequently to F major. A similar sequence can be heard in the Burt Bacharach song 'Raindrops Keep Falling On My Head', but this time in the key of Gb. A less predictable use of this descending sequence can be heard in S Club 7's 'Reach', which begins in G, progresses through Gmaj7 and G7, but then surprisingly arrives on E major.

Technique #60: the minor 7

The minor chord can also be turned into a seventh. As with the major, there are two types. The first, and by far the most common, minor 7 chord adds the note a tone (whole-step) below the root. In a major key the three minor chords (II, III, and VI) all take this form. It is written Am7, Bm7, Em7, etc. The main uses of this minor 7 are:

• to lighten the emotion of chords II, III, and VI by diluting their minor quality
• to make a progression sound mildly 'jazzy', as in Thin Lizzy's 'The Boys Are Back In Town' and 'Dancing In The Moonlight'
• to form a descending sequence
• to lighten the sound of a song in a minor key.

Because of their jazzy flavour, these minor 7s are most common in the work of professional songwriters or sophisticated jazz-inclined artists. In the 1960s Burt Bacharach and Hal David wrote many jazz-influenced songs for artists such as Aretha Franklin and Dionne Warwick.

The intro and verses of Aretha Franklin's 'I Say a Little Prayer' begin on a bar of F#m7, and progress to two bars of Bm7. These minor 7 chords, in addition to sounding jazzy, lighten the sound of the plain minor chord and contribute to the wistful nature of the song. Similarly, the Bacharach/David song 'Walk On By', this time sung by Dionne Warwick, uses Bbm7 and Eb for verses, adding Abm7 for choruses.

Examples of minor 7 chords in more recent soul music can also be found. Christina Aguilera's 'Underappreciated' is based mostly on a two-chord groove alternating between F#m7 and B7. These two chords might appear to be chord II7 and chord V7 in E, but there is no resolution to the tonic E chord in this song. Instead, at the end of the verse, there comes an interesting four-bar sequence of chords on a chromatic bassline: F#m/A for two bars, then Ab7 and G7. The G7 in this context behaves like a dominant chord to F# minor, and when the chorus begins again with the F#m7 and B7 groove there is no doubt that F# minor is the key.

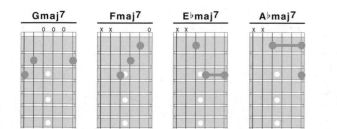

WORKING WITH CHORD TYPES

WORKING WITH CHORD TYPES

The second, rarer minor 7 is the minor/major 7. Although the name appears complex, this is simply a minor chord with the note added which is a semitone (half-step) below the root – the major seventh. It is written Am/maj7, Bm/maj7, Em/maj7, etc.

The main uses of the min/maj7 are:

- to form a descending note sequence with the ordinary minor 7
- to form part of a similar chromatic sequence in which a note is moving in semitones
- to contribute to an unsettling, tense, eerie or slightly sinister feeling.

Here is the earlier example of a bridge in G with the minor chords now minor 7s and the C7 replaced by Am7. The minor 7s give it a 'lighter' feel:

Bridge in G with minor 7s

III				VI				III				III			
Bm7	/	/	/	Em7	/	/	/	Bm7	/	/	/	Bm7	/	/	/

I				VI				IV				V			
G	/	/	/	Em7	/	/	/	C7	/	/	/	D7	/	/	/

Minor 7s can 'lighten' one of two turnarounds in a song if both turnarounds have minor chords. The stronger emotion generated by the straight minor turnaround could be reserved for the chorus while the other might go into the verse:

Minor 7 verse turnaround in G

VI				I				II				IV			
Em7	/	/	/	G	/	/	/	Am7	/	/	/	C	/	/	/ :‖

Minor 7 chorus turnaround, same song in G

I		III		IV		V	
G	/	Bm	/	C	/	D	/ :‖

Minor 7s and common tones

The minor 7 can link chords through a common tone, or even two, as shown here. The common tones are given underneath:

Minor 7 verse in G

I				II				III		V		VI			
G	/	/	/	Am7	/	/	/	Bm7	/	D	/	Em7	/	/	/ :‖
g				g				a+d		a+d		d			

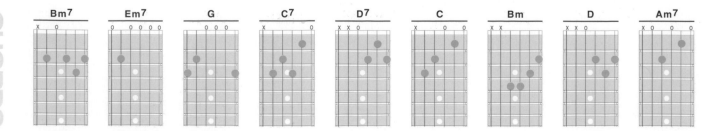

| Bm7 | Em7 | G | C7 | D7 | C | Bm | D | Am7 |

CHORDS

Minor 7s and a chromatic shift

Here is a traditional songwriter's trick with a chromatic minor 7 shift:

Verse in A

I		III	♭IIIm	II		V			
A	/	C♯m7	Cm7	‖Bm7	/	E	/	:‖	c♯

The chromatic chord is ♭IIIm, built on the flattened-third degree of the scale. It is a harmonically disruptive chord, but because it is there only for a couple of beats, is approached by step and left by step, and moves from and to the same type of chord (minor 7), it is acceptable to the ear. This change is found in jazz-influenced songs. In Section 9 we will meet more of these chromatic chords, which I call 'dark outriders'. On a guitar, such changes always involve using barre shapes. Here is a popular use of the min/maj7 with the min7 coming afterward and then returning, first on chord I and then on chord IV:

Minor 7 verse in A minor

I				I			I				I			
Am	/	/	/	‖Am/maj7/	/	/	‖Am7	/	/	/	‖Am/maj7/	/	/	‖

IV				IV			IV				IV			
Dm	/	/	/	‖Dm/maj7/	/	/	‖Dm7	/	/	/	‖Dm/maj7/	/	/	‖

This progression has a 'slinky' sound. If the chord were to descend after bar 3 it could resolve to chord VI (F) or IV (Dm) or iIV^ (D/F♯). In the next example, the min/maj7 forms part of a descending inner voice, D-C♯-C-B-B♭ and then A on the return to Dm:

Min/maj7 verse in D minor

I				I			I				IV			
Dm	/	/	/	‖Dm/maj7/	/	/	‖Dm7	/	/	/	‖G	/	Gm	/	:‖
d				c♯			c				b		b♭		

Here a first-inversion chord IV allows a return to D in the bass without chord I:

Min/maj7 verse in D minor

I				I			I				iIV			
Dm	/	/	/	‖Dm/maj7 /	/	/	‖Dm7	/	/	/	‖B♭/D	/	/	/	:‖
d				c♯			c				d				

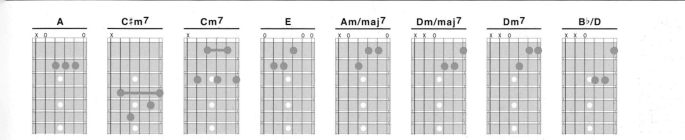

Technique #61: the major and minor 6

The major chord becomes a major 6 by adding the sixth note of the scale. Sixths can be created on chords I, IV, and V, and also on chords II^ and ♭VII without including a note which is not in the key scale. Sixths are easy on a keyboard but cause fingering problems on the guitar, where it can be hard to find a comfortable shape in some keys.

The main uses of the major 6 are:

• to add 'colour' and mild tension to major chords.
• to make a progression sound more 'jazzy' or exotic or Latin.
• to provide a 'Beatles' final chord (as in 'She Loves You').

Here is a song that uses sixths. Usually there would not be so many in a song; the effectiveness of sixths (and other exotic chords) declines the more of them there are.

Song with major 6

Intro

I		V		I		V	
A6	/	B6	/	E6	/	B7	/

Verse

I				IV				V				I				
C	/	/	/	F6	/	/	/	G6	/	/	/	C6	/	/	/	:||

VI				II				IV				III				
Am	/	/	/	Dm	/	/	/	F	/	/	/	Em	/	/	/

IV				V				I				I				
F6	/	/	/	G6	/	/	/	C	/	/	/	C6	/	/	/

The two forms of the minor 6 are rare; both add tension to a minor progression. The more common form is the raised sixth (A C E F♯), which can be related to the IV^ chord in the minor key. It lends a mildly sinister air to a progression. The Am6 chord is similar to a D7 (D F♯ A C), a similarity that can be exploited like this:

Minor 6 verse in G

IV				iI				II				V				
C	/	/	/	G/B	/	/	/	Am6	/	/	/	D7	/	/	/

In a major key, chords II and IVm form minor sixths. It would be unusual to link several minor 6 chords together in a sequence.

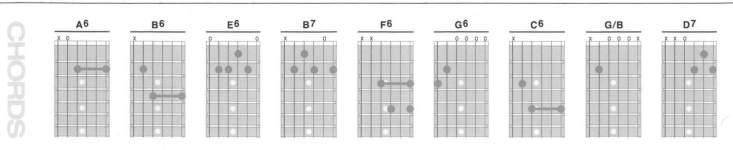

Technique #62: suspended chords

There are two kinds of suspended chord: the suspended second and the suspended fourth; these are written as Asus2 and Asus4, etc.

These chords are neither major nor minor. The note that would have indicated whether the chord is major or minor (the third) has been removed ('suspended') and replaced with either the second or fourth note above the root of the chord. To make an Asus2, the third (C♯) is replaced with B, so the chord is ABE. To make an Asus4, the third (C♯) is replaced with D, so the chord is ADE.

The sus2 has a slightly tense, empty quality; the sus4 is more focused and tense. All six primary chords in a key can be turned into suspended forms, although these are not all of the same kind if the sus4 is drawn from the scale. Although IV and ♭VII need out-of-scale notes to become sus4 chords (♭7 and ♭3 of the scale, respectively) these are common notes in blues-inflected harmony, so it is acceptable to use them.

I	II	III	IV	V	VI	♭VII
Gsus4	Asus4	Bsus4	Csus4	Dsus4	Esus4	Fsus4 (with a B♭)

The main uses of suspended chords are:

- to add tension to a progression, especially at approaches to a new section.
- to add strength to a turnaround when chord V becomes a sus4: I-III-IV-Vsus4-V.
- to prevent resolution in a turnaround when chord I becomes a sus4: Isus4-III-IV-Vsus4-V.
- to reinforce a V-I change by making chord V a sus4 first.
- to create a sense of mystery (sus2) or conflict (sus4).
- to provide sections which are tonally neutral.
- to displace and delay the major or minor chord to which they can resolve.
- to change key (see Section 8).

The coda of Cat Stevens' 'Can't Keep It In' is a very good example of using sus4 chords to make a dramatic ending. The Pretenders' 'Brass In Pocket' has many sus2/sus4s in its chord sequence.

It's important to ensure that all the harmonic instruments (guitars, keyboards, strings, backing vocals, brass) in an arrangement 'agree' with a sus4 chord. This means that the suspended note must not be present anywhere – or a horrible clash results.

In the first example an eight-bar I-IV change is made more interesting by the sus4s. The Dsus4 note (G) provides a common tone as an opportunity to insert a ♭VII chord:

Sus4 verse in A

continues on next page

WORKING WITH CHORD TYPES

IV				IV				♭VII				IV				
D	/	/	/	Dsus4	/	/	/	G	/	/	/	Dsus4	/	/	/	:‖

Using the sus4 for an intro

Sus4 chords are great for dramatic intros, especially in rock songs. Simply alternating with a straight chord I can work:

Sus4 intro in E

I				I				I				I			
E	/	/	/	Esus4	/	/	/	E	/	/	/	Esus4	/	/	/

In the next example, the Esus4 (chord V) creates a tense expectancy of the appearance of chord I (A), which finally enters at the verse. Notice in bar 4 that the suspension does not resolve on the first beat but the third. Hanging on for another two beats is more dramatic and less predictable. In the verse, a quick change to Dsus4 almost suggests a riff:

Sus4 intro in A

V				V				V				V		V	
Esus4	/	/	/	Esus4	/	/	/	Esus4	/	/	/	Esus4	/	E	/

Sus4 verse

I				IV		IV		I				I		V	
A	/	/	/	D	/	Dsus4	D	A	/	/	/	A	/	E	/ :‖

Remember that the same sus4 can resolve to a major or a minor chord. In the next example, the Esus4 in bar 3 leads eventually to Am. In bar 6 the sus4 resolves to a minor chord on the same root, and the same type of resolution occurs in the next bar. Contrast the sound of Esus4 resolving to E in bar 3 with the change to Em in bar 7. Which you use depends on the melody notes:

Sus4 verse in A minor

I				IV				V		V		I			
Am	/	/	/	Dm	/	/	/	Esus4	/	E	/	Am	/	/	/

I				IV		IVm		V		V		I			
Am	/	/	/	Dsus4	/	Dm	/	Esus4	/	Em	/	Am	/	/	/

To create additional frustration and tension in a sequence, use a sus4 without resolving it. Here the Esus4 goes straight to Am without first resolving to E. A common tone of A links all four chords:

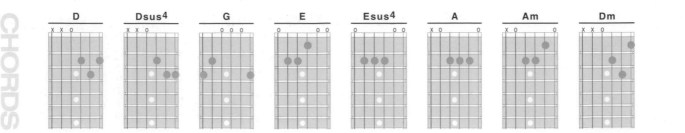

D   Dsus4   G   E   Esus4   A   Am   Dm

Sus4 verse in A minor

I				IV				V				I			
Am	/	/	/	Dm	/	/	/	Esus4	/	/	/	Am	/	/	/
a				a				a				a			

A strong effect is generated with a sus4 on chord I:

Sus4 verse in E minor

I		III		VI				V				I			
Em	/	G	/	C	/	/	/	B7	/	/	/	Esus4	/	Em	/

To smooth the integration of a sus4, find a chord to precede it which has a common tone – possibly the suspended tone itself. In this example, G is the fourth in the Dsus4, which is prepared for by the Am7 (ACEG). Instead of resolving to D and then chord I in bar 4, which would have given a sense of finality, chord VI makes for more onward movement and surprise:

Sus4 verse in G

I				II				V		V		VI			
G	/	/	/	Am7	/	/	/	Dsus4	/	D	/	Em	/	/	/
g				g				g		f♯		g			

Chord V can be a dominant 7 and a sus4 chord at the same time; in A, this chord would be E7sus4. In this chorus the chord provides a double common tone with D, which prepares the sus4. There is also a common tone provided by chord VI. Using both makes an eight-bar chorus:

Sus4 chorus in A

I				II				IV				V			
A	/	/	/	Bm	/	/	/	D	/	/	/	E7sus4	/	E7	/
								a + d				a + d		g♯ + d	

I				II				VI				V			
A	/	/	/	Bm	/	/	/	F♯m7	/	/	/	E7sus4	/	E7	/
								a				a + d		g♯ + d	

THE SUS4 AND THE PERFECT CADENCE

This next example uses two common tones to link chord II to chord V. The C in Dm7 becomes the fourth in Gsus4; the F in Dm7 becomes the seventh in G7. This formula, in which a prepared sus4 on the dominant 7 goes to chord I, is one of the most powerful conclusion cadences. It is an

WORKING WITH CHORD TYPES

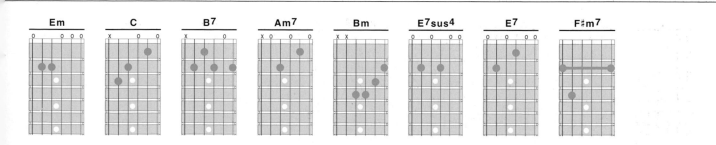

intensifier of the perfect cadence. How easy it is to finger on the guitar depends on the key – C major works well.

Sus4 verse in C

I				VI				II				-V			
C	/	/	/	Am	/	/	/	Dm7	/	/	/	G7sus4 /	G7	/	:‖
								c + f				c + f	b + f		

THE SUSPENDED SECOND

Here is an example of the sus2 adding colour and mystery to a sequence:

Sus2 verse in A

I				II				IV				V			
A	/	/	/	Bsus2	/	/	/	Dsus2	/	/	/	E	/	/	/

VI				IV				♭VII				V			
F♯m	/	/	/	Dsus2	/	/	/	Gsus2	/	/	/	Esus4 /	E	/	

The sus2 can create movement when there are only a few chords:

Sus2 verse in E

I				IV				I				IV			
E	/	/	/	Asus2 /	A	/	E	/	/	/	Asus2 /	A	/	

V				V				IV				IV			
Bsus2 /	B	/	Bsus2 /	B	/	A	/	/	/	Asus2 /	/	/	

In a minor-key sequence, the sus2 can dilute the minor effect or serve to withhold the minor chord I. Compare bars 1–4 with 5–8 in this sequence:

Sus2 verse in Dm

IV				V				I				III			
Gm	/	/	/	A	/	/	/	Dsus2	/	/	/	F	/	/	/

IV				V				I				I			
Gm	/	/	/	A	/	/	/	Dm	/	/	/	Dsus2	/	/	/

Songs written in the 'jangle' style of rock (think of The Searchers, The Byrds, R.E.M., The Smiths) sometimes link the sus2 with the sus4. Because easily playable suspended shapes are available only

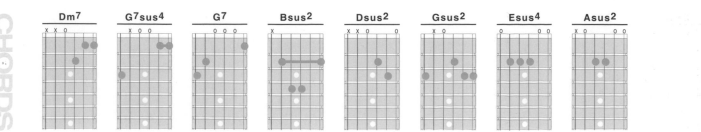

Dm7   G7sus4   G7   Bsus2   Dsus2   Gsus2   Esus4   Asus2

in a few keys on the guitar, such sequences tend to happen in those keys. Here is an example in D. Notice the sus4-sus2 variation on a simple D-G-A sequence. The Bm in bars 7–8 is important; it gives the ear a change from the established rate of chord movement by taking up six beats, and as a simple minor chord it offers a respite from the suspensions:

Sus4/sus2 verse in D

I		I		I		I		IV		IV		IV	
Dsus4	/	D	/	Dsus2	/	D	/	Gsus4	/	G	/	Gsus2	/	G	/

V		V		VI		VI		V	
Asus4	/	A	/	Asus2	/	A	/	Bm	/	/	/	Bm	/	A	/

K T Tunstall's 'Other Side Of The World' is an example of a song that uses both types of suspended chord to create interest in the introduction. Beginning on D major, we then hear Dsus2, followed by Dsus4 and Dsus2 again. This introduction returns as a brief musical interlude between the verses. It is something of a 'false intro' (see Technique #82) as this D-centred sequence should lead to G major (chord V to chord I), but the song begins in A major.

One of the best-known uses of suspended chords in rock music is The Who's 'Pinball Wizard'. After an introduction involving a series of chords over a pedal note, the music arrives on Bsus4 for one bar, which then resolves to B major for one bar. Sus4 chords, as seen here, seem mostly to want to resolve to the major chord on the same root. These two bars are then repeated four times creating an eight bar phrase which builds the suspense before the start of the vocals. The verse is then based on a series of alternating sus4 and major chords, working their way down the guitar neck one bar each, from B to A and then to G before arriving on F♯ major.

Sus4 chords can also be used to delay the arrival of the dominant chord without actually having to use a different underlying harmony. This can be heard in Taylor Swift's 'White Horse', a song with a verse based on a turnaround of chords I, IV, and VI in C major. For the four-bar link between the verse and chorus the chords are: Am-F-Gsus4-G. The Gsus4 chord adds a little tension before the arrival of the dominant which then prepares the way back to C for the start of the chorus.

Technique #63: the add-ninth major chord

The add-ninth major chord is closely related to the sus2 and is an easy way of adding strength to a simple sequence. Compare Csus2 (CDG) with Cadd9 (CEGD) – the additional note is the E, which makes it clear that the add9 chord is a major chord, not a neutral one like the sus2. This chord is called an add9 to distinguish it from the full major ninth (CEGBD). Add9 chords are more popular on the guitar than full ninths because they're easier to find in a playable shape and their sound is more suited to rock music. Here's a standard I-IV change decorated with add9s:

WORKING WITH CHORD TYPES

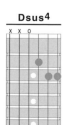

WORKING WITH CHORD TYPES

Add9 change in C

I				I				IV				IV			
Cadd9	/	/	/	Cadd9	/	/	/	Fadd9	/	/	/	Fadd9	/	/	/ :‖

Add9s are often used in situations where the ninth is a common tone with the preceding or following chord. There is a simple explanation: it means the guitarist doesn't have to lift a finger off the note!

Add9 change in D

I				bVII				IV				II			
D	/	/	/	Cadd9	/	/	/	Gsus2	/	/	/	Em7	/	/	/ :‖
d				d				d				d				

Technique #64: the minor add-ninth chord

The minor add-ninth chord is also closely related to the sus2. Compare Asus2 (ABE) with Amadd9 (ACEB) – the additional note is the C, which makes it clear that the add9 chord is a minor chord, not a neutral one like the sus2. This chord is called an add9 to distinguish it from the full minor ninth (ACEGB). The minor add9 chord is an intensifier – it makes the minor chord even more tragic and sad. This is powerfully demonstrated on Marshall Crenshaw's 'Laughter' and All About Eve's 'Martha's Harbour'. Notice its effect in these two sequences:

Minor add9 in A minor

I				VII				VI				VII			
Amadd9	/	/	/	G	/	/	/	F	/	/	/	G	/	/	/ :‖

Minor add9 in E minor

I				VI				VII				VII			
Emadd9	/	/	/	C	/	Cmaj7	/	D	/	/	/	Dsus4	/	/	/ :‖

Technique #65: the 'fifth' chord

In looking at suspended chords, we saw how both were tonally neutral because they omitted the note (the third) which defines a chord as major or minor. So what happens if this note is not replaced with another note? What remains are two notes making the interval known as a perfect fifth – for example, A and E.

Perfect fifths played on the lower strings are an integral part of rock guitar, particularly in styles such as hard rock (Thin Lizzy), heavy metal (Metallica), and grunge (Soundgarden). For the guitar-playing songwriter, it is useful to know that if these two notes are doubled or even trebled a strummable chord results. We can call this a 'fifth' chord (written C5, D5, etc). Chords I–VI, as well as bIII, bVI, and bVII can all be turned into fifth chords. These chords:

CHORDS

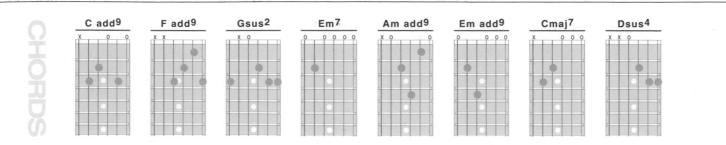

C add9   F add9   Gsus2   Em7   Am add9   Em add9   Cmaj7   Dsus4

- combine effectively with most other chords, especially suspended chords and the major add9.
- are often used for intros and links.
- can toughen a chord progression.
- can be powerful tools for contrasting one song section with another.

When used for contrast, fifth chords are an example of 'withholding' not just a single chord but the unambiguous emotion of a clear major or minor progression. Imagine, say, a turnaround heard first in fifths and then at a climactic point, such as a chorus, with major and minor chords.

Notice the stark quality that fifth chords give to a simple three-chord trick idea:

Fifth change in G

I				IV				I				V			
G5	/	/	/	C5	/	/	/	G5	/	/	/	D5	/	/	/ :‖

Bruce Springsteen is fond of taking simple primary chord changes and turning them into sequences that combine fifth chords with add9s:

Fifth change in C

I				IV				V				IV			
C5	/	/	/	Fadd9	/	/	/	Gadd9	/	/	/	Fsus2	/	/	/ :‖

This is a popular chord sequence with songwriters who play guitar:

Fifth change in D

I				♭VII				iIV				IV			
Dsus2	/	/	/	Cadd9	/	/	/	G/B	/	/	/	G5	/	/	/ :‖

Songs that use the fifth chord can be found all over rock music. For an example from classic rock, we could choose Deep Purple's 'Smoke On The Water', which begins with one of the most famous rock riffs of all time. The riff is played in fifth chords, although in this case the fifth is inverted, so that the root is on top and the fifth is below. For the verses, the song is based on G5 and F5, (chords I and ♭VII) and fifth chords are also used in the chorus, this time C5 and A♭5 (chord IV and an extremely rare ♭II).

Another famous guitar riff introduces Blur's 'Song 2'. On guitar, a fifth chord shape can be moved around fairly easily once mastered. It can consist of just a root and a fifth or a root and a fifth with the root doubled an octave higher. This song uses both types. For the intro, the two-note fifth chord is played beginning with F5 and E♭5, followed by A♭5, B♭5, and C5. For the "Woo hoo" choruses the same chords are played, mostly in a lower octave, and this time using the three note shape.

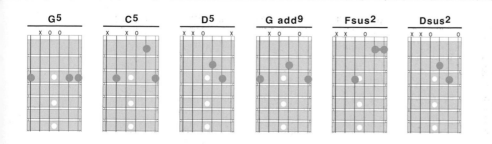

'Smells Like Teen Spirit' was the biggest hit of the grunge movement for Seattle band Nirvana. It is based entirely upon fifth chords and demonstrates how these chords can be slid around the guitar to create a repeatable and memorable guitar riff. The chords, two chords per bar, are: F5-B♭5-A♭5-D♭5. This two-bar riff is the basis for almost the entire song, although in the verses it is present only as a bassline. Notice the use of chords built on the 'rock' altered ♭III and ♭VI degrees of the F major scale.

Technique #66: the augmented chord

An augmented chord is formed when the fifth of a major triad is raised one semitone (half-step): G major is GBD; G augmented is GBD♯. An augmented chord is neither major nor minor. Its strange sound means that it almost invariably occurs in songs as a passing chord, not a chord to be dwelt on for bars at a time. The augmented note itself usually moves up a semitone; in the case of G augmented (G+), it would move from D♯ to E. Any chord with an E in it could be used to follow G+, although sometimes the step-wise movement happens on a static chord.

An augmented chord cannot be inverted, as any inversion simply makes the new bass note the root: G B D♯ is G+; B D♯ G is B+; D♯ G B is D♯+. However the three notes are arranged, there are two tones (whole-steps) between them, which defines the augmented chord. Also, a minor chord cannot have an augmented fifth, because that creates a first-inversion major chord: Am = A C E; augmenting Am = A C E♯ – but E♯ = F, making A C F, the first inversion of F major (F A C).

Sometimes the augmented chord can substitute for chord V. This is handy if the same progression leads to chord V somewhere else in the song:

Augmented chord in E

IV		V+		I		V	
A	/	B+	/	E	/	B	/

Here a ♭VI is turned into an augmented chord which shares two common tones with the chords on either side of it. In this context the augmented ♭VI is close in sound to a IVm, only tougher:

Augmented chorus in E

VI				♭VI+				I				II				
C♯m	/	/	/	C+	/	/	/	E	/	/	/	F♯m	/	/	/	:‖
e + g♯				e + g♯				e + g♯								

Augmented chorus in E as link to bridge

Chorus								Bridge								
I				I+				IV				II				
E	/	/	/	E+	/	/	/	A	/	/	/	F♯m	/	/	/	(etc)
b				b♯				c♯								

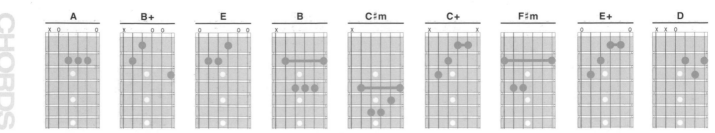

In the following examples, different ways of resolving the augmented chord are shown. In the first it is merely a variation on a chord I which stays the same for the four bars. This would make a good link or intro:

Augmented-chord verse in D (a)

I				I+				I				I+			
D	/	/	/	D+	/	/	/	D6	/	/	/	D+	/	/	/
a				a♯				b				a♯			

In example two, the augmented note rises to the root note of a new chord, Bm, before falling back:

Augmented-chord verse in D (b)

I				I				VI				I+			
D	/	/	/	D+	/	/	/	Bm	/	/	/	D+	/	/	/
a				a♯				b				a♯			

In the third example, the augmented note rises to the third of a G and then drops back to an A♯ in a reverse-polarity III^, F♯:

Augmented-chord verse in D (c)

I				I+				IV				III^			
D	/	/	/	D+	/	/	/	G	/	/	/	F♯	/	/	/
a				a♯				b				a♯			

In example four, the augmented note again rises to the fifth of an Em and the bassline continues up to C, the root of a ♭VII chord:

Augmented-chord verse in D (d)

I				I+				II				♭VII			
D	/	/	/	D+	/	/	/	Em	/	/	/	C	/	/	/
a				a♯				b				c			

Lastly, the augmented note rises to the seventh of a Cmaj7 chord and then to the C in a ♭III chord:

Augmented-chord verse in D (e)

I				I+				♭VII				♭III			
D	/	/	/	D+	/	/	/	Cmaj7	/	/	/	F	/	/	/
a				a♯				b				c			

WORKING WITH CHORD TYPES

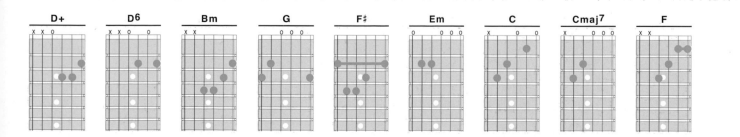

D+   D6   Bm   G   F♯   Em   C   Cmaj7   F

SECTION 7

Technique #67 : the diminished chord

The augmented chord has a partner, the diminished chord. A diminished chord is formed when the fifth of a minor triad is lowered one semitone (half-step): Gm is G B♭ D; G diminished is G B♭ D♭. The strange sound of a diminished triad means that, like the augmented chord, it functions mostly as a passing chord, not one that hangs around. It is almost never used in songs in its pure, triadic form as the unaltered chord VII of the major key or II of the minor.

To make the diminished chord more musically useful, it is often turned into a seventh. This can happen two ways, leading to either the half-diminished 7 or full diminished 7. In the G major scale the diminished triad (chord VII) is F♯ A C. To make this a seventh, add an E: F♯ A C E. This is a half-diminished 7 because the distance between the C and E is a major third; in a full diminished 7, that interval must be a minor third: F♯ A C E♭. On some chord charts, a half-diminished chord is shown by a circle with a slash through it (F⌀) and a full diminished chord by a circle (F°).

A half-diminished 7 is only one note different from a major seventh with its root a semitone below. For example, F♯ half-dim7 = F♯ A C E and Fmaj7 = F A C E. The half-diminished 7 can also be thought of as a dominant 9 that is missing its root. In the key of G the dominant (chord V) is D. Dominant 7 = D F♯ A C; dominant 9 = D F♯ A C E. Take out D and you're left with F♯ A C E, an F♯ half-diminished 7. In practical terms this means the bass could play the root note D and the guitar could play F♯ half-dim7 and the resulting composite sound would be D9.

The full diminished 7 can substitute for the dominant 7♭9 chord. In G major, F♯dim7 = F♯ACE♭; D7♭9 = is DF♯ACE♭. A full diminished 7 cannot be inverted. As was true of augmented chords, whatever note is in the bass becomes the root note. This makes it an unusually versatile chord in terms of the number of keys into which it can be inserted. The diminished 7 chord is used:

- for colouristic effect in songs with dark emotions and lyrics.
- for grandiose gestures and melodrama (see songs by Queen and Meatloaf).
- as a chromatic passing chord, adding tension and sophistication.
- in half-diminished form, as a substitute for the dominant 9 chord.
- in full diminished form, as a substitute for the dominant7♭9 chord.
- for key changing (see Section 8).

This sequence has a jazz flavour thanks to the full and half-diminished 7s and an augmented chord instead of a straight chord V:

Dim7 verse in D

I				II				VI				IV			
D	/	/	/	Edim7	/	/	/	Bm	/	/	/	G7	/	/	/

I				V+				I				II			
Dmaj7	/	/	/	A+	/	/	/	D	/	/	/	E1/2dim7	/	/	:

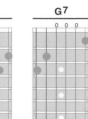
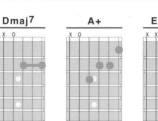

D   Edim7   Bm   G7   Dmaj7   A+   E½dim7

Diminished and augmented chords are rare in all forms of songwriting, although diminished chords are more likely to be found towards the jazzy end of the spectrum. The Amy Winehouse song 'Love Is A Losing Game' begins on an A♭ diminished 7 chord, which returns for one bar at the end of each combined verse and chorus. Each time it returns, its 'out of key' quality seems to hold the music in a moment of suspended animation. This song is well suited to this section of the book as it contains many different chord types. It is in the key of C major, but the C major chord invariably appears as a major 7. In addition it has the progression IV-IVm, in which the F minor chord is a minor 7; there are also chords of Am7, Dm7, and B♭7 in second inversion with F in the bass.

Given the rarity of diminished and augmented chords, what are the chances of finding a song that uses both? The Beatles' 'It Won't Be Long' opens with an eight-bar chorus, initially two bars of C♯ minor followed by two bars of E. The last four bars of the chorus are a bar of C♯m, a bar divided between A and A♯ diminished 7, and two bars of E. The A♯ diminished 7 chord is an unusual way to get back to chord one, but it certainly works. Arguably, the sequence has some similarity with IV-IVm in terms of its musical effect.

We have already examined the verse of this song because of its unusual alternation between I and ♭VI. The middle eight is equally intriguing. Beginning on E, it progresses to D♯ augmented, then D and C♯ major, which creates a chromatic bassline and uses the unlikely sequence of ♭VII leading to a reverse polarity chord VI. Order is restored in the last four bars, with the progression IV-V-II^-V. These are chords of A, B, F♯, and B; the latter, being the dominant, points strongly back towards the keynote E. Note also the use of the reverse polarity chord II - this is the 'dominant's dominant', and adds strength and forward motion to the chords at this point.

There are many other chord types, but the ones covered in this section are those that are most useful to songwriters. Having reached the end of Section 7 of *The Songwriting Sourcebook* we can summarise the material provided so far, and see that we have already travelled a long way from the simple three-chord trick. By now you should feel you can:

- write a major-key sequence using six primary chords (I–VI) and their inversions.
- supplement the six primary chords with ♭III, ♭VI, and ♭VII, and their inversions.
- further supplement them with the reverse-polarity chords II^, III^, IVm, and VI^, and their inversions.
- write a sequence using the composite minor-key chords I, III, IV, IV^, V, Vm, VI, and VII, and their inversions.
- add interest to the harmony by turning these chords into sevenths, sixths, suspended chords, fifths, augmented chords and diminished chords.
- construct a full song using any variation on the intro/verse/chorus/bridge formula.

The next step will add a whole new dimension to your songwriting. Every musical example so far has been in a single key – but there are many keys. What about writing a song that is in more than one key? Section 8 will show you how to go travelling ...

WORKING WITH CHORD TYPES

SECTION 8
WRITING SONGS THAT CHANGE KEY

Changing key is a powerful way to create contrast in your music. It is essential in music longer than the three or four-minute song, but even short songs can benefit from a key change. It reduces monotony and takes the listener on more of a journey.

WHAT KEY SHALL I START IN?

The key you choose for a song depends on many factors. To mention just a few:

- Sometimes a melody pops into your head, and the pitch of the notes suggests a key.
- Sometimes a chord sequence suggests the key.
- Sometimes you choose chords that are easy for you to play, and that determines the key. This is often a factor in the choice of keys by guitar-playing songwriters.
- Some keys acquire personal associations for experienced songwriters because of songs they have already written. If a writer has two atmospheric ballads in C minor, that key may quickly evoke that emotion. If the same songwriter's happiest song is in E major, that key will have an optimistic aura.
- Some keys are chosen because they suit a singer's voice.
- Some keys, such as E♭ and B♭, are popular in music where a brass section is to be used. Brass instruments are most comfortable in these flat keys. E and A are popular for the guitar at concert pitch because they allow the use of the two lowest open strings. For the same reason, E♭ and A♭ are popular keys in heavy rock songs where the guitar has been detuned by a semitone.

WHY DO SONGS CHANGE KEY?

Changing key can achieve many musical goals:

- It can refresh a section that has been heard before, usually more than once, by presenting it again at a different pitch. Traditionally it is the chorus which is most likely to move into a different key, often near the end of a song. After the last verse or bridge or solo, the chorus is heard first in the home key and then, on repetition, in a new key.

- Even more startling, the chorus can change key right after the last verse. In pop tradition, this key change is up either a semitone (half-step) or tone (whole-step).
- If a song has a repeating section, changing the key enables it to be repeated without monotony. This is handy with turnarounds.
- Key changing can contrast different parts of a song. All the verses could be in different keys but the choruses remain the same, or the bridge could be in a new key.
- As changing the key offers the listener the subjective feeling of travelling somewhere new in the music, if something in the lyric suggests a new perspective (literal or metaphorical – new love, new job, new town, new emotion) a key change can make the listener *feel* it rather than just hear about it. If your new lover makes you feel like you've never felt before (to use a lyric cliché) why not say so with a key that has not been heard before in the song? Think of Lou Reed's 'Perfect Day' (verse in B♭ minor, chorus in B♭ major), Red Hot Chili Peppers' 'Californication' (verse in A minor, chorus in C major, solo in F♯ minor), the move from wistful regret (D major intro) to desperation (A minor link) to breaking-out (C major) in Wings' 'Band On The Run', the faith symbolized by the shift of key in David Bowie's 'Word On A Wing', and the exultant sense of freedom as the music changes into the major for the chorus of The Lovin' Spoonfull's 'Summer In The City'. Key contrasts can be magnified if they also have a matching contrast of tempo, as in The Moody Blues' 'Question' where a rapidly strummed, ambiguous E♭-F-E♭-D chord sequence contrasts with a much slower middle section in a placid C major.

DOES A SONG HAVE TO CHANGE KEY?

No – but the simpler the chord progression and the more limited the number of chords, the more potentially inspiring a key change could be. This is particularly true of a three-chord trick.

DO KEY CHANGES BELONG MORE TO SOME STYLES THAN OTHERS?

No – but there is a relationship between musical sophistication and key changing. Some musical genres are more likely to have a key change than others. You will not encounter as many key changes in slow reggae tunes, Top 40 pop songs, dance music and R&B, punk, 12-bar blues, and 1950s rock'n'roll songs as you will in 'arty' genres like progressive rock.

HOW MANY KEYS ARE THERE?

There is a major key and a minor key on each of the 12 notes, giving 24 in total. However, three majors and three minors are written enharmonically as both a sharp key *and* a flat key. These keys are B major (C♭ major), F♯ major (G♭ major), and C♯ major (D♭ major), and their relative minors G♯ minor (A♭ minor), D♯ minor (E♭ minor), and A♯ minor (B♭ minor). The keys are laid out in sequence in table 5 in the Appendix, where chord I represents the major key and chord VI the relative minor. Songwriters who play guitar will tend to favour the keys which permit open-string chords: F, C, G, D, A, and E major. Playing in other keys is often facilitated by using a capo to eliminate tiring barre chords.

So, if a song starts in any major or minor key, there are 23 other keys to which it could change. But some are related to the home key because they have many notes and chords in common, and others are not related because they have few notes and chords in common.

WHAT IS A NEAR KEY?

A *near key* is one that can be reached relatively easily from the home key. It requires a minimal adjustment of accidentals in the melody, and the change will not perturb the listener. It requires only one chord to reach an important chord in a near key. It is easy to return from this key to the home key.

WHAT IS A DISTANT KEY?

A *distant key* is one that can be reached from the home key only with some ingenuity. It will require considerable adjustment of accidentals in the melody, and it will sound unusual to the listener, even unsettling if not adequately prepared. It requires several chords to reach an important chord in the new key and likewise to get back again.

WHAT CHORDS CAN BE USED IN THE NEW KEY?

Once you are in a new key, all eight or 13 chords (depending on whether it is minor or major) are potentially available – these are the equivalents to the 'pool' you can draw from in the home key. To make this clear, imagine a song that starts in E major and changes key to C major for its bridge. The available chords are:

I	II	III	IV	V	VI	bVII	bIII	bVI	II^	III^	IVm	VI^
E	F#m	G#m	A	B	C#m	D	G	C	F#	G#	Am	C#
C	Dm	Em	F	G	Am	Bb	Eb	Ab	D	E	Fm	A

This key change involves a significant journey, travelling past A major, D major, and G major to get to C major. In the verses and choruses, the song draws on the 13 available chords in E major. The bridge in C major could potentially draw on the equivalent 13 in that key. In practice, establishing the new key and contrasting it with the home key requires that you limit yourself to those chords that are more characteristic of the new key. When changing key you must get rid of any harmonic ambiguity or the music will be confused and the new key will not be well established. This means that chords I to VI will be the primary chords for the section in the new key.

Compare chords I-VI in E major and C major. There are no common chords. Bring in the other seven of E major and we find three chords (G, C, and Am) which are among C major's primary chords. It takes experience to know how to use those after the key change without undermining the new key. In thinking about the examples in this section and working with your own key changes, consult tables 5 and 6 in the Appendix to see where chords are found in each key.

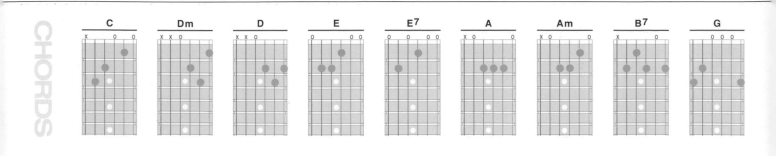

Technique #68: methods for changing key

A new key is established most securely by the use of a V–I (preferably V7–I) chord change in the new key- a perfect cadence. Other options include IV–I (which is less assertive), IVm–I (which is more emotive), or using the diminished 7 for a VII–I change.

V–I key change, C major to A major

I				II		II^ [IV]		V				I			
C	/	/	/	Dm	/	D	/	E	/	E7	/	A	/	/	/

IV–I key change, C major to E major

I				VI				VI^ [IV]		I		V		I	
C	/	/	/	Am	/	/	/	A	/	E	/	B7	/	E	/

IVm–I key change, C major to D major

I				V				V^ [IVm]		I		V		I	
C	/	/	/	G	/	/	/	Gm	/	D	/	A7	/	D	/

In the next example, chord VII in C major is turned into a full diminished 7 (Bdim7 = B D F A♭); this is the same chord as the full diminished 7 built on chord VII in the key of E♭ major (Ddim7 = D F A♭ C♭). They are the same notes, just in a different order (C♭ = B), so the key change is smooth:

VII–I key change, C major to Eb major

I				II				VII	[VII]			I			
C	/	/	/	Dm	/	/	/	Bdim7	[Ddim7]	/	/	E♭	/	/	/

Modulating (as key changing is also called) involves finding a chord common to the two keys to act as a 'stepping stone' and then using one of the above four chord changes.

Think of the other keys as clubs, which will let you in only if you're dressed in appropriate clothes. 'Appropriate' means looking as though you are a member of the club – which means being one of chords I–VI. Let's say we belong to the club C major and want to infiltrate the club called A major. There isn't a common 'cloak' – no chord is found in both keys, although G, chord V in C major, is the ♭VII of A. Unfortunately, that won't really establish the new key on its own. But chord II in C major (Dm) is the IVm of A, so we could make the change in a single step. If this is done, it can be followed by a perfect cadence in the new key, to cement the change:

IVm–I key change, C major to A major

I				V				II [IVm]		I		V		I	
C	/	/	/	G	/	/	/	Dm	/	A	/	E7	/	A	/

Gm   A⁷   Bdim⁷   E♭

WRITING SONGS THAT CHANGE KEY

Here is a table in which the chords of the home key are placed down the left-hand side. In addition to the six primary chords, ♭VII is present; this is the only degree of the scale that has been altered. Also present are the four reverse-polarity chords: II, III, and VI as majors, IV as a minor. Across the top are the numbers that represent harmonic function. With key changing it is crucial to remember that any single chord can have many such functions. Spotting these is the way to find a stepping stone. Reading horizontally across the table, you can see the key in which the chord has a new harmonic role. To take the first column, C is chord IV in G, chord V in F, and chord ♭VII in D.

TABLE OF STEPPING STONES

No. in new key:	II	III	IV	IVm	V	VI	♭VII
Home key:							
I	C		G		F		D
II	Dm		B♭		A		F
IImaj	D		A		G		E
III	Em	D		B		G	
IIImaj	E		B		A		F♯
IV	F				B♭		G
IVm	Fm	E♭	D♭			A♭	
V	G		D				A
VI	Am	G	F	E			
VImaj	A		E		D		B
♭VII	B♭		F		E♭		

The table shows that a number of major keys can be reached from C major, just by shifting the harmonic function of a chord. The easiest keys to change to are represented by the five primary chords, aside from chord I. Here are the keys with their technical names and examples in C and D major:

		Key of C major	Key of D major
Chord II	supertonic	D minor	E minor
Chord III	mediant	E minor	F♯ minor
Chord IV	subdominant	F major	G major
Chord V	dominant	G major	A major
Chord VI	submediant	A minor	B minor

Technique #69: using chords I, IV, and V to change key

Chord V (the dominant) can't be chord V of any major key other than the one you're in, though it can be chord V of the tonic minor, as this key change illustrates:

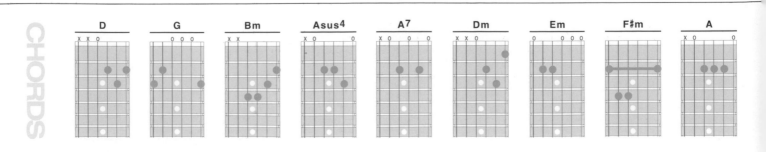

D   G   Bm   Asus⁴   A7   Dm   Em   F♯m   A

Chord V as gate to the tonic minor (D major to D minor)

I				IV				I				IV		VI	
D	/	/	/	G	/	/	/	D	/	/	/	G	/	Bm	/

I				V				V [V]				I			
D	/	/	/	Asus4	/	/	/	A7	/	/	/	Dm	/	/	/

Chord V can be treated as chord IV of another key – a stepping stone to the new key's chord V. This will always take the music into the key a tone higher:

Chord V as chord IV in key change (D major to E major)

I				IV		II		I				IV		II	
D	/	/	/	G	/	Em	/	D	/	/	/	G	/	Em	/

III				V [IV]				V				I			
F♯m	/	/	/	A	/	/	/	B	/	/	/	E	/	/	/

Chord IV can be treated as chord V of the key which is a tone (whole-step) below the one you're in. This is a smooth and easy transition. To strengthen this, turn IV into a dominant 7 chord. In this example, chord IV in the new key comes soon after, to cement the change:

Chord IV as chord V in key change (D major to C major)

I				VI				I				IV			
D	/	/	/	Bm	/	/	/	D	/	/	/	G	/	/	/

IV [V]				I				IV		V		I			
G7	/	/	/	C	/	/	/	F	/	G	/	C	/	/	/

Here is the same sequence leading into C minor:

Chord IV as chord V in key change (D major to C minor)

I				VI				I				IV			
D	/	/	/	Bm	/	/	/	D	/	/	/	G	/	/	/

IV [V]				I				IV		V		I			
G7	/	/	/	Cm	/	/	/	Fm	/	G	/	Cm	/	/	/

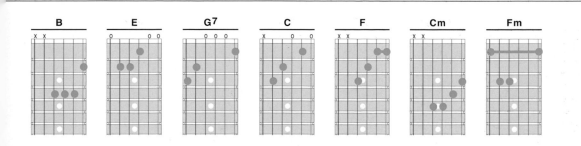

Chord I offers two key-changing opportunities. It could be treated as chord IV of a new key. This will take the music into the key a fifth above:

Chord I as chord IV in key change (D major to A major)

I				VI				I [IV]				V			
D	/	/	/	Bm	/	/	/	D	/	/	/	E7	/	/	/

I			
A	/	/	/

Or chord I could become chord V if turned into a dominant 7. This takes the music into the major or minor key a fourth below:

Chord I as chord V in key change (D major to G major)

I				VI				I [V]				I			
D	/	/	/	Bm	/	/	/	D7	/	/	/	G	/	/	/

Chord I as chord V in key change (D major to G minor)

I				VI				I [V]				I			
D	/	/	/	Bm	/	/	/	D7	/	/	/	Gm	/	/	/

Technique #70: the reverse-polarity gate

It is possible to treat a reverse-polarity chord as chord V of the new key. This is an abrupt but effective way to change key. Here are the reverse-polarity chords in D major and the keys they will take you to:

Chord II^ as gate to the dominant key (D major to A major)

IV				IV				I				I			
G	/	/	/	G7	/	/	/	D	/	/	/	D7	/	/	/

II^ [V]				V				I				[V]			
E	/	/	/	E7	/	/	/	A	/	/	/	A7	/	/	/

Notice how the bar of A7 signals that the A chord is now functioning as chord V again, to return to D major. It is as if the train has stopped – but not long enough to do more than wind down a window, breath the fresh air, and watch the porters messing about.

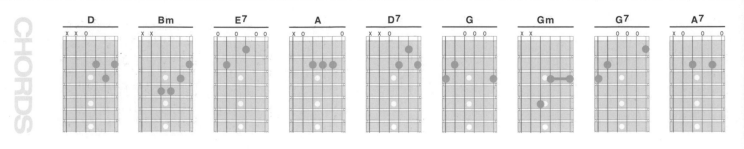

Chord III^ as gate to the submediant key (D major to B major or B minor)

IV				IV				I				I			
G	/	/	/	Gmaj7	/	/	/	D	/	/	/	Dmaj7	/	/	/

III^ [V]				V				I				I [VI]			
F#	/	/	/	F#7	/	/	/	B	/	/	/	Bm	/		/

Chord VI^ as gate to the supertonic key (D major to E major or E minor)

IV				V				I				I			
G	/	/	/	A	/	/	/	D	/	/	/	Dmaj7	/	/	/

VI^ [V]				V				I				I		[II]	
B	/	/	/	B7	/	/	/	E	/	/	/	E	/	Em	/

Technique #71: using IVm to change key

One reverse-polarity chord is different: IVm. It can't function as chord V of another key because it isn't a major chord. But there are two ways of approaching it that enable it to be a stepping stone to a new key. The first is to treat it as one of the normal minor chords of a major key – II, III, or VI – and from there move to chord IV and V (or even just V) of the new key, before resolving to the new chord I. Here are three examples:

Chord IVm as II in the flattened mediant key (D major to F major)

I				IVm [II]				V				I			
D	/	/	/	Gm	/	/	/	C	/	/	/	F	/	/	/

Chord IVm as III in the flattened supertonic key (D major to E♭ major)

I				IVm [III]				IV		V		I			
D	/	/	/	Gm	/	/	/	A♭	/	B♭	/	E♭	/	/	/

Chord IVm as VI in the flattened submediant key (D major to B♭ major)

I				IVm [VI]				V				I			
D	/	/	/	Gm	/	/	/	F	/	/	/	B♭	/	/	/

The second method is to take the three minor chords of the key you're in – II, III and VI – and locate the keys in which they play the harmonic role of IVm:

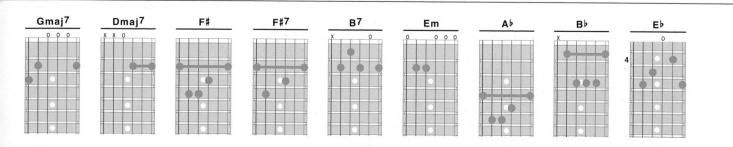

Chord II as IVm in the submediant key (D major to B major)

I				IV				II [IVm]				I			
D	/	/	/	G	/	/	/	Em	/	/	/	B	/	/	/

Chord III as IVm in the leading-note key (D major to C♯ major)

I				IV				III [IVm]				I			
D	/	/	/	G	/	/	/	F♯m	/	/	/	C♯	/	/	/

Chord VI as IVm in the mediant key (D major to F♯ major)

I				IV				VI [IVm]				I			
D	/	/	/	G	/	/	/	Bm	/	/	/	F♯	/	/	/

Having looked at some examples of how to 'travel' by changing key, we can now survey some of the more popular 'places to visit'.

Technique #72: key change to the dominant (V)

The change to the dominant key (a near key) is one of the most common modulations in popular songwriting. To use the railway analogy, this is a 'one-stop' key change. It often happens at the start of the bridge, or at the end of it, as here:

Key change from G major to D major, bridge

IV				IV				I				I			
C	/	/	/	C	/	/	/	G	/	/	/	G7	/	/	/

II^ [V]				V				I				I [V]			
A	/	/	/	A	/	/	/	D	/	/	/	D	/	/	/

This example would fit a four-chord song in which the verse had been dominated by chords I and V with minimal use of chord IV:

Key change from C major to G major, bridge

IV				IV				I				I			
F	/	/	/	F	/	/	/	C	/	/	/	C	/	/	/

II^				II^ [V]				I				[V]			
D	/	/	/	D7	/	/	/	G	/	/	/	G7	/	/	/

WRITING SONGS THAT CHANGE KEY

CHORDS D G Em B F♯m C♯ Bm F♯ C

To create the expectation of this key change, but then deny it, place chord IV immediately after II^ to cancel it:

Unfulfilled key change from C major to G major, bridge

IV				IV				I				I			
F	/	/	/	F	/	/	/	C	/	/	/	C	/	/	/

II^				II^ [V]				IV				V			
D	/	/	/	D7	/	/	/	F	/	/	/	G7	/	/	/

In the following example, F#m is the stepping-stone chord: III in D, it becomes VI in A and leads to the new key's chord V, E. This change could be immediately undermined if the A were an A7 or if an extra bar of A7 were added. That would create what might be termed a 'not-stopping' modulation, like a train that goes through a station instead of stopping. This is a feature of many bridges – they change key to the dominant only for a moment before heading back to the home key in the next verse or chorus.

Dominant key change, D major to A major

IV				IV				I				I			
G	/	/	/	G7	/	/	/	D	/	/	/	D7	/	/	/

IV				III [VI]				V				I			
G	/	/	/	F#m	/	/	/	E7	/	/	/	A	/	/	/

This is a bridge for a song in G. It modulates to the dominant (D), and then modulates to the next dominant key (A) before using dominant 7 chords to cancel out the changes and return to G major. G itself acts as the first stepping stone, as chord I and IV of the new key.

Dominant key change, G major to D major, bridge

I				I [IV]				V				V			
G	/	/	/	Gmaj7	/	/	/	A	/	/	/	A7	/	/	/

I				I [IV]				V				I [V]		I [V]	
D	/	/	/	Dmaj7	/	/	/	E7	/	/	/	A7	/	D7	/

In the following example, we expect that the music is about to change to E major, the dominant of A, because of the appearance of its chord V (B7) replacing A's chord II (Bm). However, the D# present in B7 (the extra sharp which E major requires) is cancelled by the following D chord, and the E7 confirms we are still in A major. There is no key change.

WRITING SONGS THAT CHANGE KEY

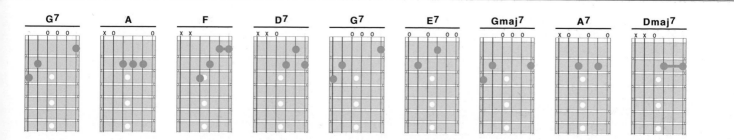

Bridge in A major

VI				II^ [V]				IV				V			
F#m	/	/	/	B7	/	/	/	D	/	/	/	E7	/	/	/

If a modulation to the dominant finishes on chord I as a seventh, the new key is not firmly established. This is because in traditional harmony a dominant 7 chord cannot occur on chord I. If the song is a blues, the listener may accept that there has been a key change if the I7 is emphasised enough. In popular music, with its blues and modal influences, this chord can be a form of chord I, so the effect is not as undermining as it would otherwise be.

These types of modulations also apply to the dominant minor, although that is a more distant key. In the next example, notice how the Dm7 prepares for the D7 which will return the song to G major if chord I follows at or near the start of the next song section, because they have the note C as a common tone.

Key change from G major to D minor, bridge

IV				IV				I				VI			
C	/	/	/	C	/	/	/	G	/	/	/	Em	/	/	/

II^ [V]				V				I				I		[V]	
A	/	/	/	A	/	/	/	Dm	/	/	/	Dm7	/	D7	/

Dominants and dominant 7s can be chained into sequences that suggest new keys but never establish them, as here:

Bridge

I				III^ [V]				I [V]				I [VI]			
C	/	/	/	E7	/	/	/	A7	/	/	/	Dm	/	/	/

V				I [V]				I [♭VII]				V			
C7	/	/	/	F7	/	/	/	B♭	/	/	/	G	/	/	/

The music touches on the keys of A major, D minor, F major, and B♭ major, but none is established.

Technique #73: key change to the subdominant (IV)

The key can also change to the subdominant key (IV). This has a gentler feel than the change to the dominant – it's not as bold.

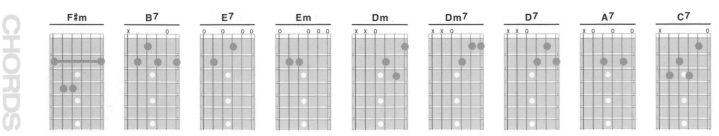

F#m   B7   E7   Em   Dm   Dm7   D7   A7   C7

Key change to subdominant key (G major to C major to F major)

I				I				I [V]				I			
G	/	/	/	Gmaj7	/	/	/	G7	/	/	/	C	/	/	/
g				f♯				f				e			

I				I				I [V]				I			
C	/	/	/	Cmaj7	/	/	/	C7	/	/	/	F	/	/	/
c				b				b♭				a			

I				I				I [♭VII]				V			
F	/	/	/	Fmaj7	/	/	/	F7	/	/	/	D7	/	/	/
f				e				e♭				d			

Here the sequence takes the music into C major and F major, with a falling note in the two kinds of seventh chords. The F7 could in turn lead into another key, B♭, but the I-Imaj7-I7 idea becomes less effective the more it is used. To get back to G major, the F7 functions as a ♭VII in G . The E♭ note drops a semitone (half-step) to the root of chord V (D).

The next example shows that if chord V is turned into a major 7 there is immediate ambiguity about the key. This is because the major 7 on chord V has the ♯4 of the scale. The presence of this ♯4 implies the key which is a fifth higher – a step on the table of keys (from G to D major). Change chord V into a maj7 only if you want this kind of unsettling effect.

Verse in G

I				IV				V				IV			
G7	/	/	/	C7	/	/	/	Dmaj7	/	/	/	C7	/	/	/

I				IV				V				V		IV	
G7	/	/	/	C7	/	/	/	Dmaj7	/	/	/	Dmaj7	/	C7	/

The key change to the subdominant has a gentler feel than the change to the dominant partly because it represents a step back in the cycle of fifths. (One accidental is lost if the home key is above C major on table 5; thereafter, one flat is gained.) The change is easy because the two keys have four chords in common, five if the ♭VII is counted; the ♭VII becomes chord IV of the new key. The simplest change merely uses the dominant 7 on the tonic:

I				I [V]				I				I			
C	/	/	/	C7	/	/	/	F	/	/	/	F	/	/	/

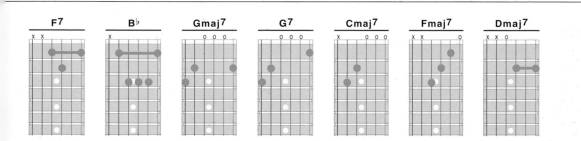

F7 B♭ Gmaj7 G7 Cmaj7 Fmaj7 Dmaj7

WRITING SONGS THAT CHANGE KEY

The ♭VII can strengthen the basis for this move:

I				♭VII [IV]				I [V]				I			
C	/	/	/	B♭	/	/	/	C7	/	/	/	F	/	/	/

Perhaps the most powerful way to change key is to make chord V into a minor chord. This reverse polarity rapidly undermines the home key. In C major, changing G to Gm makes it chord II of F major:

I				V				V [II]		V		I			
C	/	/	/	G	/	/	/	Gm	/	C7	/	F	/	/	/

The next example is a song with an eight-bar verse and a two-bar link. The second verse ignores the link and goes straight into a seven-bar bridge which makes a brief modulation to F. F is quickly cancelled by turning it into its tonic minor:

Key change to subdominant

Verse 1

I				III				II				V			
C	/	/	/	Em	/	/	/	Dm	/	/	/	G	/	/	/ :|

Link

I				IV		V		
C	/	/	/	F	/	G	/	

Verse 2

I				III				II				V			
C	/	/	/	Em	/	/	/	Dm	/	/	/	G	/	/	/ :‖

Bridge

I				I [V]				I				I [IVm]			
C7	/	/	/	C7	/	/	/	F	/	/	/	Fm7	/	/	/

IVm				I		II		IV		V		
Fm7	/	/	/	C	/	Dm	/	F	/	G	/	

Technique #74: key change to the supertonic (II)
This might sound complicated, but a key change to the supertonic simply means moving up a tone (whole-step). This is probably the most popular modulation in popular songs. It is often heard in

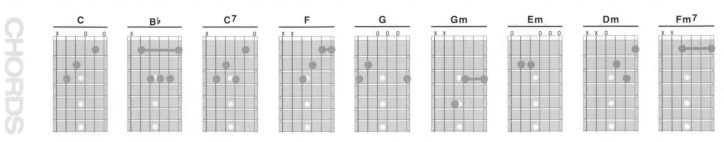

the last chorus, where it adds excitement by lifting the pitch of a section which has been heard before. Compare these turnaround choruses:

Chorus

I				III				IV				II		V [IV]		
C	/	/	/	Em	/	/	/	F	/	/	/	Dm	/	G	/	:‖

Chorus after key change

I				III				IV				II		V		
D	/	/	/	F♯m	/	/	/	G	/	/	/	Em	/	A	/	:‖

When a song changes key it does not have to repeat the chord sequence from an earlier section. If it does, this is called *transposition*. In the above example the entire progression is raised a tone (whole-step). The melody would go up a tone with it. If the chorus were first heard in C major and instead of repeating went straight into D major, the G chord (V in C) would function as IV in D. This IV–I change (plagal cadence) makes for a smooth modulation. The IV–I cadence is strengthened if IV becomes a major 7.

The supertonic key can also be reached by any of these common chords, marked in bold, the priority going to those that are primary chords (I–VI):

I	II	III	IV	V	VI	♭VII	♭III	♭VI	II^	III^	IVm	VI^
D	**Em**	F♯m	**G**	A	Bm	**C**	F	B♭	E	F♯	Gm	B
G												
C	Dm	**Em**	F	**G**	Am	B♭	E♭	A♭	D	E	Fm	**A**

Tone (whole-step) keychanges can be very dramatic, especially when, as is usually the case, they are 'unprepared'. The Taylor Swift song 'Love Story' uses just four chords: D, G, A, and Bm. The song is solidly in D major throughout, but the final chorus and outro are in E major, an unprepared key change that boosts the emotional moment at the end of the song as the hero proposes marriage.

An even more remarkable key change happens for the final choruses of 'I Will Always Love You' in the Whitney Houston version of the Dolly Parton song. The music stops, there is a single drum beat, and Whitney enters a tone higher, with the lyric "and I ...". The key change here is A major to B major, and given the power of Whitney Houston's voice it can be a dramatic moment on first hearing.

David Bowie's 'Quicksand' also shifts a whole tone, but with a prepared change in an unusual place. The song begins in C major after an intro based on G and Am7 chords. The verses mainly use C and G, but offer cameo appearances to Cm and F, the unusual 'tonic minor' and the more commonplace chord IV. At the end of the first verse the intro chords return briefly, and then the Am7 chord becomes A major via Asus2: G-Am7-Am-Asus2-A. This sets up the modulation to D major for the second verse as A is chord V in D major. Key changes this early in a song are rare.

WRITING SONGS THAT CHANGE KEY

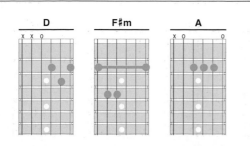

SECTION 8

Technique #75: key change to the relative minor (VI)

The practical use of a modulation to the relative minor is to contrast a section, such as a verse or bridge or prechorus, with a chorus that is in the major key. With care, however, it is possible to present a chorus – same melody, same words – in the relative minor by using chord substitution. The quickest route to the relative minor in its classical form is to use reverse polarity on chord III, as III^ is chord V of the minor. The modal minor shares all the chords of the relative major, so that poses no problem at all – except that it may not sound as though you have changed key.

Here is an example showing a key change from the home major key to the relative minor (in this case, G major to E minor). One verse is given a slightly different ending: the final bar uses chord III changed to its major form, making a perfect cadence (V–I) into the E minor of the bridge. Even if this E minor bridge uses Bm as its chord V, it still makes sense to use III^ (B) to achieve the key change. The effect is heightened by making III^ a dominant 7 chord (B7). Another good preparation for this B7 would be a straight III (Bm) in the preceding bar.

End of verse in G major, key change to E minor bridge

First time

IV				V				I		V		IV			
C	/	/	/	D	/	/	/	G	/	D	/	C	/	/	/

Second time

IV				V				I		V		III^[V in E minor]			
C	/	/	/	D	/	/	/	G	/	D	/	B7	/	/	/

Technique #76: key change to the tonic minor

Moving to the tonic minor can be achieved by simple reverse polarity: chord I of a major key becomes minor. Chord V is also chord V of this new key, but a minor form of chord IV would help to consolidate the change. Imagine a song that starts with this chorus in C major and a verse in C minor follows – the effect is dramatic:

Chorus in C major

I				IV				VI				V		V	
C	/	/	/	F	/	/	/	Am	/	/	/	Gsus4	/	G	/ :||

Verse in C minor

I				VI				IV				IV			
Cm	/	/	/	A♭	/	/	/	Fm	/	/	/	Fm	/	/	/

First time

I				VI				IV				V			
Cm	/	/	/	Ab	/	/	/	Fm	/	/	/	G7	/	/	/ :‖

Second time

I				VI				IV		V		IV [IVm]			
Cm	/	/	/	Ab	/	/	/	Fm	/	G	/	Fm	/	/	/

A perfect cadence takes the song into C minor for the verse. The verse goes eight bars, hits a repeat sign, goes back to repeat bars 1–4 and then goes to the last four bars (marked 'second time'). This is a method for structuring a song section which we can call the *second time option*. This enables the verse to end on a chord IV which functions as IVm to take the music back to C major for the next chorus, using a minor version of the plagal cadence (IVm–I).

Technique #77: the semitone key change

Like the tone (whole-step) shift, the semitone (half-step) key change is heard in many popular songs, often for the last chorus. Motown songs such as 'Heaven Help Us All', 'I'll Pick A Rose For My Rose', and 'I Hear A Symphony' all change key by a semitone – in the case of these songs, even earlier than the last chorus and in the latter two more than once!

The semitone modulation is a musical oddity. From a player's perspective, it seems a small shift: the guitarist moves chord shapes up one fret; the pianist goes a little way up the keys; the singer transposes the melody up a bit. But from the theoretical aspect, to use our railway metaphor, this key change is almost like going to the end of the line. Check this for yourself by referring to table 5 in the Appendix. Locate C major and then see how far away C♯ major is!

The semitone modulation takes you to a distant key with no common chords or notes. Going there usually mean changing to another key first; in other words, you must do it in stages. Yet hit records put a premium on a song's length – they are structurally impatient. They want to just leap to the new key when that last chorus comes around. They don't want to spend time going through even a four-bar link to reach a distant key. As a consequence, many songs that move up a semitone do so without any preparation. There is a key change, but no modulation. Play the following chorus:

Chorus in C major, moving up in semitones

I				IV				VI				V		V	
C	/	/	/	F	/	/	/	Am	/	/	/	Gsus4	/	G	/ :‖

I				IV				VI				V		V	
C♯	/	/	/	F♯	/	/	/	A♯m	/	/	/	G♯sus4	/	G♯	/

continues on next page

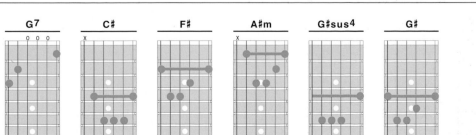

G7   C#   F#   A#m   G#sus4   G#

WRITING SONGS THAT CHANGE KEY

I				IV				VI				V		V	
D	/	/	/	G	/	/	/	Bm	/	/	/	Asus4	/	A	/

The second line transposes the turnaround up a semitone to C♯ major, and then it moves up another semitone to D major. Neither is prepared. In fact, if you listen carefully, the changes from G to C♯ and G♯ to D are awkward-sounding because the chords are unrelated. Instead of a V–I cadence, we're getting ♭V (♯IV of the new key)–I, a discord. Hit songs do this and get away with it by steamrolling through such changes. A quick tempo, a strong rhythm, a melodic hook and a noisy production usually serve to hide the grisly secret!

So how would such a change be prepared? Let's imagine going from E♭ to E major:

I	II	III	IV	V	VI	♭VII	♭III	♭VI	II^	III^	IVm	VI^
E♭	Fm	Gm	A♭	B♭	Cm	D♭	G♭	C♭	F	G	A♭m	C
B♭												
F												
C												
G												
D												
A												
E	F♯m	G♯m	A	B	C♯m	D	G	C	F♯	G♯	Am	C♯

At first glance, there seems to be very little in common. This is where the art of thinking enharmonically comes in. Every flat note is also a sharp note with a different letter: G♯ is also A♭, so IVm in E♭ (A♭m) is actually chord III (G♯m) in E major. Here are some other connections:

Key E♭			E	
G♭	(♭III)	=	F♯	(II^)
A♭	(IV)	=	G♯	(III^)
C♭	(♭VI)	=	B	(V)
C	(VI^)	=	C	(♭VI)
D♭	(♭VII)	=	C♯	(VI^)

None of these chords will make for a smooth transition or establish the new key in themselves, but they can act as stepping stones to the new key.

Technique #78: changing key with a diminished 7

Another way of making a key change is to use the diminished 7 chord, first mentioned in Section 7. Remember that this is a seventh chord based on chord VII of the major key. In E♭ it is Ddim7

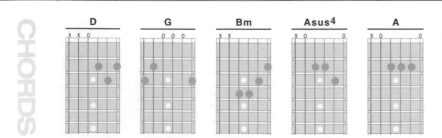

D   G   Bm   Asus4   A

(D F A♭ C♭). Though they are enharmonically disguised, this chord has two notes in common with an E major chord (E G ♯B). Using enharmonic equivalents, Ddim7 could be spelled D F G♯ B. The common notes G♯ and B (A♭ and C♭) allow a transition to chords I, III, and VI as minor 7 chords in E major. From one of those, the music could move to a perfect cadence to establish E major as the new key.

A second possibility is to think about VII in E major, the key to which we want to go. Its diminished 7 is D♯dim7 (D♯ F♯ A C). D♯ is the same note as E♭, so this diminished 7 chord has a root note which is the same as the root note of the home key. Instant connection! The full respelling of D♯dim7 as E♭dim7 is E♭ G♭ B♭♭ D♭♭ – '♭♭' means double-flat, when a note is lowered by a tone (whole-step). This strange formulation is correct because the chord notes must proceed alphabetically by every other note from the one where you start. Enharmonically, E♭ = D♯, G♭ = F♯, B♭♭ = A, and D♭♭ = C.

So what? Well, remember that to establish a new key a perfect cadence (V7–I) is desirable, which here would be B7–E. The notes of B7 are B D♯ F♯ A – and our respelt E♭dim7 is D♯ F♯ A C. Three notes the same! In other words, E♭dim7 is very close to chord V (B7) in the new key. This opens the door for a chord sequence like this:

Verse change from E♭ major to E major

I				I	[VII]		V				I				
E♭	/	/	/	E♭dim7	[D♯dim7]	/	B7	/	/	/	E	/	/	/	:‖

There isn't another chord quite like the diminished 7 in this respect. Its magic power is that it acts as a gate that can take you into seven other keys, because each of its four notes can be interpreted as the *leading note* (the seventh degree of the scale) of a major or minor key. As a consequence, it will always have three notes in common with chord V of that other key. Here's how it works:

Verse change from E♭ major to G major

I				I [VII]			V				I				
E♭	/	/	/	E♭dim7	[F♯dim7]	/	D7	/	/	/	G	/	/	/	:‖

Verse change from E♭ major to B♭ major

I				I [VII]			V				I				
E♭	/	/	/	E♭dim7	[Adim7]	/	F7	/	/	/	B♭	/	/	/	:‖

Verse change from E♭ major to D♭ (or C♯) major

I				I [VII]			V				I				
E♭	/	/	/	E♭dim7	[Cdim7]	/	A♭7	/	/	/	D♭	/	/	/	:‖

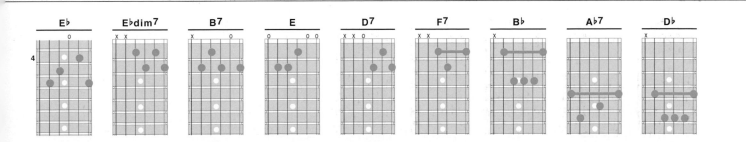

To complete Section 8, here is a full song with several keys used in the different sections.

Full song in G major with modulations

Intro

IV				V				iIV				iV			
C	/	/	/	D	/	/	/	C/E	/	/	/	D/F♯	/	/	/

Verse

I				V				IV				IV			
G	/	/	/	D	/	/	/	C	/	/	/	Cadd9	/	/	/

I				V				IV				IV [VI]		V	
G	/	/	/	D	/	/	/	C	/	/	/	Cmaj7	/	B7	/

Prechorus

I				IV				V				I			
Em	/	/	/	Am	/	/	/	B7	/	/	/	Em	/	/	/

I				I				I				IV [II]		V	
Em	/	/	/	Em/maj7/		/	/	Em7	/	/	/	Am	/	D7	/

Chorus

I		IV		V		V		I		IV		V			
G	/	C	/	Dsus4	/	D	/	G	/	C	/	Dsus4	/	/	/ :‖

Repeat verse, prechorus and chorus

Bridge

II				IV				V				I			
Dm	/	/	/	F	/	/	/	G7	/	/	/	C	/	/	/

II				IV				V		I		II [IVm]			
Dm	/	/	/	F	/	/	/	G	/	C	/	Dm	/	/	/

Last chorus

I		IV		V		V		I		IV		V			
A	/	D	/	Esus4	/	E	/	A	/	D	/	Esus4	/	/	/ :‖

C   D   C/E   D/F♯   G   C add9   Cmaj7   B7   Em

Note:

- This song features the keys of G major, E minor, C major and A major.
- The intro uses inversions to build a rising bassline to chord I in the verse.
- The verse is in G major.
- The prechorus is in the relative minor, E minor, reached via a IV=VI-V-I sequence.
- The chorus returns to G major via IV=II-V-I.
- The second chorus's last Dsus4 resolves unexpectedly onto Dm at the start of the bridge. Dm is II of C major, the subdominant key, reached after the G7.
- This same chord II (Dm) becomes IVm of the key which is a tone (whole-step) above the home key. The last chorus(es) are in A major, the supertonic key.

Not every song needs a key change, and most of the time you may feel you need only to journey to a near key. But always remember how effectively a key change can bring a new dimension to a song and to a lyric's theme. This is one aspect of songwriting which is truly inexhaustible. If some of this material seems overly technical, don't worry. Always trust your ears when you're putting a sequence together. They will tell you whether an attempted key change sounds right or not.

It is possible to construct chord changes that cannot be found in any single key. The verse of The Doors' 'Light My Fire' is a good example: it uses two minor chords a minor third apart, which can never ordinarily happen in any key. Nor can a key have two minor chords two tones (whole-steps) apart. Such progressions tend not to figure in commercial songwriting, but the odd nature of such changes was something The Doors could carry off because it fit the dark quality of some of their music.

WRITING SONGS THAT CHANGE KEY

| Am | Em/maj7 | Em7 | D7 | Dsus4 | Dm | F | G7 | Esus4 |

SECTION 9

A MISCELLANY OF TECHNIQUES

Now that we've covered all the basic ground for putting together chord sequences, let's consider some songwriting strategies that will stimulate your creativity and give your songs extra polish. To begin, we'll look at the parts of a song that often don't get as much attention as verses and choruses, starting with the intro. In commercial songwriting intros tend to be short – sometimes only a bar or two – but even a brief intro can be vital in setting the mood and grabbing the listener's attention.

Technique #79: the recycled intro

A recycled intro is one that is part (or all) of a later section, such as the chorus. It is instrumental. It has the advantage that, when the first chorus proper is reached, the listener has already heard the sequence so it is half-familiar. This gives the first chorus a sense of returning to something rather than being a new thing. Another option is to recycle the bridge as the intro. If you wish to contrast them, use the same chord sequence but transposed to a different key.

Back in Section 1 we mentioned Blondie's 'Dreaming' as a song which use the same music for the intro as for the chorus: a recycled intro. The Police's 'Every Breath You Take' uses the music of the verse as an intro, allowing the distinctive guitar riff to set the mood of the song. Other songs mentioned in Section 2, such as ' I'm Yours', 'Hey, Soul Sister', and 'With Or Without You' also use the chords from a section of the song, or in the case of 'With or Without You', the four-bar pattern that is used for the entire song. On balance, the majority of intros are constructed from existing sections of a song; false intros (see below) are relatively less common.

Technique #80: the free-time intro

A free-time intro is one that has no regular beat – it's 'out of time'. Chords are played, often arpeggiated on the piano or guitar and left to ring, while a few vocal phrases are sung with small pauses between them. This emphasises the meaning of the words. In more kitsch songs, the words might be spoken. Think of The Beatles' 'I'm A Loser', The Miracles' 'Shop Around', Jeff Buckley's 'Lilac

Wine', or Don McLean's 'American Pie', which has an intro so long it almost constitutes a free-time verse. The free-time intro creates suspense by withholding the beat. When the percussion instruments enter in regular time, the song seems to lift off. This technique lends itself to melodrama and even comedy – as in the case of British radio comedy act The Goons and their 'Ying Tong Song'.

Technique #81: the false intro

A false intro is not one that is 'wrong' – it is one that deliberately misleads the listener, to enhance the impact of what follows. A false intro makes the listener think he or she knows what sort of a song it will be, only to find it turns out quite different. In the broadest sense, a false intro could start in one musical style but reveal its 'true' style upon reaching the verse. Them Crooked Vultures' 'Elephants' has a false intro which suddenly doubles the tempo after about 10 seconds.

You can create a false intro by starting at a different tempo or time signature from the one in the first verse. Or the intro could be in a different key, as in this example where the intro is in A major but the verse in F major:

False intro in A

I		VI		II		V		I		VI		V		IVm [VI]	
A	/	F#m	/	Bm	/	E	/	A	/	F#m	/	E	/	Dm	/

Verse

I			
F	/	/	/

In advanced songwriting, the idea that the intro should say something truthful about the song can be turned upside-down with a false intro. It is possible to create an expectation and then defeat it. For example, R.E.M.'s 'Shiny Happy People' starts with a slow waltz-like rhythm which gives no clue about the uptempo 4/4 pop song that follows.

We mentioned K T Tunstall's 'Otherside' in Section 7 as a song with a false intro. The Red Hot Chili Peppers' 'Under The Bridge' is an example of a song with a very distinctive false intro. It is a guitar solo and cycles between two chords, D and F#, in an eight-bar section. When the verse of the song begins, however, it is in the key of E major. The concluding choruses of this song are in A major, proving that once the sense of key in a song has become less than certain it is possible to change key quite freely without the song lacking a sense of conclusion at the end.

Technique #82: the sus4 false intro

Sus4 chords are great for false intros, as the next example shows. The Esus4 (chord V) creates a tense expectancy of the eventual appearance of chord I (A or Am), which enters at the start of the verse. To frustrate the expectation simply substitute any chord which includes the note A but not as the root: F, F#m, D and Dm are the prime possibilities.

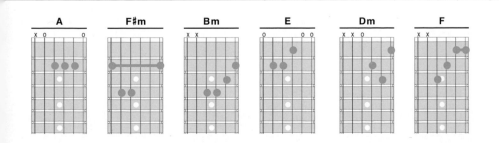

A MISCELLANY OF TECHNIQUES

False intro in A

V				V				V				V		V [III^]	
Esus4	/	/	/	Esus4	/	/	/	Esus4	/	/	/	Esus4	/	E	/

IV				V				I				III		III^	
F	/	/	/	G	/	/	/	C	/	/	/	Esus4	/	E	/ :‖

In this instance, Esus4 turns out not to be V of A or A minor but III^, resolving unexpectedly to IV of C major. This is a classic example of displacement: we have a I-III^-IV-V turnaround which has been displaced to put chord I in its third bar.

Technique #83: the false intro (guitar version)

There is a version of the false intro that is specific to the guitar. This technique exploits the contrast between the 'closed' sound of barre chords and the more resonant tone of open-string chords. Find a set of barre chords which are in a different key from the main part of the song and use those chords only for the intro. It won't matter if they're tiring to play, because they are only going to be played for a few bars. This example starts in the barre-laden key of C♯ major but ends up in A major at the verse:

False intro with barre chords

II				♭II				I				VI			
D♯m	/	/	/	D	/	/	/	C♯	/	/	/	A♯m7	/	/	/

II				♭II				I [VI^]		V		I [V]		V	
D♯m	/	/	/	D	/	/	/	C♯	/	B	/	Esus4	/	E	/

Verse

I			
A	/	/	/

Technique #84: the false keynote intro

One beautifully elegant method for teasing people's ears is to sound just a single note – not a chord – at the start of a song, with or without a beat. By default the listener will assume this is the keynote (root). So if the note A is heard, the listener will assume the key to be A (or possibly A minor). Then harmonize this note with any chord to which it can belong *except* A or A minor. Here is a list of possible chords and the function of A in each:

CHORDS

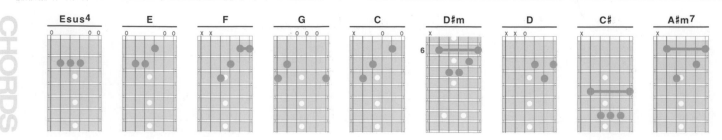

Third of a major	F
Third of a minor	F#m
Fifth of a major or minor	D or Dm
Sixth of a major	C6
Seventh of a dominant 7	B7
Seventh of a major 7	B♭maj7
Seventh of a minor 7	Bm7
Seventh of a min/maj7	B♭m/maj7
add 9	Gadd9
minor 9	Gm9

This causes a mild shock because the listener has to recompute the musical meaning of the note. Paul McCartney's band Wings had a hit called 'My Love' which starts with the single note A. When the first chord is played, this A turns out to be the seventh of a B♭maj7 chord – and the song itself is in F!

Technique #85: the turnaround bridge

Now let's turn our attention to the bridge. If a song doesn't have a turnaround sequence anywhere else, putting one in the bridge is a great method for making the bridge more of a hook – it's almost like a second chorus. This one has the turnaround I-III-II-V and lasts for only six bars:

Bridge in E

I		III		II		V		I		III		II		V	
E	/	G#m	/	F#m	/	B	/	E	/	G#m	/	F#m	/	B	/

IV		II		V			
A	/	F#m	/	B	/	/	/

Technique #86: the bridge avoiding chord I

This bridge is centred on chord VI and sounds best if VI is avoided elsewhere. Notice the avoidance of chord I to contrast with the rest of the song:

Bridge in E

VI				V				VI				II			
C#m	/	/	/	B	/	/	/	C#m	/	/	/	F#m	/	/	/

VI				III				V				V			
C#m	/	/	/	G#m	/	/	/	B	/	/	/	B7	/	/	/

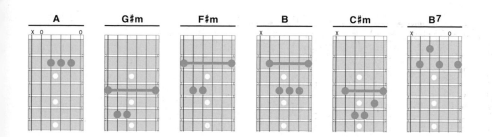

A special instance of avoiding chord I would be to avoid the home key. This next bridge is from a song with a verse in A minor. It moves into the tonic major A and uses dominant 7s to create less certainty about the key, and then has a chromatic semitone (half-step) shift back to the next verse. The last four chords are linked by the common tone of A.

Bridge using tonic major

I				IV				II^ [V]				I [V]			
A	/	/	/	D	/	/	/	B7	/	/	/	E7	/	/	/

I				IV				II^				bII			
A	/	/	/	D	/	/	/	B7	/	/	/	Bbmaj7	/	/	/

Technique #87: the minor bridge

A shift into a minor key at the bridge can be an effective contrast. Try composing a song that has a 12-bar verse with dominant 7 chords and no minor chords, and then move to a bridge with minors, like this one:

Minor bridge

III				VI				I				II			
Em	/	/	/	Am	/	/	/	C7	/	/	/	Dm7	/	/	/

III				VI				II				IV			
Em	/	/	/	Am	/	/	/	Dm	/	/	/	F	/	/	/

Imagine a song with a 12-bar verse in G and then the bridge below, which changes key to E minor. Listen for the effect of the Vm chord, the key-challenging G7 and the two-chord bars (bars 3 and 8):

Minor bridge

III^ [V]				I				IV		Vm		III			
B7	/	/	/	Em	/	/	/	Am	/	Bm	/	G7	/	/	/

V				I				VI				Vm [III]		V	
B7	/	/	/	Em	/	/	/	C	/	/	/	Bm	/	D	/

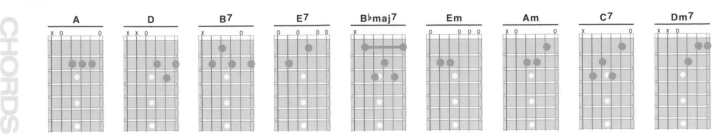

Technique #88: the through-composed bridge

Here's a through-composed bridge of 14 bars with a two-bar link. In bar 9 the music passes through C major (the F in G7 cancels out the F♯ that belongs to E minor and the home key of G major); the tonic C in turn becomes part of a IV-V-I into G major. Bars 15–16 are the link to the rest of the song.

Through-composed bridge

I				VI				III				V			
Em	/	/	/	C	/	/	/	G	/	/	/	B7	/	/	/

I				I				III				III [V]			
Em	/	/	/	Em	/	/	/	G	/	/	/	G7	/	/	/

I [IV]				V				I				II			
C	/	/	/	D7	/	/	/	G	/	/	/	Am	/	/	/

IV				V				I		V		IV			
C	/	/	/	D	/	/	/	G	/	D	/	C	/	/	/

Technique #89: the middle eight that isn't eight

It's fun to occasionally do something unpredictable with a bridge. You might, for instance, change the length from the expected eight bars to another number. Here are some examples.

First, a bridge is lengthened by adding a two-bar link with no vocals. Notice the extra bar of Am, second time, which pushes the Bm one bar forward. It would have been easier (and lazier) to repeat the first line's pattern, but this is more interesting. The sequence II-III-I-VI could be a displaced turnaround (of I-VI-II-III), but this expectation is defeated in bars 5–8:

10-bar bridge in G

II				III				I				VI			
Am	/	/	/	Bm	/	/	/	G	/	/	/	Em	/	/	/

II				II				III				V			
Am	/	/	/	Am	/	/	/	Bm	/	/	/	D	/	/	/

VI				V			
Em	/	/	/	D7	/	/	/

This 11-bar bridge features a II^ chord that suggests the music is about to change key from C major to G major – but the next chord cancels that impression:

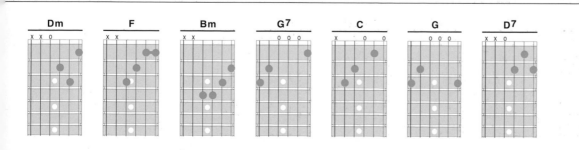

11-bar bridge in C

III				VI				III				VI			
Em	/	/	/	Am	/	/	/	Em	/	/	/	Am	/	/	/

VI				II^				IV				♭VII			
Am	/	/	/	D7	/	/	/	F	/	/	/	B♭	/	/	/

V				IV				V			
Gsus4	/	/	/	F	/	/	/	G	/	/	/

This 12-bar bridge creates the expectation of a key change from G major to D major, but again this is not fulfilled:

12-bar bridge (6 x 2)

I				I				VI				II^			
G	/	/	/	G	/	/	/	Em	/	/	/	A	/	/	/

IV				V				
C	/	/	/	D7	/	/	/	:‖

Technique #90: the coda

A song does not have to have a coda. It could fade on a repeat of the chorus, or end on the chorus's last chord. Some codas use an instrumental version of the chorus over which the singer (and/or soloist) can ad lib. A coda might also use any links in the song, or the intro – which gives the song a neat circularity. This example is a typical use of a down-escalator sequence as an ending:

Coda for song in C

V				IV				II				I	
G	/	/	/	F	/	/	/	Dm	/	/	/	C	‖

Another approach that allows you to end with finality but a twist is to treat the penultimate chord as V, IV, or IVm of a new key:

Coda for song in C, ending on A

V				IV				II [IVm]				I	
G	/	/	/	F	/	/	/	Dm	/	/	/	A	‖

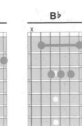
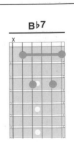

Em   Am   D7   B♭   Gsus4   Dm   Gm   Bm   B♭7

Coda for song in C, ending on B♭

V				I				IV [V]				I	
G	/	/	/	C	/	/	/	F	/	/	/	Bb	‖

This works best at a slower tempo. In the following example we expect to end on F; instead, the Gm becomes a IVm to land on the unexpected D major:

Coda modulation

II				I				II [IVm]				I	
Gm	/	/	/	F	/	/	/	Gm	/	/	/	D	‖

Another way to end in the home key is to link the chords by common notes and add a chromatic chord. Here the common link note through the first three chords is D. The F♯ in A6 is a common note with the final D:

Coda for song in D

VI		♭VI		V		V		I					
Bm	/	Bb7	/	Asus4	/	A6	/	D	/	/	/		‖

The next example uses the ♭III and ♭VI to introduce an element of surprise:

Coda for song in E

I		♭III		♭VI		V		I	
E	/	G	/	C	/	B	/	E	‖

Here's another chromatic approach to chord I held together by the common note E:

Coda for song in E

III		♭III		II		♭II		I	
G♯m		G6	/	F♯m7	/	Fmaj7	/	E	‖
e		e		e		e		e	

This last coda has quite an exotic descending progression:

Coda for song in E

IVm		♭III		II		I	
Am		G	/	F♯m	/	E	/	‖

Asus4   A6   G♯m   G6   F♯m7   Fmaj7   F♯m

Technique #91: the final cadence

If a song does not fade out, it will end with a final cadence comprising the last two chords. The most emphatic final change is the perfect cadence (V-I). The plagal cadence (IV-I) is not as forceful, and its minor version (IVm-I) stresses a melodramatic sadness or resignation. You can also try II-I and III-I, though these are rarer and usually need to be 'decorated' as sevenths to sound like a cadence. For a more unusual ending, try VII-I where VII is a diminished 7.

FORMS OF CHORD I

Most songs end on chord I. This can be a root-form major or minor triad, but you can add extra colour to the ending by using a more complex chord. A first or second inversion will make it less stable; it could also be played as a dominant 7, major 7, minor 7, sixth, sus4 or sus2, ninth, etc, each of which has its own effect. Compare these endings:

Coda for song in C

II				IV		V		I	
Dm	/	/	/	F	/	G	/	Cadd9	

Coda for song in C

II				IV		V		I	
Dm	/	/	/	F	/	G	/	Cmaj7	

OTHER FINAL CHORDS

Apart from chord I, the most likely final chords are V and IV. Neither will sound as finished as ending on chord I, but that might be what a song demands. The lyric content of some songs dictates that ending on chord I would result in a feeling of false consolation. Chord IV sometimes sounds good if turned into a major 7 for an expressive ending.

Ending a major-key song on any of its three minor chords will sound unsettling – it's a bit like putting your foot into what you thought was a hot bath and finding it's cold. The Beatles' 'Ask Me Why' finishes on chord III, while 'A Hard Day's Night' is unusual in ending on the ♭VII chord. If a song is in a minor key, there is a well-known trick of turning the final chord I to the tonic major; for example, a song in A minor would end on an A major chord.

Technique #92: implied chords

Implied chords are excellent for creating variations on sequences that have already happened in a song. Imagine a song in which Dsus4-D-Dsus2-D has been played as a link or part of a verse. Instead of repeating it for the coda, you can give it a new dimension by having the bass play different notes. This results in an implied harmony that exists because of the combination of instruments, not one instrument alone:

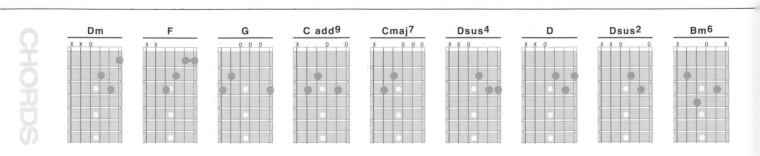

Coda in D, guitar part with bass

I				I				I				I			
Dsus4	/	D	/	Dsus2	/	D	/	Dsus4	/	D	/	Dsus2	/	D	/
d				d				b				b			

I				I				I			
Dsus4	/	D	/	Dsus2	/	D	/	D			
g				g				d			

Here are the chords the listener would be likely to hear from this combination:

Coda in D, implied chords

I				I				VI				VI			
Dsus4	/	D	/	Dsus2	/	D	/	Bm6	/	Bm	/	Bm7add4	/	Bm	/

IV				IV				I			
Gsus2	/	Gmaj9	/	G6/9	/	Gmaj9	/	D			

The chord sequence is close enough to its earlier form to be recognized, but sufficiently different to avoid the feeling of mere repetition.

Shifting notes in the bass part is a powerful tool. Bass notes are crucial to harmony, and the ear relies on them to identify chords. Changing the root note can not only make an inversion, it can change the harmony. Try this chord sequence, which would fit anywhere in a song, with the bass playing the root notes:

Chorus in C

I				VI				IV				I			
C	/	/	/	Am	/	/	/	F	/	/	/	C	/	/	/ :||

Then try the same chord sequence with different bass notes:

Implied chords, chorus in C

I				VI				IV				I			
C	/	/	/	Am	/	/	/	F	/	/	/	C	/	/	/ :||
c				f				d				c			

These bass notes turn Am into Fmaj7 and F into Dm7, as though it were a I-IV-II-I sequence. However, this sequence has a sound of its own. If the whole harmony played the implied chords, the effect would not be as startling. The choice of bass notes is governed here by reverse polarity:

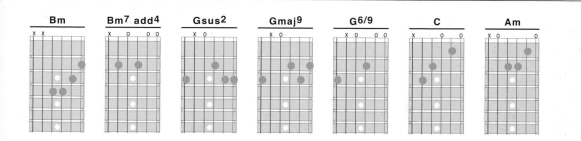

Bm   Bm7 add4   Gsus2   Gmaj9   G6/9   C   Am

a minor chord with a bass note a major third lower becomes a major chord (Am/F = Fmaj7); a major chord with a bass note a minor third lower becomes a minor chord (F/D = Dm7).

THE IMPLIED TURNAROUND

The trailer bassline (see Section 2) is one way of implying a turnaround before its proper form is heard. This is done by replacing chords with reverse-polarity inversions, to 'preview' the turnaround's bassline. A more radical method is to play the bassline but hold one of the chords static above it. The resulting chords are not necessarily inversions – only if the bass note coincides with either of the chord's upper notes will an inversion result.

Let's do this with the turnaround I-II-IV-V in D major: D-Em-G-A. The bassline is thus D-E-G-A under a held D chord:

Implied turnaround

I				I				I				iiI			
D	/	/	/	D/E	/	/	/	D/G	/	/	/	D/A	/	/	/

Only the last chord (D/A) is an inversion. Such a technique generates more harmonic tension than first or second inversions because the relationship between the bass note and the chord may be more complex. Here is a 16-bar verse in which the bassline repeats four times but each chord has its turn to remain for four bars:

I				I				I				iiI			
D	/	/	/	D/E	/	/	/	D/G	/	/	/	D/A	/	/	/

II				II				iiII				II			
Em/D	/	/	/	Em	/	/	/	Em/G	/	/	/	Em/A	/	/	/

iiIV				IV				IV				IV			
G/D	/	/	/	G/E	/	/	/	G	/	/	/	G/A	/	/	/

V				iiV				V				V			
A/D	/	/	/	A/E	/	/	/	A/G	/	/	/	A	/	/	/

It is as if we have a four-chord turnaround disguised, stretched out to four bars a chord. Within it the four-note bassline D-E-G-A keeps repeating. As a result, no chord repeats – there are 16 different, if related, chords in this verse. It begins with a root chord and ends on chord V, the perfect chord to lead into a chorus turnaround beginning with chord I. When the bass note and the root note of a chord coincide, a root chord results – a sudden moment of stability in an otherwise shifting sequence. The root chords form a diagonal line on the chart, appearing in bars 1, 6, 11, and

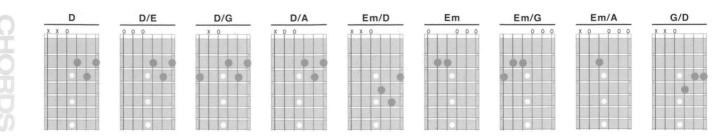

D   D/E   D/G   D/A   Em/D   Em   Em/G   Em/A   G/D

16. The D, G, and A chords all appear as second inversions; Em does not because there isn't a B in the bass.

Now let's take the first four bars of this 16-bar verse and use them as the intro for a song. This song will have only four chords, but we will get more from them by changing the bass notes. Notice that the verse is an elongated version of the turnaround in the chorus:

Song in D major, turnaround I-II-IV-V

Intro

I				I				I				iiI				
D	/	/	/	D/E	/	/	/	D/G	/	/	/	D/A	/	/	/	:‖

Verse

I				I				II				II				
D	/	/	/	D	/	/	/	Em	/	/	/	Em	/	/	/	

IV				IV				V				V				
G	/	/	/	G	/	/	/	A	/	/	/	A	/	/	/	

Link

I				I				I				iiI				
D	/	/	/	D/E	/	/		D/G	/	/	/	D/A	/	/	/	

Chorus

I		II		IV		V		x3	IV				IV				
D	/	Em	/	G	/	A	/	:‖	G	/	/	/	G	/	/	/	

Bridge

II				IV				V				iI				
Em	/	/	/	G	/	/	/	A	/	/	/	D/F♯	/	/	/	

II				IV				V				V				
Em	/	/	/	G	/	/	/	A	/	/	/	A	/	/	/	

Technique #93: the implied dominant 11

Here's a neat trick for making your harmony sound more sophisticated, especially when chord V appears in the run-up to a chorus. Eleventh chords are hard to play on the guitar – but there is an easy way to mimic them. The trick is to play chord IV and then stay on it instead of going to chord V, but change the bass note to the root of chord V. In the key of C, G dominant 11 is G D B F A C.

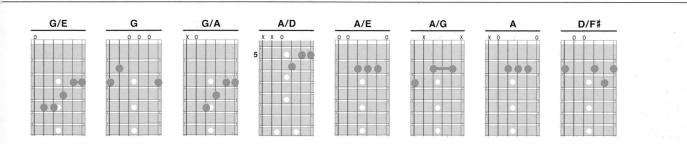

A MISCELLANY OF TECHNIQUES

The top three notes are F A C, an F major triad. By playing the F/G chord, it is as if you are playing the root, seventh, ninth and 11th of the G dominant 11 chord. It may be incomplete, but at least it can be fingered on the guitar. The F/G can resolve to the straight chord V if you have enough room. Compare these three versions of a prechorus:

Prechorus in C

II				III				IV				V			
Dm	/	/	/	Em	/	/	/	F	/	/	/	G	/	/	/ :||

Prechorus in C with implied dominant 11

II				III				IV				IV			
Dm	/	/	/	Em	/	/	/	F	/	/	/	F/G	/	/	/ :||

Prechorus in C with implied dominant 11-V

II				III				IV		IV		IV		V	
Dm	/	/	/	Em	/	/	/	F	/	F/G	/	F/G	/	G	/ :||

Technique #94: asymmetry

Asymmetry is the deliberate cultivation of moments of irregularity in a song. This often involves the insertion of odd numbers – either for a section length or the number of repeats. It covers anything that gets the song away from the boring predictability of everything going in fours – the 'tyranny of four'. Effectively done, asymmetry can be beautiful and carry much emotion. Listen to the phrasing of the melody on Peter Gabriel's 'Intruder', where the asymmetry is used to heighten the sinister atmosphere. Here are some areas where it can be applied:

ASYMMETRICAL TURNAROUNDS

Turnarounds tend to be two or four bars in length. They often repeat four times and have four chords. You can introduce asymmetry by adding a fifth chord within four bars, or making the turnaround last five bars, or have an extra bar every second or fourth time through. Or you can construct a three-bar turnaround and play it four times: 4 x 3 = 12 bars, a standard symmetrical structure.

ASYMMETRICAL SECTIONS

Write a verse, bridge or chorus that is built on odd numbers (3, 5, 7, 9, 11, etc). This one has a descending bassline:

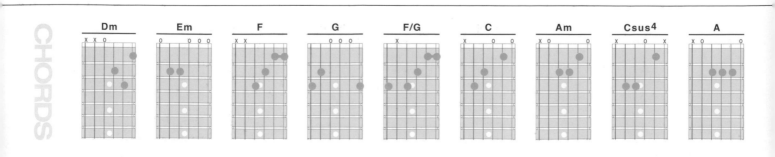

Three-bar verse

I		VI		IV		II	V	I				x4
C	/	Am	/	F	/	Dm	G	C	Csus4	C	/	:‖
c	b	a	g	f	e	d		c				

Seven-bar verse

I				I				I [V]				I			
A	/	/	/	A	/	/	/	A7	/	/	/	D	/	/	/

I				I [IV]				I		V	
D	/	/	/	D	/	/	/	A	/	E	/

The easiest way to arrive at one of these odd lengths is to chop one bar off a four-, eight- or 12-bar section. I call such sections 'curtailed'. This one has a descending note in it:

Curtailed verse in G

I				I				I				IV			
G	/	/	/	Gmaj7	/	/	/	G7	/	/	/	C	/	/	/
g				f♯				f				e			

IV				IV				II		V		
Cmaj7	/	/	/	C7	/	/	/	Am	/	D7	/	:‖
b				b♭				a				

The cut doesn't have to be at the end. Consider an eight-bar verse which has two melodic phrases, in bars 1–3 and 5–7, with bars 4 and 8 acting as pauses. Why not chop out bar 4, so the second phrase starts a bar earlier than you expected? There is a brilliant example of a curtailed verse like this in The Beatles' 'It Won't Be Long'.

Asymmetrical time signature

All the examples in this book assume a time signature of 4/4. But there's nothing to stop you from having a bar in a section which has more or fewer beats – for emphasis, a bar of 2/4 might be inserted. This 2/4 bar could also be used to extend a 4/4 bar into six beats for the sake of the melody – useful if your lyric line won't fit in a single bar of 4/4. To add asymmetry, try bars of 3/4, 5/4 and 7/4.

A MISCELLANY OF TECHNIQUES

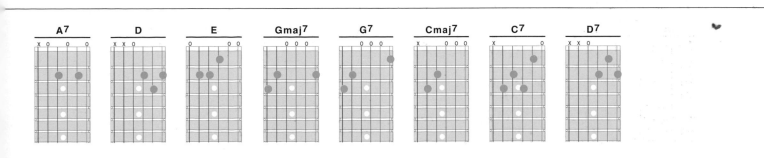

SECTION 9

Technique #95: duration – how long is your song?

The length of any section is extremely variable, but there are certain favourite structures, just as there are favourite chord progressions that everybody uses and will go on using. How many sections will fit into a song is chiefly determined by how long you want it to last. Songs designed for broad appeal tend to run from about 2.00 to 4.30. Longer songs are usually edited for release as singles; the album version might remain at seven minutes. There have been some notable exceptions: The Beatles' 'Hey Jude', T.Rex's 'Hot Love', Queen's 'Bohemian Rhapsody', Don McLean's 'American Pie', and Radiohead's 'Paranoid Android' were all unusually long for singles but became enormous hits. Their success was not due to their length, however.

Duration is determined by the speed (tempo) of the song. A fast song gets through more bars in its four minutes than a slow one; therefore, the fast song could have more verses and choruses. For this reason, always check the length of your song before you record it. To do this, you will need a metronome to determine the number of beats per minute (bpm). Divide this figure by four if you have four beats in a bar; that gives you the number of bars in a minute. Let's block out a simple song structure and do this calculation:

Intro	Verse	Chorus	Link	Verse 2	Chorus 2	Bridge	Verse 3	Chorus 3	Chorus 4	Coda
4	16	8	4	16	8	8	16	8	8	8

This song has 104 bars. At 96bpm, there are 24 4/4 bars per minute – so this song would take about 4 minutes and 30 seconds. If you felt this was too long, then cut sections to make it shorter. For example, you could cut the third verse to save 40 seconds, bringing the song in under four minutes. The structure would now be:

SONG EDIT #1

Intro	Verse	Chorus	Link	Verse 2	Chorus 2	Bridge	Chorus 3	Chorus 4	Coda
4	16	8	4	16	8	8	8	8	8

Another possibility would be to shorten verse 2 to eight bars. This is a popular technique because it brings the second chorus round that much earlier. Doing this *and* the previous edit shortens the song by a minute to 3.30:

SONG EDIT #2

Intro	Verse	Chorus	Link	Verse 2	Chorus 2	Bridge	Chorus 3	Chorus 4	Coda
4	16	8	4	8	8	8	8	8	8

With this version you might be concerned about the predominance of the number 8 as a structuring device. If this makes the song too predictable, some other changes might be needed to introduce more variety to the length of sections. Here is a third way the song could be re-ordered:

SONG EDIT #3

Intro	Verse	Chorus	Link	Bridge	Verse 2	Chorus 2	Chorus 3	Coda
4	16	8	4	8	16	8	8	8

This song is now 80 bars, clocking in at 3.20. The structure is less obvious because one of the choruses has been cut and the bridge is in the middle of the song. There is no repetition of a section until the second verse is reached. Something like this idea was used for the single edit of Boston's celebrated 1970s hit 'More Than A Feeling'. It is worth comparing this with the original album version and seeing which you think is punchier and less predictable.

'MORE THAN A FEELING' (SINGLE EDIT)

Intro • Verse • Link 1 • Chorus • Bridge • Solo • Link 2 [intro] • Verse • Link 3 • Link 1 • Chorus [repeat to fade]

If all this talk of cutting sections, bpm, metronomes and calculations seems ruthless ... well, that's what is sometimes required, not only to make a song commercial but to bring it to its most satisfying form. *Always err on the side of brevity*. If you finish a three-minute song and your listeners think, Hell, that was great – why did it stop so soon? the chances are they'll either ask you to sing it again (live) or play it again (on record) – which is just what you want.

Develop the objectivity to separate the pleasure you get from playing and singing a song from the demands of the song itself, in terms of finding its best length. You may well feel like pouring your heart out in that passionate chorus by tacking six repeats onto the end. Your listeners may tire of it sooner. Don't let that happen. The time for six repeats of the chorus is live, in front of a hysterical audience willing to sing along almost forever. In the recording studio, don't get carried away by what you enjoy playing and thus spoil the song by making it drag on. This also applies to instrumental solos – they're great fun to play, but watch for the critical point when the solo starts to detract from the onward progress of the song, its emotion and story.

There is another aspect to structure which goes beyond verses and choruses. We can call it *deep structure*. It expresses itself through aspects of an arrangement like the number of instruments playing, tempo changes, dynamics, etc. An example would be U2's 'With Or Without You': The surface structure of the song is unremarkable. After the intro, a number of verses follow, one after another. These verses use the same four-bar, four-chord sequence as the intro and, with one notable interruption after the song's climax, continue unchanged throughout. There is hardly a structure to speak of, but the song works because it makes a gradual arch toward the climax via the carefully planned inclusion of more instruments and an increase in volume. This expresses its deep

A MISCELLANY OF TECHNIQUES

structure. The same might also be said of 'Stairway To Heaven'. This is an advanced area of songwriting, but bear in mind that it exists.

Refer to the Appendix for a table of song structures that will give you an idea of the many permutations on the verse/chorus/bridge format songwriters have developed.

Technique #96: the enharmonic common tone

Just as a chord can have many harmonic functions, so a note can have more than one function. If you think of the note A♯ as a sharp note alone, you will tend to use it with chords that belong to the sharp keys, such as B, F♯ and C♯. However, it can also be treated as B♭, which opens up its use in some of the flat keys and their chords. Try to remember the double function of the 'black' notes, because that will suggest new musical possibilities both in chord changes and key changes. In this verse idea, a common note is three times 'absorbed' into a new chord by being enharmonically redefined from A♯ to B♭:

Verse in D

I				I				IVm				V			
D	/	/	/	D+	/	/	/	Gm	/	/	/	A	/	/	/
a				a♯				(a♯) b♭				a			

I				I				♭VI				III^			
D	/	/	/	D+	/	/	/	B♭	/	/	/	F♯	/	/	/
a				a♯				(a♯) b♭				(b♭) a♯			

Technique #97: pedal effects

Can you recall songs such as 'Substitute', 'I Can See For Miles', and 'Pinball Wizard' by The Who, or the chorus of Van Halen's 'Jump'? All of these made use of a device known as a pedal. A *pedal* is a bass note that remains the same while chords move above it. (The term is derived from organ pedals, which are used to play bass notes.) A tonic pedal uses the keynote, and a dominant pedal uses the fifth of the scale. These are the most common pedals. On the guitar, pedal notes tend to be E, A and D, the lowest open strings, because they leave the fingers free to move around the neck to play different chords. Pedals are an excellent way to get extra mileage from a chord sequence. Through an intro or verse, a sequence might be played over a pedal; the same sequence could then be used for a chorus with moving root notes in the bass.

Sometimes inversions are used to get the right chord over the pedal note. Let's say you are playing an A pedal. Here is an intro that makes use of inverted forms of ♭VI and IV in A major to sustain a pedal effect:

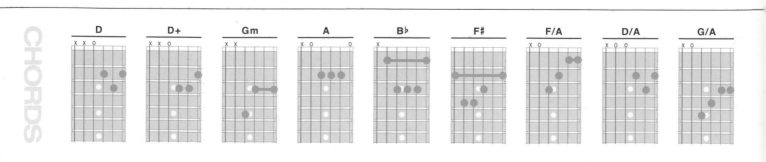

D   D+   Gm   A   B♭   F♯   F/A   D/A   G/A

Tonic pedal Intro in A major

I				♭VI				iiIV				♭VI			
A	/	/	/	F/A	/	/	/	D/A	/	/	/	F/A	/	/	/
a				a				a				a			

In the example above, the pedal note A belongs to each chord – but this need not be the case. The next example is a classic of 1960s soul and Motown songs. A I-♭VII-IV three-chord turnaround is suspended over a tonic pedal:

Tonic pedal in A major

I				♭VII				iiIV				I			
A	/	/	/	G/A	/	/	/	D/A	/	/	/	A	/	/	/ :‖
a				a				a				a			

Compare the musical effect of the same sequence over a dominant pedal, where the pedal note belongs to only one of the chords:

Dominant pedal in A major

iiI				♭VII				IV				iiI			
A/E	/	/	/	G/E	/	/	/	D/E	/	/	/	A/E	/	/	/ :‖
e				e				e				e			

Technique #98: the prechorus

Remember that a prechorus is a section which comes between the verse and the chorus. It is identifiable because the lyric should stay the same. Here are four popular strategies for handling a prechorus:

Escalator prechorus in G

II				III				IV				V			
Am	/	/	/	Bm	/	/	/	C	/	/	/	D	/	/	/

Escalator inversion prechorus in G

II				iI				IV				V			
Am	/	/	/	G/B	/	/	/	C	/	/	/	D	/	/	/

IV-V prechorus in G

IV				V				IV				V			
C	/	/	/	D	/	/	/	C	/	/	/	D	/	/	/

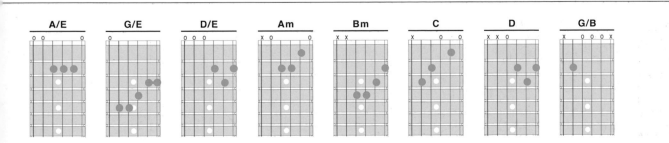

A/E   G/E   D/E   Am   Bm   C   D   G/B

continues on next page

A MISCELLANY OF TECHNIQUES

A MISCELLANY OF TECHNIQUES

IV-V inversion prechorus in G

IV				V				iIV				iV			
C	/	/	/	D	/	/	/	C/E	/	/	/	D/F♯	/	/	/

Technique #99: descending basslines

The descending bassline is an appealing musical idea. This section gives examples of the many ways of harmonizing such a bassline. To begin, we will work with the notes that lie between the keynote and the fifth of the scale in D major, namely D-C♯-B-A, before moving on to examples that use the bass notes D-C-B-A, D-C♯-C-B-A, and D-C♯-B-B♭-A.

Descending bassline (a)

I				I				iIV				V			
D	/	/	/	D/C♯	/	/	/	G/B	/	/	/	A	/	/	/

Descending bassline (b)

I				iV				iIV				V			
D	/	/	/	A/C♯	/	/	/	G/B	/	/	/	A	/	/	/

Descending bassline (c) – open-ended

I				iV				iIV				iIII			
D	/	/	/	A/C♯	/	/	/	G/B	/	/	/	F♯m/A	/	/	/

Descending bassline (d)

I				iV				iiII				V			
D	/	/	/	A/C♯	/	/	/	Em/B	/	/	/	A	/	/	/

Descending bassline (e)

I				iiIII				iIV				V			
D	/	/	/	F♯m/C♯	/	/	/	G/B	/	/	/	A	/	/	/

Descending bassline (f)

I				iiIII				VI				V			
D	/	/	/	F♯m/C♯	/	/	/	Bm	/	/	/	A	/	/	/

Descending bassline (g)

I				iiIII				iiII				V			
D	/	/	/	F♯m/C♯	/	/	/	Em/B	/	/	/	A	/	/	/

CHORDS

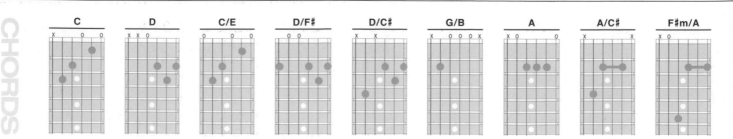

Descending bassline (h) – chromatic VII

I				VII^				iIV				V			
D	/	/	/	C♯	/	/	/	G/B	/	/	/	A	/	/	/

Descending bassline (i) – ♭VII

I				♭VII				iIV				V			
D	/	/	/	C	/	/	/	G/B	/	/	/	A	/	/	/

Descending bassline (j) – ♭VII

I				♭VII				VI				V			
D	/	/	/	C	/	/	/	Bm	/	/	/	A	/	/	/

Descending bassline (k) – static chord I

I				I				I		iIV		V			
D	/	/	/	D/C♯	/	/	/	D/C	/	G/B	/	A	/	/	/

Extended chromatic bassline (a)

I				iiIII				VI				♭VI			
D	/	/	/	F♯m/C♯	/	/	/	Bm	/	/	/	B♭	/	/	/

iiI				V			
D/A	/	/	/	A	/	/	/

Extended chromatic bassline (b)

I				iiIII				VI				iIVm			
D	/	/	/	F♯m/C♯	/	/	/	Bm	/	/	/	Gm/B♭	/	/	/

iiI				V			
D/A	/	/	/	A	/	/	/

Extended chromatic bassline (c)

I				iiIII				♭VII				VI			
D	/	/	/	F♯m/C♯	/	/	/	C	/	/	/	Bm	/	/	/

iIVm				iiI				V				I			
Gm/B♭	/	/	/	D/A	/	/	/	A	/	/	/	D	/	/	/

A MISCELLANY OF TECHNIQUES

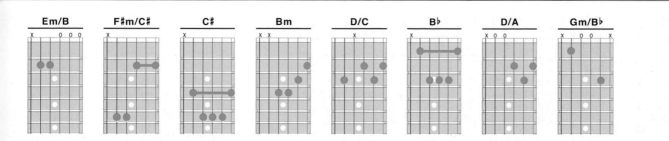

Em/B   F♯m/C♯   C♯   Bm   D/C   B♭   D/A   Gm/B♭

A MISCELLANY OF TECHNIQUES

Extended chromatic bassline (d)

I				iiIII				VI				iIVm			
D	/	/	/	F#m/C#	/	/	/	Bm	/	/	/	Gm/B♭	/	/	/

iiI				V			
D/A	/	/	/	A	/	/	/

Adding a bar of D creates a seven-bar verse with an unexpected return to chord I (inverted):

Descending bassline verse

I				I				bVII				VI			
D	/	/	/	D/C#	/	/	/	C	/	/	/	Bm	/	/	/

iIVm				iiI				V			
Gm/B♭	/	/	/	D/A	/	/	/	A	/	/	/

This bassline travels even further down the scale:

Descending bassline

I				I				iiV				V			
D	/	/	/	D/C#	/	/	/	G/B	/	/	/	A	/	/	/

IV				III				II				V			
G	/	/	/	F#m	/	/	/	Em	/	/	/	A	/	/	/

For a softer bar 8, substitute G; for an emotional intensifier try IVm (Gm) or a return to III or VI, since the B note was harmonized with a first-inversion chord IV.

Descending bassline – inversions but no minors

I				iV				iiV				V			
D	/	/	/	A/C#	/	/	/	G/B	/	/	/	A	/	/	/

IV				iI				iiV				IV			
G	/	/	/	D/F#	/	/	/	A/E	/	/	/	G	/	/	/

F#m/C# Bm Gm/B♭ D/A D/C# G/B F#m Em A/C#

Descending bassline – minors and inversions

I				iiIII				iiII				iIII			
D	/	/	/	F#m/C#	/	/	/	Em/B	/	/	/	F#m/A	/	/	/

iII				iVI				II				iIII			
Em/G	/	/	/	Bm/D	/	/	/	Em	/	/	/	F#m/A	/	/	/

This sequence intensifies the minor aspect and contrasts with the much happier effect of harmonizing the bass with only majors. It is more usual to find them in balance, so choose your minors to go where you feel they have the most effect – this may be determined by your lyric.

Descending bassline – mixed

I				iV				VI				iIII			
D	/	/	/	A/C#	/	/	/	Bm	/	/	/	F#m/A	/	/	/

IV				iI				II				V			
G	/	/	/	D/F#	/	/	/	Em	/	/	/	A	/	/	/

Descending bassline – quicker rate of change

I		iiIII	iIV		V		iII		iI		II		IV	
D	/	F#m/C#	G/B	/	A	/	Em/G	/	D/F#	/	Em	/	G	/

Descending bassline – fall and rise

I			iV	VI			IV					V		iIV	iV
D	/	/	A/C#	Bm	/	/	Bm/A	G	/	/	/	A	/	G/B	A/C#

VI				iII^		IV		III^				V			
Bm	/	Bm7/A	/	E/G#	/	G	/	F#	/	/	/	A	/	/	/ :||

STATIC CHORD V OVER A DESCENDING BASSLINE

Here's another way to use a descending bassline for an intro: keep chord V static and have the bassline move down the scale from the fifth note to the fifth note an octave lower. You can hear this at the start of The Kinks' classic 'Waterloo Sunset'. This creates an interesting tension and expectation. To increase the anticipation, double the rate of change to one chord a bar. Notice how the addition of a dominant 7 helps to differentiate it from the chord V at the start and also leads powerfully to the much-anticipated chord I.

A MISCELLANY OF TECHNIQUES

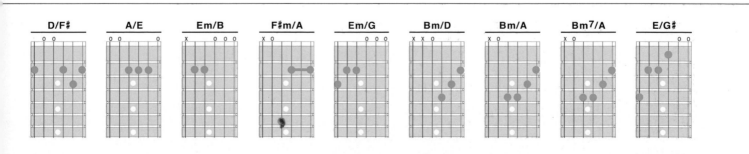

Descending bass intro in D

V		iiiV7		V		iiV		V		iV		V		V	
A	/	A/G	/	A/F♯	/	A/E	/	A/D	/	A/C♯	/	A/B	/	A7	/

The same approach could be applied to any of the other chords in the key. After chord V, the subdominant (chord IV) is probably the next favourite:

Descending bass intro in D

IV		iiiIVmaj7		IV		iiiIV		IV		iIV		IV		IV	
G	/	G/F♯	/	G/E	/	G/D	/	G/C♯	/	G/B	/	G/A	/	G	/

A nice dramatic twist here would be to turn the final G into Gm. (Note: both of these static-chord examples include third-inversion chords, with the seventh note in the bass. Playing four-note chords provides this additional type of inversion.) Both sequences require another instrumentalist to play the bass notes; they are too awkward to play alone on guitar.

DESCENDING BASSLINES FROM A MINOR CHORD

See Section 6 (minor-key progressions) for a list of descending basslines from a minor chord. Here is a famous one that uses a chromatic transformation of chord I:

Descending bassline in E minor

I				I				I				iIVmaj			
Em	/	/	/	Em^7	/	/	/	Em7	/	/	/	A/C♯	/	/	/

Technique #100: chromatic chords – the 'dark outriders'

We have now looked at all the basic chords of the songwriter's craft. Using a progressive approach, gradually more chords have been added to the list, rather like a painter starting with seven colours and then obtaining more and more shades. Our journey has gone like this:

Stage 1: writing with the three major chords of the key: I, IV, and V. Total:	3
Stage 2: adding the three minor chords: II, III, and VI.	6
Stage 3: adding the ♭VII chord	7
Stage 4: adding two more flattened chords: ♭III and ♭VI	9
Stage 5: using reverse-polarity: II, III, and VI as majors, IV as a minor	13

By stage five the songwriter has 13 basic chords (and their inversions) to use in any song in a major key. Are there any chords that we have not yet considered? How many basic chords are there in total? There are 12 notes, so there must be 12 major chords and 12 minor chords. The total is 15 each

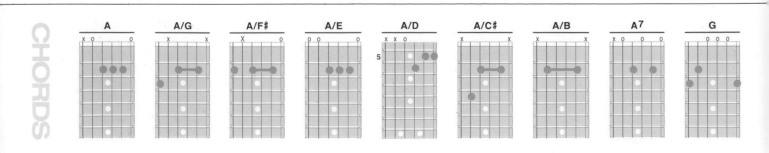

if the enharmonic chords are counted twice (B = C♭, F♯ = G♭, C♯ = D♭), but in terms of actual sound the total remains 24. We have covered 13 of the 24 – just over half of all the basic chords related in some way to the home key.

The 13 chords are divided into two groups: group one is the primary chords I to VI. They can be used however you like and the sense of key will remain strong. The other seven must be added to the mixture in such a way that they won't conflict with each other or overwhelm the home key (unless that is the effect you want). It is exceedingly unlikely that you would use all seven in a song – unless the song is longer than usual, in which case a key change would probably be more effective.

What about the remaining chords? Many of these are too distant to be used without inflicting a high degree of harmonic disturbance. There is one chord, though, which can be brought in because it naturally belongs to a major key. It's the one we've avoided so far: the original chord VII.

STAGE 6: CHORD VII AS A DIMINISHED 7 FORM

In most popular songs after the rock'n'roll era, the VII chord is replaced by the ♭VII chord. As we've seen, the reason for this is that VII is a diminished triad – it is neither major nor minor. The trick is to turn it into a diminished 7. In C major, Bdim = B D F and Bdim7 = B D F A♭. This chord has a variety of uses: it can be used as a substitute for chord V. It can act as a doorway into other keys. Each of its notes can be a root note or act as the leading note of a new key. (We have looked at these functions in Sections 7 and 8.)

One simple device is to treat the major form of VII as a chromatic passing chord between I and a ♭VII. You can hear this in Elvis Costello's 'Pump It Up' (B-B♭-A) and more recently in the main riff of 'No One Loves Me And Neither Do I' by Them Crooked Vultures.

THE 'DARK OUTRIDERS'

Here are the remaining chords – the ones I call the 'dark outriders' of the home key:

I	II		III	IV		V		VI		VII
C		Dm		Em	F		G		A		Bdim
	C♯					F♯					B
Cm	C♯m		D♯m			F♯m	Gm	G♯m		A♯m	Bm

Any of these chords will disrupt the key. Notice that seven of them relate directly to the three pillars of the key - scale degrees 1, 4, and 5 - either sharping them (C♯, C♯m, F♯, F♯m, G♯m) or reversing their polarity (Cm). If the song lyrics suggest a dark emotion of some kind, then it may be appropriate to use one of these chords. But beware: these chords exert a powerful influence on their musical surroundings - they stick out. Their very strangeness means that few popular songs use them, because they tend to express colours and emotions which the audience does not recognize. This complicates matters if you are trying to write a hit. Pull it off - use a strange chord

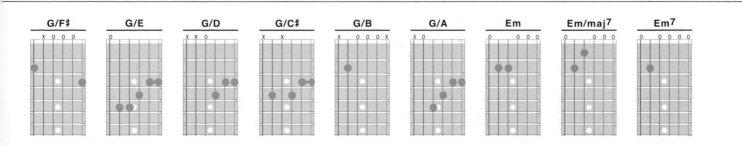

A MISCELLANY OF TECHNIQUES

but make it work – and you will have a song that doesn't sound like anyone else's, pretty much ever! But it isn't easy. The dark outriders are not the stuff of hit singles – album tracks and experimental B-sides, maybe. One exception is Elvis Costello's 'I Want You' which is in Em. The bitterness of the lyric is expressed by an unrelated D♯m chord that stabs the music every few verses. If you wish to experiment with these chords, here are some tips for making them blend a little better:

- Insert one between two chords that are a tone (whole-step) apart. This effect is heightened if the chords have the same form – pure chromaticism. Here is a chord sequence often heard in 1920s jazz-age popular songs (also mentioned in Section 7 under minor 7 chords):

Verse in A

II		V		I		III	♭III	II		V		I			
Bm	/	E	/	A	/	C♯m7	Cm7	Bm7	/	E	/	A	/	/	/

- Approach the root from a scale degree and move to another degree of the scale.
- Approach the root chromatically or as part of a descending or ascending bassline:

Verse in G (VII^)

I		VII^		VI				I		II		III		V	
G	/	F♯	/	Em	/	/	/	G	/	Am	/	Bm	/	D	/

- Dilute the chord by turning it into a seventh or sixth, or even a suspended chord.
- Create a common tone on either side of the dark outrider, so one note doesn't change. In this example, the basic progression is V-IV-III-II-I, as might be found in the coda or at the end of a major section. Three dark outriders have been inserted into this sequence to create a chromatic bassline moving in semitones (half-steps) down from G to C: G-F♯-F-E-E♭-D-D♭-C. In order to integrate them better, they are played as sevenths. The additional note provides a common tone with the scale and the chords before and after. The common tone is a thread which the ear can follow, to make the chords sound more linked.

Verse in C

V		♯IV		IV				III		♭III		II		♭II	
G6	/	F♯7	/	Fmaj7	/	/	/	Em7	/	E♭maj7	/	Dm7	/	D♭maj7	
e		e		e				e+d		d		d+c		c	

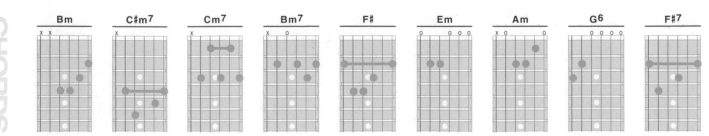
Bm C♯m7 Cm7 Bm7 F♯ Em Am G6 F♯7

Here is an example where the common tone B links the chromatic chord with the G that precedes it in bars 1 and 3, and the Bm that succeeds it in bar 4:

Verse in G (♯IV)

I		♯IV		V				I		♯IV		III			
G	/	C♯7	/	D	/	/	/	G	/	C♯7	/	Bm	/	/	/
b		b						b		b		b			

• Change the chromatic chord to a type which has a common note with the home key:

Verse in C (♯IV)

III				V			iII^	III				V			
Em	/	/	/	G	/	/	D/F♯	Em	/	/	/	G	/	/	/

♯IV				VI			
F♯7	/	/	/	Am	/	/	/

Fmaj7   E♭maj7   Dm7   D♭maj7   C♯7   D/F♯

SECTION 10
A GUIDE TO THE CD

The 20-song CD that accompanies *The Songwriting Sourcebook* has chord sequences in a variety of musical styles. These are missing only a melody and a lyric to be complete songs. The chord charts for these examples are provided on the following pages, just like the full-song examples in Sections 1–9 – only this time you can hear what they sound like.

To save space, each section of a song is given once and then referred to as a verse, chorus, etc, when repeated. There is a brief annotation for each track, explaining some of the techniques used and providing listening tips. Where there is real ambiguity about the key of a song or song section, an approximate harmonic analysis is provided.

The CD is a multi-purpose learning tool. It illustrates many aspects of harmony and song structure that are discussed in the book. You can also use it as a source for arranging ideas by listening to the type and number of instruments on each track and where they are placed in the stereo field. You can also play along – or sit back and enjoy the music.

Track 1: You Can't Run

Intro

I				VI				I				VI			
E	/	/	/	C♯m	/	/	/	E	/	/	/	C♯m	/	/	/

Verse

I				II				III				VI			
E	/	/	/	F♯m	/	/	/	G♯m	/	/	/	C♯m	/	/	/ :‖

IV				IV				V				V			
A	/	/	/	A	/	/	/	B	/	/	/	B	/	/	/

I				VI				I				VI			
E	/	/	/	C♯m	/	/	/	E	/	/	/	C♯m	/	/	/

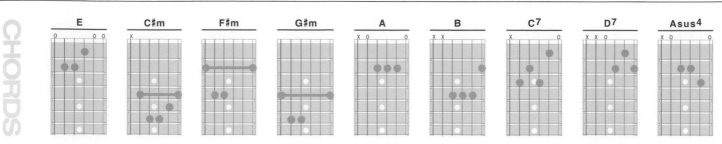

E	C♯m	F♯m	G♯m	A	B	C7	D7	Asus4

Verse

Bridge

bVI				bVI				bVII				bVII			
C7	/	/	/	C7	/	/	/	D7	/	/	/	D7	/	/	/

IV				bVI				bVI				bVII			
Asus4	/	A	/	C7	/	/	/	C7	/	/	/	D7	/	/	/

bVII				IV				IV				bIII			
D7	/	/	/	Asus4	/	A	/	Asus4	/	A	/	Gsus4	/	G	/

V			
B7	/	/	/

Verse

Bridge

Verse

Coda

I				VI				I
E	/	/	/	C#m	/	/	/	E

Notes:

- 'You Can't Run' is loosely modelled on The Beatles' early verse/bridge songs which have no separate chorus. The lyric hook is inside the verse.
- The 16-bar verse has three components: a rising I-II-III-VI progression which uses the three minor chords of the key (twice), a second four-bar section, and a third section which recycles the I-VI change from the intro.
- The bridge creates a necessary contrast by avoiding minor chords, avoiding chord I, and using chords bVI and bVII in dominant 7 forms that include a note foreign to the scale of E major. This has a tougher feeling than the verse.
- The bridge is asymmetrical, consisting of a five-bar phrase and an eight-bar phrase, making 13 bars in total.

Gsus4

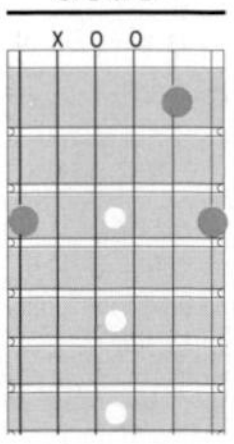

B7

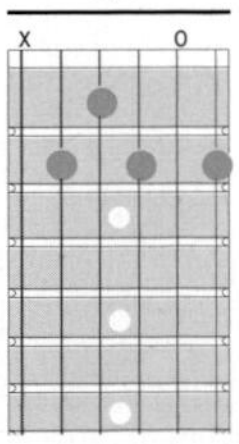

Track 2: A Postcard In Winter

Intro

I				Vm				I				Vm			
C	/	Cmaj7	/	Gm	/	/	/	C	/	Cmaj7	/	Gm	/	/	/

I			
C	/	Cmaj7	/

Verse

II				III				IV				V			
Dm	/	/	/	Em	/	/	/	F	/	/	/	G	/	/	/

VI				iiI				iiII^				ii♭VII			
Am	/	/	/	C/G	/	/	/	D/F♯	/	/	/	B♭/F	/	/	/

IVm				iI			
Fm	/	/	/	C/E	/	/	/ :‖

Verse

Coda

Vm				I		I		x3	Vm				Vm	
Gm9	/	Gm	/	C	/	Cmaj7	/ :‖		Gm9	/	Gm	/	Gm9 ‖	

Notes:

- This song is an example of a miniature (hence 'postcard'), clocking in under two minutes and with only a single verse, which is through-composed. The verse is repeated. The lyric hook would go at the end of the verse or in the coda.
- The harmony is ambiguous. The intro appears to start in C major, but there is a Gm instead of the expected chord V (G). Perhaps this is V-II in F major … but in F major chord V would be C7, not C*maj*7. (For this chart, I have analyzed the chords as though the key were C major.)
- The verse could be in C major or modal A minor for the first eight bars.
- The bassline of the verse makes an arch: it climbs to A and then descends to E.
- Notice the unexpected ♭VII-IVm change and the use of inversions.
- In the coda, a minor ninth intensifies the emotion. The song ends, unresolved, on this chord. The postcard, it seems, awaits a reply.

Cmaj7 Gm Dm Em Am C/G D/F♯ B♭/F Fm

Track 3: Central Circle Bakerloo

Intro/riff

I		bVII		IV				x4
Asus4	A	Gsus4	G	D	/	/	/	:‖

Verse

I				bVII				V		bVII		V			
A	/	/	/	A	/	/	/	G	/	E	/	G	/	E	/ :‖

VI				VI				II				II			
F#m	/	/	/	F#m	/	/	/	Bm	/	/	/	Bm	/	/	/

IV				IV				V				IV	V		
D	/	/	/	D	/	/	/	E	/	/	/	D	E	/	/

Chorus

IV				I				V				I	V		
D	/	/	/	A	/	/	/	E	/	/	/	A	E	/	/ :‖

Riff
Verse
Chorus

Guitar solo

I				I				bVII				bVII				x3
A	/	/	/	A	/	/	/	G/A	/	/	/	G/A	/	/	/	:‖

V				V				V				V			
E	/	/	/	E7sus4	/	/	/	E	/	/	/	E7sus4 /	/	/

Verse
Chorus twice
Riff

Notes:
- This is an uptempo power-pop/punk song in the style of UK's The Jam.
- The intro features a chordal riff made up of tense sus4s. This serves as a link throughout.
- Notice the effect of using only minor chords for bars 9–12 of the verse.
- Predictably for a rock track, bVII puts in an appearance.

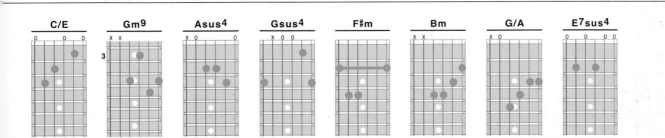

C/E   Gm9   Asus4   Gsus4   F#m   Bm   G/A   E7sus4

- Chords often occur on adjacent beats to create rhythmic 'punches'.
- During the guitar solo, the I-♭VII change creates something of a breather. It is followed by four bars of V to make a powerful return to chord I in the last verse.

Track 4: The First September

Intro/riff

I				IV		V		
D	/	/	/	G	/	A	/	:‖

Verse

I				II				IV				V			
D	/	/	/	Em	/	/	/	G	/	/	/	A	/	/	/

I				IV		V		x2	VI				V			
D	/	/	/	G	/	A	/	:‖	Bm	/	/	/	A	/	/	/

Riff for 2 bars

iI				IV				VI				V			
D/F♯	/	/	/	G	/	/	/	Bm	/	/	/	A	/	/	/

III				IV				V				V			
F♯m	/	/	/	G	/	/	/	Asus4	/	/	/	A	/	/	/

Chorus

I				V				IV				IV			x4
D	/	/	/	A/	/	/		G	G/F♯	G/E	/	G	G/F♯	G/E	/	:‖

II				V			
Em	/	/	/	A	/	/	/

Riff

Verse

Chorus

Coda

I				IV		V		I		VI		II		V	
D	/	/	/	G	/	A	/	D	/	Bm	/	Em	/	A	/ :‖ to fade

Riff for 2 bars   Riff for 2 bars

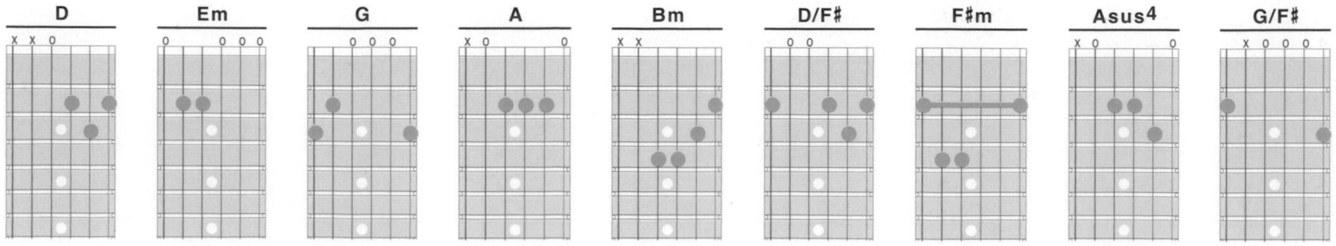

D   Em   G   A   Bm   D/F♯   F♯m   Asus4   G/F♯

Notes:

- This arrangement is in the style of 1960s folk-rockers The Byrds, featuring the 12-string picking style pioneered by Roger McGuinn.
- The verse uses a four-bar vocal phrase followed by the two-bar riff.
- Notice how D/F♯ and F♯m are used in the verse to create different colours over the same bass note.
- The chorus's I-V-IV is a variation on the I-IV-V of the intro.
- The coda couples the original two-bar riff with a further two bars which use chord substitution. The D bar now includes the relative minor (Bm) and the G of the second bar becomes its relative minor (Em).

Track 5: Corngold Moonsilver

Intro and verse

IV				VI				IV				VI			
Dmaj7	/	/	/	F♯m	/	/	/	Dmaj7	/	/	/	F♯m	/	/	/

I				I								
A	/	/	/	Amaj7	/	/	/	:‖				

IV				VI				IV				VI			
Dmaj7	/	/	/	F♯m	/	/	/	Dmaj7	/	/	/	F♯m	/	/	/

Prechorus

IV				IV				IV				IV			
D	/	/	/	D	/	/	/	D	/	/	/	D	/	/	/

I				I				I				I			
A	/	/	/	A	/	/	/	A	/	/	/	A	/	/	/

IV				IV				IV				IV			
D	/	/	/	D	/	/	/	D	/	/	/	D	/	/	/

Chorus

I				VI				IV				V			x3
A	/	/	/	F♯m	/	/	/	D	/	/	/	E	/	/	/ :‖

continues on next page

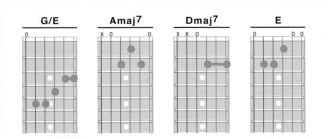

G/E   Amaj7   Dmaj7   E

Verse 2

IV				VI				IV				VI			
Dmaj7	/	/	/	F#m	/	/	/	Dmaj7	/	/	/	F#m	/	/	/

I				I			
A	/	/	/	Amaj7	/	/	/ :||

Prechorus

Chorus 2

I				VI				IV				V				x3
A	/	/	/	F#m	/	/	/	D	/	/	/	E	/	/	/ :||	

V			
E	/	/	/

Bridge

IV				VI				IV				IV			
‖: D	/	/	/	F#m	/	/	/	D	/	/	/	D	/	/	/ :‖
c#				(2nd time) b	c#	d	e	f#							

IV				VI				IV				IV			
‖: D	/	/	/	F#m	/	/	/	D	/	/	/	D	/	/	/ :‖
								b	c#	d	e	f#			

IV				IV				V				V			
D	/	/	/	D	/	/	/	E	/	/	/	E	/	/	/
b	c#	d	e	f#											

Chorus: as chorus 2 but ‖x4 instead of :‖x3

Coda

IV				IV				IV				IV			
D	/	/	/	D	/	/	/	D	/	/	/	D	/	/	/
d		c#		b		a		g#		f#		e		d	

II			
Bm9	/	/	/ :‖
b			

Notes:

- In the intro, the bass is delayed to bar 5 so the IV-VI change is less rooted.

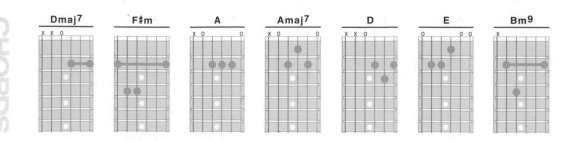

Dmaj7   F#m   A   Amaj7   D   E   Bm9

- In the prechorus, notice the entry of the drums and the use of pedal D and A in bass and guitar as the 12-string guitar plays rising chords.
- The chorus uses a I-VI-IV-V turnaround with an extra bar of E when it goes to the bridge.
- In the bridge, the bassline changes the colour of the chords even though the basic change is the same as the verse.
- Listen for the descending bassline in the coda.

Track 6: Elizabeth

Intro

I		VII		IV^				I		VII		IV^		Vm	
Dm	/	C	/	G	/	/	/	Dm	/	C	/	G	/	Am7	/

I		VII		IV^				Vm				Vm			
Dm	/	C	/	G	/	/	/	Am7	/	/	/	Am7	/	/	/

Verse

bIII				IV				I				I			
Eb	/	/	/	F	/	/	/	C	/	/	/	C	/	/	/

bIII				IV				I				bVI			
Eb	/	/	/	F	/	/	/	C	/	/	/	Abmaj7	/	/	/

bIII				IV				I				I			
Eb	/	/	/	F	/	/	/	C	/	/	/	C	/	/	/

II^				II^				IV				IV [III^]			
Dsus4	/	D	/	Dsus2	/	D	/	Fadd9	/	F	/	Fmaj7	/	/	/

Chorus = Intro
Verse

Chorus 2

I		VII		IV^				I		VII		IV^		Vm	
Dm	/	C	/	G	/	/	/	Dm	/	C	/	G	/	Am7	/

I		VII		IV^				IV^				[drum fill]			
Dm	/	C	/	G	/	/	/	G					/	/	/

continues on next page

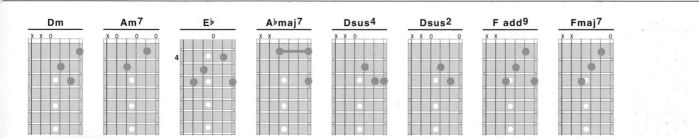

Dm   Am7   Eb   Abmaj7   Dsus4   Dsus2   F add9   Fmaj7

Bridge

I	VII	♭VII^	VII
Gm6 / / /	F#m7 / / /	Fm/maj7 / / /	F#m7 / / /
e	e	e	e

I [VII]	IV	V	V [II^]
Gm6 / / /	Dmaj9 / / /	Esus4 / / /	E / / /
e	e	e	e

Chorus 3

Chorus 4

I	VII	IV^		I	VII	IV	Vm
Dm /	C /	G / / /		Dm /	C /	G /	Am7 /

I	VII	IV^	Vm	III
Dm /	C /	G / / /	Am7 / / /	Fmaj7 / / /

Coda

Vm	III	x3	I	VII	IV	Vm	I
Am7 / / /	Fmaj7 / / /	:‖	Dm /	C /	G /	Am7	Dm ‖

Notes:

- This track is harmonically ambiguous. The chords have been analyzed as though the home key was a modal D minor with Vm, but with a verse in C major.
- The intro is recycled as the chorus.
- The intial Dm-C-G change is given a different ending in bars 4 and 7–8.
- There is a sense of surprise at the start of the verse because of the ♭III chord, and ♭VI appears in bar 8 for an additional twist.
- The verse ends with a sus4/sus2 change that arouses the expectation of a key change, possibly to G, which is then cancelled by the following F chords.
- The highly chromatic bridge provides substantial contrast to the verse and chorus. There is no sure feeling of key here. (The analysis shows it moving from G minor to A major.) Throughout the eight bars, the note E is a common tone linking the chords. Listen for the Esus4-E change, which is unexpected and creates a new approach to the Dm chord that begins the chorus.

A GUIDE TO THE CD

CHORDS

Gm6   F#m7   Fm/maj7   Dmaj9   Esus4   Dm   C   G   Am7

Track 7: Much Ado About Something

Intro

I				VI				II				IV			V	
D	/	/	/	Bm	/	/	/	Em7	/	/	/	G	/	/	A6	:‖

Link

VI				VII^		♭VII		VI				VII^		♭VII	
Bm	/	/	/	C♯7♭9	/	C9	/	Bm	/	/	/	C♯7♭9	/	C9	/

♭VII			
C9	/	/	/

Verse

I				III^				IV				II^			
D	/	/	/	F♯	/	/	/	G	/	/	/	E7	/	/	/

♭VII				V				VI				IV			
C	/	/	/	A7	/	/	/	Bm	/	/	/	G6	/	/	/ :‖

Chorus = Intro

Bridge

II				II				II				II			
Em	/	/	/	Em	/	/	/	Em	/	/	/	Em	/	/	/

II				II		V		x4 II			
‖: Em	/	/	/	Em	/	A	/	:‖ Em	/	/	/

Link (four bars only)
Verse
Chorus twice

Coda = Link

I				II^		♭II		x3 I	
Bm	/	/	/	C♯7♭9	/	C9	/	:‖ Bm	‖

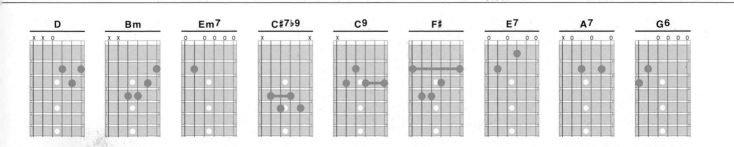

D   Bm   Em7   C♯7♭9   C9   F♯   E7   A7   G6

Notes:
- A two-bar unaccompanied drum break starts the song.
- The song is in D major but has a strong leaning toward its relative minor, B minor.
- The link features an unusual chromatic chord change and voicings of C♯ and C chords.
- The verse uses two reverse-polarity chords, II^ and III^, but neither acts as a doorway to another key.
- The chorus has a I-VI-II-IV turnaround with chord V sneaked in at the very end.
- There are only two chords in the bridge, and it stays on Em for quite a while in order to create a breather.
- The song ends unexpectedly on the relative minor.

Track 8: From Celtic Roots

Capo II

Intro

IV		IV		IV				x3	I				VI			
Am	/	Am7	/	Am/F♯	/	/	/	:‖	Em	/	/	/	C	/	/	/

I				VI			
Em	/	/	/	C	/	/	/

Verse = Intro

Chorus

I				Vm				VI				VI			
Em	/	/	/	Bm6	/	/	/	Cmaj7	/	/	/	Cmaj7	/	/	/

I				Vm				VI				IV			
Em	/	/	/	Bm6	/	/	/	Cmaj7	/	/	/	Am	/	/	/

VII				VII			
D7	/	/	/	D7	/	/	/

Verse twice

Chorus

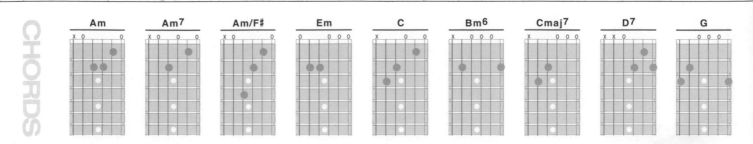

| Am | Am7 | Am/F♯ | Em | C | Bm6 | Cmaj7 | D7 | G |

Bridge/guitar solo

I		III	IV		VI			
Em	/	/	G	Am	/	C	/	:‖

I		III	IV		VI		x3	VII				VII			
Em	/	/	G	Am	/	C	/	:‖	D /	/	/	D /	/	/	/

I		III	IV		VI		x3	VII				VII			
Em	/	/	G	Am	/	C	/	:‖	D /	/	/	D /	/	/	/

I		III	IV		VI		x3
Em	/	/	G	Am	/	C	/	:‖

Last verse

IV		IV		IV			x3	I				VI			
Am	/	Am7	/	Am/F♯	/	/	/	:‖	Em	/	/	/	C	/	/	/

I				VI			
Em	/	/	/	C	/	/	/

Coda

I				VI				I	
Em	/	/	/	C	/	/	/	:‖ Em	‖

Notes:

- 'From Celtic Roots' is a slow rock ballad in E minor with a punchier bridge and contrasting dynamics. The actual chords are a tone higher; use a capo at II.
- The song uses triple repeats and 10-bar sections.
- The intro is recycled as the verse.
- The chorus centres on chord I, uses Vm and extends to 10 bars.
- The last Am-D7 change of the chorus creates the expectation of a possible key change to G – but the music returns to the Am chord.
- The bridge is preceded by a silent bar. It is a I-III-IV-VI rising turnaround with two bars of D that act as a breather from the turnaround's motion.

Track 9: She Paints The Picture

Verse

VI				III				II^				II			
Am	/	/	/	Em	/	/	/	D	/	/	/	Dm	/	/	/

I				IV				I				II		V [IV]	
C	/	/	/	F	/	/	/	C	/	/	/	Dm	/	G	/ :‖

Chorus

I		II		VI		V		x3 I		V		IV		V	
D	/	Em	/	Bm	/	A	/	:‖ D	/	A	/	G	/	A	/

I		V		VI^							
D	/	A	/	B	/	/	/

Verse

Chorus

Bridge 1

iiI				VI				IV				II			
E♭/B♭	/	/	/	Cm	/	/	/	A♭	/	/	/	Fm	/	/	/

iiV				III [IVm]				I				I [♭VII]			
B♭/F	/	/	/	Gm	/	/	/	Dsus4	/	/	/	D	/	/	/

Bridge 2

I				I				IV				IV			x2
E	/	/	/	E	/	/	/	A7	/	/	/	A7	/	/	:‖

I				I				IV				V			
E	/	/	/	E	/	/	/	A	/	/	/	B	/	/	/

Verse 3

VI				III				II^				II			
Am	/	/	/	Em	/	/	/	D	/	/	/	Dm	/	/	/

I				IVm				I				II		V	
C	/	/	/	Fm	/	/	/	C	/	/	/	Dm	/	G	/ :‖

Am   Em   D   Dm   C   F   G   Bm   A

A GUIDE TO THE CD

Chorus 3

I		II		VI		V		x3	I		V		IV		V	
D	/	Em	/	|Bm	/	A	/	:||	D	/	A	/	|G	/	A	/	|

I		V		♭III				
D	/	A	/	|F	/	/	/	|

Chorus repeat to fade

Notes:

- 'She Paints The Picture' is written and arranged in the style of the mid-1960s Beach Boys. This comes across in the harmonic contrasts, use of inversions and instrumentation.
- There is no intro.
- The song begins in C major, though chord I is not reached until bar 5. It contrasts a verse in C, a chorus in D, and bridges in E♭ and E.
- The chorus links two turnarounds: I-II-VI-V has minor chords, I-V-IV-V does not. The first chorus ends on B (VI^) but chorus 3 ends on F (♭III).
- The key changes are managed as follows: IV-I into D (chorus) is a plagal cadence. The change into the bridge is smoothed out because the bass moves a semitone (half-step) down from B to B♭, while the chord E♭ is enharmonically D♯, and D♯ is a note in a B major chord. Bridge 1 moves a tone (whole-step) to get to E major. Notice the contrast between the complexity of bridge 1 and the far more straightforward bridge 2.
- Listen for verse 3's reverse polarity in bar 6: IV becomes IVm, giving an extra emotional twist to this final verse.

Track 10: Strike The Bridge

Intro

II				iiVI				IV				II		V		
Am	/	/	/	|Em/B	/	/	/	|C	/	/	/	|G/B	/	/	/	|

Verse

IV				IV				IV				III^				
C	/	/	/	|C	/	/	/	|C	/	/	/	|B7	/	/	/	:||

Chorus

II		III		IV		III		II		III		I		VI		
Am	/	Bm	/	|C	/	Bm	/	|Am	/	Bm	/	|G	/	Em	/	|

continues on next page

B	E♭/B♭	Cm	A♭	B♭/F	Gm	Dsus4	A7	Em/B

Link

iiI				VI			
A/E	/	/	/	F#m7	/	/	/

Verse

Chorus 2

II		III		IV		III		II		III		I		VI	
Am	/	Bm	/	C	/	Bm	/	Am	/	Bm	/	G	/	Em	/

II		III		IV		III		II		V		I		VI	
Am	/	Bm	/	C	/	Bm	/	Am	/	D	/	G	/	Em	/

Bridge

iiV		V		iiIV		IV		iiV		V		iiVm [II]		II	
B/F#	/	B	/	A/E	/	A	/	B/F#	/	B	/	Bm/F#	/	Bm	/

VI				II^ [V]				II				III			
F#m	/	/	/	B	/	/	/	Fm	/	/	/	Gm	/	/	/

IV				V				iiIV				iV			
Ab	/	/	/	Bb	/	/	/	Ab/C	/	/	/	Bb/D	/	/	/

Verse (no repeat)

Chorus 3

II		III		IV		III		II		III		I		VI	
Am	/	Bm	/	C	/	Bm	/	Am	/	Bm	/	G	/	Em	/

II		III		IV		III		II		V		III			
Am	/	Bm	/	C	/	Bm	/	Am	/	D	/	Bm	/	/	/

VI							
Em	/	/	/	repeat and fade			

Notes:

- This song is also based on the mid-1960s *Pet Sounds*-era Beach Boys.
- Notice the use of inversions at various points, such as the intro and bridge.
- The key is G major, but the root G chord is withheld until the chorus.

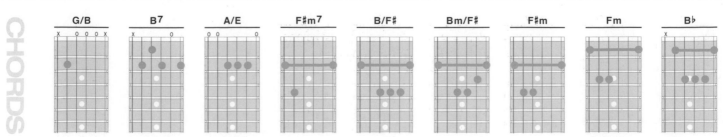

G/B   B7   A/E   F#m7   B/F#   Bm/F#   F#m   Fm   Bb

- The bass notes of the intro are similar to the chorus but harmonized differently.
- In chorus 1 many of the chords are heard over a pedal A. In chorus 2 this happens only the first time; on the repeat, the bass moves with the chords, giving a fresh sound to the sequence.
- The bridge is harmonically ambiguous. The first half has been analyzed as though it were in E major although chord I never appears. The Bm-F♯m change momentarily suggests A major until the B reappears. The Fm signals an abrupt drop down a semitone (half-step) to the key of E♭. The inversions allow the bassline to slowly ascend through almost a complete E♭ major scale (from F to D) although the E♭ is withheld.
- Verse three has been edited down to four bars.
- The last chorus has two new minor chords at the end.

Track 11: Too Much Sun

Intro

I		IV		I			I				I			
[A]	/	[D]	/	[A]		:‖	A	/	/	/	A	/	/	/ ‖

riff

Verse

I				I				I				I			
A	/	/	/	A	/	/	/	A	/	/	/	A	/	/	/ ‖

IV				IV				I				I			
D9	/	/	/	D9	/	/	/	A7	/	/	/	A7	/	/	/ ‖

V				IV				I		♭VII		I			
E	/	/	/	D	/	/	/	A	/	G	/	A7	/	/	/ ‖

Riff (two bars)
Verse
Riff twice (four bars)

Guitar solo

IV				IV				I				I			
D	/	/	/	D	/	/	/	A	/	/	/	A	/	/	/ ‖

V				IV				V				IV			
E	/	/	/	D7	/	/	/	E7	/	/	/	D7	/	/	/ ‖

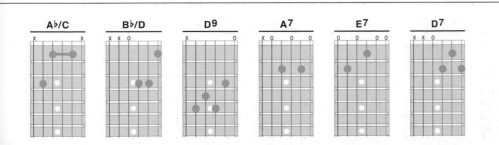

A♭/C   B♭/D   D9   A7   E7   D7

Verse

Riff

Guitar solo 2

IV				IV				I				I			
D	/	/	/	D	/	/	/	A	/	/	/	A	/	/	/

Last verse

V				IV				I		♭VII		I			
E	/	/	/	D	/	/	/	A	/	G	/	A7	/	/	/

Coda (riff once)

Notes:

- This song evokes mid-1950s rock'n'roll.
- It shows several ways of adapting a basic 12-bar to make a song which does not simply consist of a succession of 12-bar verses one after the other.
- The verse is an adapted 12-bar – notice the ♭VII chord in bar 11.
- The guitar solo uses bars 5–10 of the verse but repeats 9–10 to delay the return of chord I.
- The second guitar solo and last verse are bars 5–12 of the initial verse.

Track 12: Trouble

Intro

V				V				V				IVm			
B7	/	/	/	B7	/	/	/	B7	/	/	/	Am	/	/	/

Verse

I				VI				II		V		IV		V	
E	/	/	/	C#m	/	/	/	F#m	/	B	/	A	/	B	/

♭VII				IV				I	V		I	I	V	I	
D	/	/	/	A	/	/	/	E	B	E	/	E	B	E	/

♭VII				IV				VI	III	VI		VI	III	VI	
D	/	/	/	A	/	/	/	C#m	G#m	C#m	/	C#m	G#m	C#m	/

Chorus

IV				IV				I				VI			
A	/	/	/	A	/	/	/	E	/	/	/	C#m	/	/	/

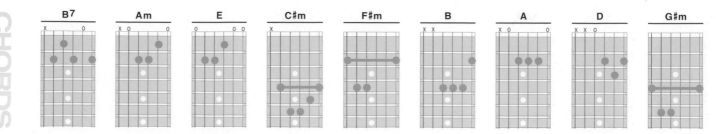

II		V		IV		V	
F♯m	/	B	/	A	/	B	/

Link

I				V				I				V			
E	/	/	/	B7	/	/	/	E	/	/	/	B7	/	/	/

Verse

Chorus

Link

Bridge

III^				III^				IV		I		IV		I	
G♯	/	/	/	G♯	/	/	/	A	/	E	/	A	/	E	/ :‖

II^				II^				II				II			
F♯	/	/	/	F♯	/	/	/	F♯m	/	/	/	F♯m	/	/	/

♭VII				iIV				V				V			
D	/	/	/	A/C♯	/	/	/	B	/	/	/	B	/	/	/

Verse

Chorus

Chorus 2

I				V				II		V		IV		V	
E	/	/	/	B7	/	/	/	F♯m	/	B	/	A	/	B	/

III				VI				II		V		IV		V	
G♯m	/	/	/	C♯m	/	/	/	F♯m	/	B	/	A	/	B	/

Coda

I				V				I				V			x3
E	/	/	/	B7	/	/	/	E	/	/	/	B7	/	/	/ :‖

I				V				I
E	/	/	/	B7	/	/	/	E ‖

G♯   F♯   A/C♯

Notes:

- 'Trouble' is a New Wave number in the style of Elvis Costello & the Attractions as they sounded around the time of their second album in 1979.
- The key is unambiguously E major.
- The intro avoids chord I but throws in the mildy exotic IVm.
- Notice the rate of chord change. It is sometimes two to a bar or even three to a bar when the chords are strongly accented. This kind of rhythmic touch pays off live. Golden rule: make the songs exciting when you *write* them.
- Don't rely on making them exciting when playing live just because it's louder and rawer. If the song is exciting in the first place, the volume and dynamics of live performance will double the impact.
- The division between verse and chorus is blurred.
- The bridge adds contrast by using III^ and II^ reverse-polarity chords.
- Listen for the minor-chord substitution in the last chorus (the melody remains the same over these chords).
- The coda's I-V change is about sheer energy rather than harmonic interest.

Track 13: Falling Under Heaven

Intro

III^				III^				II				II			
G♯	/	/	/	G♯	/	/	/	F♯m	/	/	/	F♯m	/	/	/

I				iI				IV				IV				
‖: E	/	/	/	E/G♯	/	/	/	A	/	/	/	A	/	/	/	:‖

Verse

I				iI				IV				IV				x3
E	/	/	/	E/G♯	/	/	/	A	/	/	/	A	/	/	/	:‖

I				iI				III^				V				
E	/	/	/	E/G♯	/	/	/	G♯	/	/	/	B	/	/	/	

Link

I				VI				IV				I				
E	/	/	/	C♯m	/	/	/	A	/	/	/	E	/	/	/	

Verse

Link

G♯   F♯m   E   E/G♯   A   C♯m   B   D   G

Verse
Link (four times)

Link 2

III^				III^				II				II			
G♯	/	/	/	G♯	/	/	/	F♯m	/	/	/	F♯m	/	/	/

I				iI				IV				IV			
E	/	/	/	E/G♯	/	/	/	A	/	/	/	A	/	/	/

Coda = Link (repeat to fade)

Notes:
- 'Falling Under Heaven' is based on classic mid-1980s U2.
- The song structure is very simple, and the harmonic material is limited to the key of E major. Listen for how the arrangement gradually builds tension as more instruments enter, until the drums finally let loose a standard rock beat. After this there is a lull, dynamically quieter, which reprises the intro's first four bars.
- The intro contrasts III^ with the in-key II before setting up a three-chord turnaround that becomes the basis of the verse. The G♯ bass note in the verse is harmonized with a first-inversion chord I and III^.
- Chord VI is saved for the link.
- The song does not have a chorus as such. The lyric hook would go in the link.

Track 14: Oh Mrs Peel

Capo IV

Intro

I				IV		V		I				IV		V	
D	/	/	/	G	/	A	/	D	/	/	/	G	/	A	/

Verse

I				I				VI				iI			
D	/	/	/	D	/	/	/	Bm6	/	/	/	D/A	/	/	/
d				c♯				b				a			

IV				iI				IV				♭VII			
G	/	/	/	D/F♯	/	/	/	G	/	/	/	Cmaj7	/	/	/
g				f♯				g				c			

continues on next page

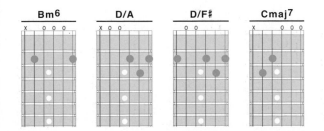

Bm6   D/A   D/F♯   Cmaj7

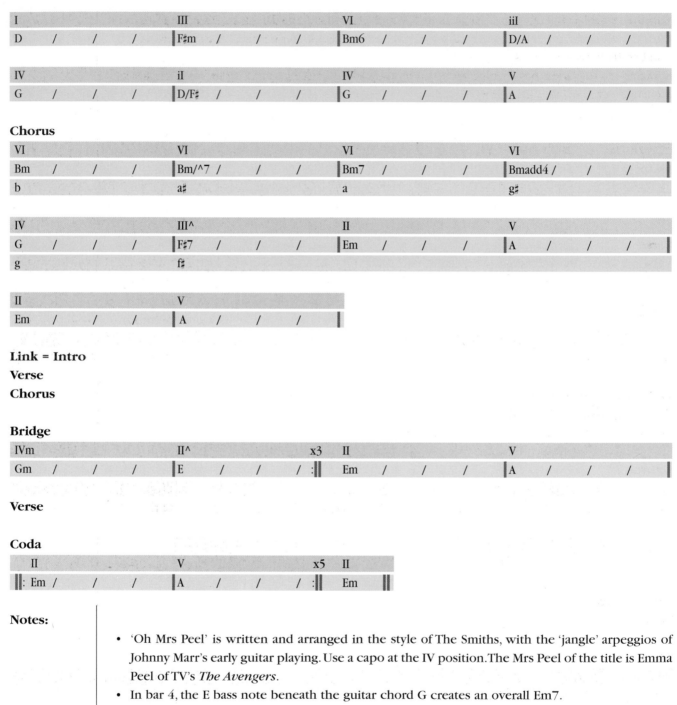

I				III				VI				iiI			
D	/	/	/	F#m	/	/	/	Bm6	/	/	/	D/A	/	/	/

IV				iI				IV				V			
G	/	/	/	D/F#	/	/	/	G	/	/	/	A	/	/	/

Chorus

VI				VI				VI				VI			
Bm	/	/	/	Bm/^7	/	/	/	Bm7	/	/	/	Bmadd4	/	/	/
b				a#				a				g#			

IV				III^				II				V			
G	/	/	/	F#7	/	/	/	Em	/	/	/	A	/	/	/
g				f#											

II				V			
Em	/	/	/	A	/	/	/

Link = Intro
Verse
Chorus

Bridge

IVm				II^			x3	II				V			
Gm	/	/	/	E	/	/	:||	Em	/	/	/	A	/	/	/

Verse

Coda

II				V			x5	II	
||: Em	/	/	/	A	/	/	:||	Em	||

Notes:

- 'Oh Mrs Peel' is written and arranged in the style of The Smiths, with the 'jangle' arpeggios of Johnny Marr's early guitar playing. Use a capo at the IV position. The Mrs Peel of the title is Emma Peel of TV's *The Avengers*.
- In bar 4, the E bass note beneath the guitar chord G creates an overall Em7.
- The verse has a descending bassline going down the D major scale. This is complemented by the popular descent from the minor chord VI in the chorus.

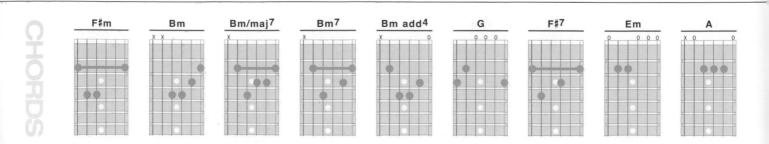

F#m   Bm   Bm/maj7   Bm7   Bm add4   G   F#7   Em   A

- In the verse, bar 8 features ♭VII as a major 7, which removes the usual 'blues' effect of a ♭VII chord. When the sequence returns to a point where we would expect to hear this chord again, in bar 16, it becomes an A.
- Many songs by The Smiths have a creepy or angst-ridden moment – so it is right to put a weird change in the bridge, going from IVm to II^.

Track 15: I Can't Tell You

Intro

IV				III				IV				I			
D	/	/	/	C♯m	/	/	/	D	/	/	/	A	/	/	/

Verse

IV				I				IV				♭VII [V]			
D7	/	/	/	A7	/	/	/	D7	/	/	/	G7	/	/	/

                                               1st time -------------------------

I				V		II^ [IV]		V				V			
C	/	/	/	G7	/	D7	/	E7	/	/	/	E7	/	/	/ :‖

2nd time-------------------------

I			
A	/	/	/

Chorus

VI				III				VI				III		I	
F♯m	/	/	/	C♯m	/	/	/	F♯m	/	/	/	C♯m	/	A	/

IV				II				I			
Dmaj7	/	/	/	Bm	/	/	/	A	/	/	/

Link = Intro
Verse

Chorus 2

VI				III				VI				III		I	
F♯m	/	/	/	C♯m	/	/	/	F♯m	/	/	/	C♯m	/	A	/

continues on next page

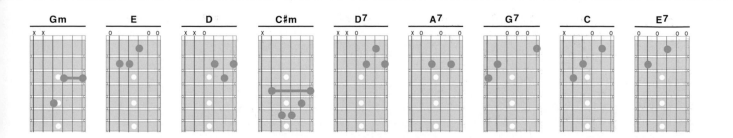

Gm   E   D   C♯m   D7   A7   G7   C   E7

A GUIDE TO THE CD

IV				II				I				I			
Dmaj7	/	/	/	Bm	/	/	/	A	/	/	/	A7	/	/	/

Bridge

bVII				bVII				V				V			
Fmaj7	/	/	/	Fmaj7	/	/	/	D7	/	/	/	D7	/	/	/

bVII				II				III [II]				V			
Fmaj7	/	/	/	Am	/	/	/	Bm	/	/	/	E	/	/	/

Verse, no repeat (second time option)

Chorus 3

VI				III				VI				III		I	
F#m	/	/	/	C#m	/	/	/	F#m	/	/	/	C#m	/	A	/

IV				II				I				VII^			
Dmaj7	/	/	/	Bm	/	/	/	A	/	/	/	G#	/	/	/

Chorus as chorus 1

Coda (link)

IV				III				IV				I			
D	/	/	/	C#m	/	/	/	D	/	/	/	A6	/	/	/

Notes:

- 'I Can't Tell You' is another power-pop song with a slight Beatles influence (notice the sixth chord at the end).
- The verse avoids minor chords and has plenty of dominant 7s. These take the progression briefly to C major from the home key of A. Watch for the second-time option, which changes the chord in the last bar.
- The chorus has lots of minor chords and initially only seven bars – a bit of asymmetry.
- The second chorus adds a breather bar of A7 to make a transition to the bridge.
- The bridge is best thought of as in G major, though that key is never confirmed. A II-V change prepares the move back to A major for the last verse.
- Chorus 3 also has eight bars. A dark outrider (VII^) appears, suggesting a possible key change, but that idea is quickly snuffed out.

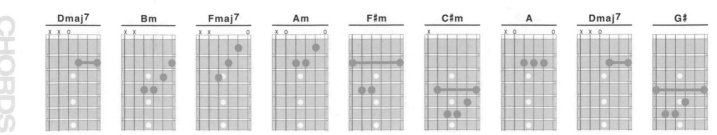

Track 16: Happy Ever After

Intro (after free-time guitar phrase)

I		IV	III	I		IV	III
E	/	Amaj7	G#m	E	/	Amaj7	G#m

Verse

I				IV		V		I				IV		V	
E	/	/	/	A	/	B	/	E	/	/	/	A	/	B	/

III				VI				II				bVII		V	
G#m	/	/	/	C#m	/	/	/	F#m	/	/	/	D	/	B	/

Verse

Bridge

II^				IV		I		II^				IV		bIII	
F#7	/	/	/	A	/	E	/	F#7	/	/	/	A	/	Gmaj7	/

6/8 bar, two beats

II		V			
F#m	/	B6	/	/	/

Verse
Bridge

Verse 4

I				IV		V		I				IV		V	
E	/	/	/	A	/	B	/	E	/	/	/	A	/	B	/

III				VI				II				bVII		VI^	
G#m	/	/	/	C#m	/	/	/	F#m	/	/	/	D	/	C#	/

II				bVII		V	
F#m	/	/	/	D	/	B	/

Coda

I		IV	III	x3		I	
E	/	Amaj7	G#m	:||		E	

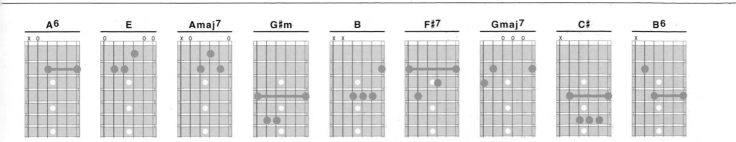

A6   E   Amaj7   G#m   B   F#7   Gmaj7   C#   B6

Notes:

- This slow ballad is in 12/8 time. There are four beats in a bar but each beat divides into three, creating a waltz-like rhythm.
- The tempo allows for a higher frequency of chord changing in a bar, like the first bar of the intro, without losing a sense of the harmony.
- Listen for the descending major scale in the bass under chord I in the first bar of the verse.
- The 12-bar verse ends with a classic ♭VII-V change.
- Coming out of verse 2 into the bridge, a sense of surprise is created by having the bridge start with II^7 – this suggests an imminent key change to B, which doesn't happen. The II^ is followed by an A instead. Further surprise is created by the appearance of a ♭III major 7 chord, whose F♯ acts as a connection to the next F♯m (chord II), and a bar of 6/8.
- There is another surprise in the last verse. The anticipated chord V at the end is replaced with VI^ (V of F♯ minor); then the same two bars repeat, this time going to the expected change. The coda brings the song full circle by recycling the intro.

Track 17: Here There Be Dragons

False intro

I				I		IV	V	x5
C	/	/	/	C	/	F	G	:‖

Intro (riff)

III^				III^				IV				II				
F♯	/	/	/	F♯	/	/	/	G	/	/	/	Em	/	/	/	:‖

Verse

I				iV				VI				VI			
G	/	/	/	D/F♯	/	/	/	Em	/	/	/	Em	/	/	/

I				iiIII				VI^				VI^ [V]				
G	/	/	/	Bm7/F♯	/	/	/	E	/	/	/	E	/	/	/	:‖

Chorus

I				I				IV				IV				
A	/	/	/	A	/	/	/	D	/	/	/	D	/	/	/	:‖

Intro as link (no repeat)
Verse
Chorus

CHORDS

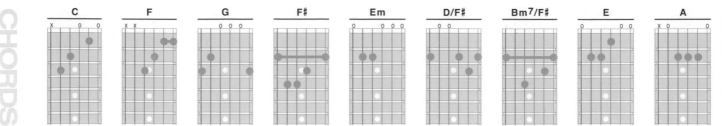

C   F   G   F♯   Em   D/F♯   Bm7/F♯   E   A

Bridge

VI				III		I		IV				IV				
Em	/	/	/	Bm	/	G	/	C	/	/	/	Cmaj7	/	/	/	:]]x4

IV		V		IV		V [IV]		
C	/	D	/	C	/	D	/	

Chorus twice

Coda

III^				III^				IV				II				
F♯	/	/	/	F♯	/	/	/	G	/	/	/	Em	/	/	/	

III^				III^				II		V		VI		V		
F♯	/	/	/	F♯	/	/	/	Em	/	A	/	Bm	/	A	/	:||

II		V		VI		V		III^	
Em	/	A	/	Bm	/	A	/	F♯	

Notes:
- 'Here There Be Dragons' is a rock song with a twin lead-guitar riff and a number of surprises. Listen for the backward guitar at the end of the false intro.
- The false intro is in C major (not the home key) and straight 4/4 time. The 'true' intro is in 12/8 (or a swung 4/4), creating the illusion of a tempo change, and it is harmonically ambiguous. This four-bar riff has been analyzed as though it were in D major, which is one way to make sense of the chords. (There is an argument for seeing F♯ as chord I, but it's too complicated to explain!).
- The verse settles into G major, carrying over the last chord of the riff as chord I. A perfect cadence takes the music into a chorus in A major.
- At the bridge, the music changes back to straightahead 4/4 and G major (though chord I appears only briefly). A IV-I plagal cadence sends the music back into A major for the last choruses.
- The coda develops the riff by adding two bars to it.
- The song ends unresolved on F♯ – a III^ in D major.

A GUIDE TO THE CD

D   Bm   Cmaj7

Track 18: Mucha's Girl

Intro

I				x4	
A	/	/	Asus2	:‖	
riff					

Verse

I				II				iIV				I				
A	/	/	Asus2	Bm7	/	/	/	D/F♯	/	/	/	Asus4	/	A	/	:‖
V				IV				I				I				
E	/	/	/	D	/	/	/	A	/	/	Asus2	A	/	/	Asus2	‖

Verse

Bridge

I		VII		VI		V		x3	IV [II]				
F♯m	/	E	/	D	/	C♯+	/	:‖	Bm	/	/	/	‖

Verse
Bridge

Guitar solo

I				I				IV				I				
A	/	/	Asus2	A	/	/	Asus2	D	/	/	/	A	/	/	Asus2	:‖

Bridge 2

I		VII		VI		V		
F♯m	/	E	/	D	/	C♯+	/	‖

Guitar solo 2

I		III		VI		II^ [V]		x3	
Am	/	C	/	F	/	B	/	:‖	

I				I [V]				
Esus4	/	/	/	Esus4	/	E	/	‖

Verse 3

A GUIDE TO THE CD

CHORDS

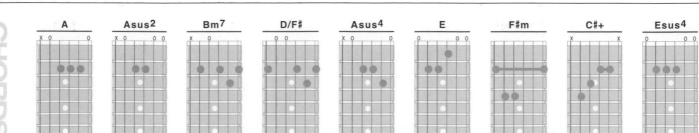

A   Asus2   Bm7   D/F♯   Asus4   E   F♯m   C♯+   Esus4

Coda

V				IV	
E	/	/	/	‖ Dmaj7	‖

Notes:

- 'Mucha's Girl' has a soul-influenced rock groove and a touch of 007. Imagine Marc Bolan's T.Rex holed up in a studio with John Barry. Result: funky glam-rock. The title refers to the Czech-born artist Alphonse Mucha (1860–1939), famous for his art nouveau posters.
- The song starts with a one-bar riff using A and Asus2 chords. This riff also appears in the 12-bar verse. The hook is in the verse, not a separate chorus.
- The bridge changes key to F♯ minor, the relative minor of A major, the home key. Notice the C♯ augmented chord that confirms it (chord V in the classical minor key).
- The first guitar solo is based on a simplified version of bars 1–4 of the verse. After the harmonic complexity of the bridge, it is good to have something clear and simple to freshen the ear.
- After this solo, the predictable move would be to go to the verse. Instead, the music goes to another bridge – but we hear only two bars, then the music jumps to the key of A minor *and* changes to a startling turnaround of I-III-VI-II^ in the minor key for a second solo. This intensifies the music. The return to A major for the last verse is achieved because II^ in A minor is V of V (B-E-A).
- Notice the romantic, unresolved ending on chord IV as a major 7.

Track 19: The One Behind It All

Intro

I		Vm		III		V		
Bm	/	F♯m/maj7/		‖ D7	/	F♯+	/	:‖

Verse

I				IV		V		I				I		V	
Bm	/	/	/	‖ Em	/	F♯	/	‖ Bm	/	Bm6	/	‖ Bmadd4	/	F♯+	‖

I				IV		♭VII		V				ii♭VII [IV^]		iv	
Bm	/	/	/	‖ Em	/	A	/	‖ F♯	/	F♯7	/	‖ A6/E	/	B7/D♯	/	‖

I [III]				V				I				IV [I]			
Em	/	/	/	‖ A	/	/	/	‖ Dmaj7	/	/	/	‖ Gmaj7	/	/	/	‖

1st time-------------------------

IV				II				VII^ [V]				Vm			
Cmaj7	/	/	/	‖ Am	/	/	/	‖ F♯	/	/	/	‖ F♯m	/	/	/	:‖

continues on next page

Dmaj7 Bm F♯m/maj7 D7 F♯+ F♯ Bm6 Bm add4 A6/E

2nd time----------------------------

V				
F#sus4 /	/	/		

Bridge (double-time feel)

IV			x8	
Em7♭5 /	/	/	:‖	

Link = Intro (no repeat)
Verse 1–12 only

Coda

IV			II [IVm]			I				
Cmaj7 /	/	/	‖Am /	/	/	‖E /	/	/	‖	

bIII	iiVm		I				x3 ♭III	iiVm		
‖: G /	Bm/F# /		‖E /	/	/	:‖	G /	Bm/F# /	‖	

Notes:

- The James Bond film soundtracks have spawned their own distinct style of song. So here's a song to get you thinking about glamorous women, nasty villains and a missing nuclear device.
- To play along with this track, detune by a semitone (half-step). The actual pitch is B♭ minor, but it is played as if it were B minor. (There is a tradition of Bond songs being pitched in extreme flat keys.)
- For this type of song, a punchy intro is needed. Notice the F#m/maj7 chord and the F# augmented.
- The verse would have a vocal over bars 1–2 and 5–6 but not 3–4 or 7–8. The latter bars rework the intro with the same rhythm but different chords.
- The second half of the verse is smoother (notice the major 7s) but drifts away from the home key of B minor – first to E minor (bar 9), D major (bar 11) and then G major, though none really get established.
- Verse 2 uses a second-time option to change the chord in bar 16 from F#m first time around to F#sus4. This creates tension going into the bridge.
- Because there are so many chord changes in the verse, we need contrast in the bridge – so it is eight bars on a single chord, Em7♭5. The minor 7♭5 is a variation on the minor 7 (see Section 7); it has a distinctly jazzy flavour. Notice that the rhythm shifts to a double-time feel here, as though there were now two beats in the same time one beat took in the verse. The music isn't faster, but it creates the illusion that it is.

A GUIDE TO THE CD

CHORDS

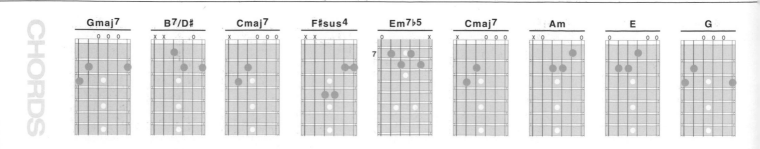

• The last verse has an altered ending. Bars 15–16 are replaced by a key change to E major (via a slushy IVm-I cadence). The coda has an exotic bIII-Vm-I turnaround, complete with a second inversion, and ends dramatically on the Bm chord, not the E. This makes a dramatic sudden ending and reminds us of the B minor key that dominated the rest of the song.

Track 20: Pocket Symphony

Capo II

Intro 1 (free-time, backward guitars)

Intro 2

I				I			
G	/	G6	/	Gmaj7	/	G6	/ :‖
riff							

Verse

I				I				I				I			
G	/	G6	/	Gmaj7	/	G6	/	G	/	G6	/	Gmaj7	/	G6	/

IV				IV			
C	/	C6	/	Cmaj7	/	C6	/ :‖

Prechorus

III		iVI		V		iVI		III		iVI		V			
Bm	/	Em/G	/	D	/	Em/G	/	Bm	/	Em/G	/	D	/	/	/

Chorus

I				bVI				I				bVI			
G	/	/	/	E♭	/	/	/	G	/	/	/	E♭	/	/	/

I		iV		VI				II		VI		IV		V	
G	/	D/F♯	/	Em	/	/	/	Am	/	Em	/	Cmaj7	/	D	/

Verse
Prechorus
Chorus

continues on next page

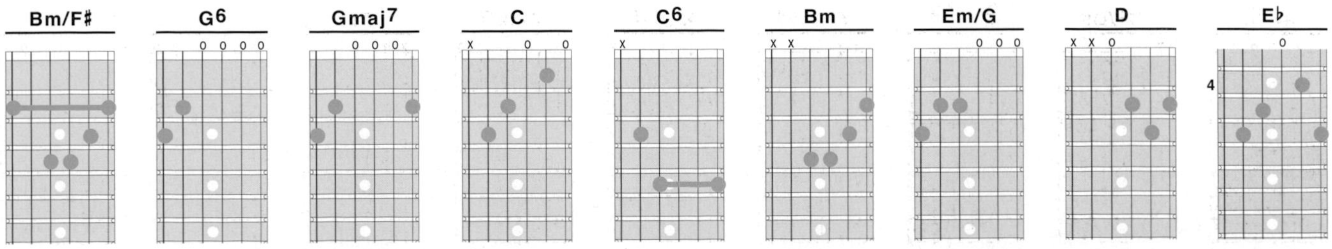

A GUIDE TO THE CD

Bm/F♯   G6   Gmaj7   C   C6   Bm   Em/G   D   E♭

Bridge/guitar solo

VII^ [III^]			I	II	x3 III^			I	V
F♯7add11 /	/	/	‖ Dmaj7 /	Em /	:‖ F♯7add11 /	/	/	‖ Dmaj7 /	A / ‖

I	II	III^	♭VII	Vm [last time II] x4
‖: Dmaj7 /	Em /	‖ F♯7add11 /	C	Am :‖

Riff once
Shortened verse 3 – starts with bar 4
Prechorus
Chorus
Chorus with repeat of last four bars

Coda 1

III	iVI	V	iVI	III
Bm /	Em/G /	‖ D /	Em/G /	:‖ Bm ‖

Coda 2 (free-time, Celtic drone guitar)

Notes:
- 'Pocket Symphony' is an example of a more complicated extended-form song. The title alludes to Brian Wilson's famous quote about wanting to write three- or four-minute songs that would be like miniature ('pocket') symphonies. This can only be possible if you use the term 'symphony' in an imprecise way – but it is still a nice phrase!
- To play along, put a capo at fret II. The true key is A major.
- The song has a free-time intro and outro using instrumental effects such as backward guitars and a secret technique I call 'Celtic drone guitar'.
- The second intro brings in a two-bar riff on G. This is used in the verse and transposed over a C chord. The verse is a six-bar phrase repeated.
- The chorus combines a I-♭VI change with more familiar changes in bars 5–8.
- The two-part bridge begins with the ambiguous chord VII^7, V as a major 7 (C♯ does not belong in G major). The second part of the bridge is in D major, but this is complicated by the 'rogue' chords III^, ♭VII and Vm. Notice the recycling of the F♯-D-Em sequence from a displaced to a non-displaced form. The return to G major for the last verse is achieved through C-Am (IV-II in G).
- The last verse is edited from 12 bars to six bars.
- Coda 1 uses the prechorus.
- The final chord is III – a minor ending to a mostly major song. This hint of mystery leads to the ambient coda (outro).

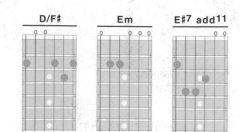

D/F♯   Em   E♯7 add11

appendix

TABLE 1: the changing roles of a C chord in the major keys

I	II	III	IV	V	VI	bVII	bIII	bVI	II^	III^	IVm
C#	D#m	E#m	F#	G#	A#m	B	E	A	D#	E#	F#m
F#	G#m	A#m	B	C#	D#m	E	A	D	G#	A#	Bm
B	C#m	D#m	E	F#	G#m	A	D	G	C#	D#	Em
E	F#m	G#m	A	B	C#m	D	G	C	F#	G#	Am
A	Bm	C#m	D	E	F#m	G	C	F	B	C#	Dm
D	Em	F#m	G	A	Bm	C	F	Bb	E	F#	Gm
G	Am	Bm	C	D	Em	F	Bb	Eb	A	B	Cm
C	Dm	Em	F	G	Am	Bb	Eb	Ab	D	E	Fm
F	Gm	Am	Bb	C	Dm	Eb	Ab	Db	G	A	Bbm
Bb	Cm	Dm	Eb	F	Gm	Ab	Db	Gb	C	D	Ebm
Eb	Fm	Gm	Ab	Bb	Cm	Db	Gb	Cb	F	G	Abm
Ab	Bbm	Cm	Db	Eb	Fm	Gb	Cb	Fb	Bb	C	Dbm
Db	Ebm	Fm	Gb	Ab	Bbm	Cb	Fb	Bbb	Eb	F	Gbm
Gb	Abm	Bbm	Cb	Db	Ebm	Fb	Bbb	Ebb	Ab	Bb	Cbm
Cb	Dbm	Ebm	Fb	Gb	Abm	Bbb	Ebb	Abb	Db	Eb	Fbm

TABLE 2: the changing roles of a C chord in the minor keys

I	bII	III	IV	V	VI	VII	IV^	V^
A#m	B	C#	D#m	E#m	F#	G#	D#	E#
D#m	E	F#	G#m	A#m	B	C#	G#	A#
G#m	A	B	C#m	D#m	E	F#	C#	D#
C#m	D	E	F#m	G#m	A	B	F#	G#
F#m	G	A	Bm	C#m	D	E	B	C#
Bm	C	D	Em	F#m	G	A	E	F#
Em	F	G	Am	Bm	C	D	A	B
Am	Bb	C	Dm	Em	F	G	D	E
Dm	Eb	F	Gm	Am	Bb	C	G	A
Gm	Ab	Bb	Cm	Dm	Eb	F	C	D
Cm	Db	Eb	Fm	Gm	Ab	Bb	F	G
Fm	Gb	Ab	Bbm	Cm	Db	Eb	Bb	C
Bbm	Cb	Db	Ebm	Fm	Gb	Ab	Eb	F
Ebm	Fb	Gb	Abm	Bbm	C	Db	Ab	Bb
Abm	Bbb	Cb	Dbm	Ebm	Fb	Gb	Db	Eb

TABLE 3: the changing roles of an Am chord in the major keys

I	II	III	IV	V	VI	♭VII	♭III	♭VI	II^	III^	IVm
C♯	D♯m	E♯m	F♯	G♯	A♯m	B	E	A	D♯	E♯	F♯m
F♯	G♯m	A♯m	B	C♯	D♯m	E	A	D	G♯	A♯	Bm
B	C♯m	D♯m	E	F♯	G♯m	A	D	G	C♯	D♯	Em
E	F♯m	G♯m	A	B	C♯m	D	G	C	F♯	G♯	Am
A	Bm	C♯m	D	E	F♯m	G	C	F	B	C♯	Dm
D	Em	F♯m	G	A	Bm	C	F	B♭	E	F♯	Gm
G	Am	Bm	C	D	Em	F	B♭	E♭	A	B	Cm
C	Dm	Em	F	G	Am	B♭	E♭	A♭	D	E	Fm
F	Gm	Am	B♭	C	Dm	E♭	A♭	D♭	G	A	B♭m
B♭	Cm	Dm	E♭	F	Gm	A♭	D♭	G♭	C	D	E♭m
E♭	Fm	Gm	A♭	B♭	Cm	D♭	G♭	C♭	F	G	A♭m
A♭	B♭m	Cm	D♭	E♭	Fm	G♭	C♭	F♭	B♭	C	D♭m
D♭	E♭m	Fm	G♭	A♭	B♭m	C♭	F♭	B♭♭	E♭	F	G♭m
G♭	A♭m	B♭m	C	D♭	E♭m	F♭	B♭♭	E♭♭	A♭	B♭	C♭m
C♭	D♭m	E♭m	F♭	G♭	A♭m	B♭♭	E♭♭	A♭♭	D♭	E♭	F♭m

TABLE 4: the changing roles of an Am chord in the minor keys

I	♭II	III	IV	V	VI	VII	IV^	V^
A♯m	B	C♯	D♯m	E♯m	F♯	G♯	D♯	E♯
D♯m	E	F♯	G♯m	A♯m	B	C♯	G♯	A♯
G♯m	A	B	C♯m	D♯m	E	F♯	C♯	D♯
C♯m	D	E	F♯m	G♯m	A	B	F♯	G♯
F♯m	G	A	Bm	C♯m	D	E	B	C♯
Bm	C	D	Em	F♯m	G	A	E	F♯
Em	F	G	Am	Bm	C	D	A	B
Am	B♭	C	Dm	Em	F	G	D	E
Dm	E♭	F	Gm	Am	B♭	C	G	A
Gm	A♭	B♭	Cm	Dm	E♭	F	C	D
Cm	D♭	E♭	Fm	Gm	A♭	B♭	F	G
Fm	G♭	A♭	B♭m	Cm	D♭	E♭	B♭	C
B♭m	C♭	D♭	E♭m	Fm	G♭	A♭	E♭	F
E♭m	F♭	G♭	A♭m	B♭m	C	D♭	A♭	B♭
A♭m	B♭♭	C♭	D♭m	E♭m	F♭	G♭	D♭	E♭

TABLE 5: 13 songwriting chords in a major key

I	II	III	IV	V	VI	♭VII	♭III	♭VI	II^	III^	IVm	VI^
C#	D#m	E#m	F#	G#	A#m	B	E	A	D#	E#	F#m	A#
F#	G#m	A#m	B	C#	D#m	E	A	D	G#	A#	Bm	D#
B	C#m	D#m	E	F#	G#m	A	D	G	C#	D#	Em	G#
E	F#m	G#m	A	B	C#m	D	G	C	F#	G#	Am	C#
A	Bm	C#m	D	E	F#m	G	C	F	B	C#	Dm	F#
D	Em	F#m	G	A	Bm	C	F	B♭	E	F#	Gm	B
G	Am	Bm	C	D	Em	F	B♭	E♭	A	B	Cm	E
C	Dm	Em	F	G	Am	B♭	E♭	A♭	D	E	Fm	A
F	Gm	Am	B♭	C	Dm	E♭	A♭	D♭	G	A	B♭m	D
B♭	Cm	Dm	E♭	F	Gm	A♭	D♭	G♭	C	D	E♭m	G
E♭	Fm	Gm	A♭	B♭	Cm	D♭	G♭	C♭	F	G	A♭m	C
A♭	B♭m	Cm	D♭	E♭	Fm	G♭	C♭	F♭	B♭	C	D♭m	F
D♭	E♭m	Fm	G♭	A♭	B♭m	C♭	F♭	B♭♭	E♭	F	G♭m	B♭
G♭	A♭m	B♭m	C	D♭	E♭m	F♭	B♭♭	E♭♭	A♭	B♭	C♭m	E♭
C♭	D♭m	E♭m	F♭	G♭	A♭m	B♭♭	E♭♭	A♭♭	D♭	E♭	F♭m	A♭

TABLE 6: nine songwriting chords in a minor key

I	♭II	III	IV	V	VI	VII	IV^	V^
A#m	B	C#	D#m	E#m	F#	G#	D#	E#
D#m	E	F#	G#m	A#m	B	C#	G#	A#
G#m	A	B	C#m	D#m	E	F#	C#	D#
C#m	D	E	F#m	G#m	A	B	F#	G#
F#m	G	A	Bm	C#m	D	E	B	C#
Bm	C	D	Em	F#m	G	A	E	F#
Em	F	G	Am	Bm	C	D	A	B
Am	B♭	C	Dm	Em	F	G	D	E
Dm	E♭	F	Gm	Am	B♭	C	G	A
Gm	A♭	B♭	Cm	Dm	E♭	F	C	D
Cm	D♭	E♭	Fm	Gm	A♭	B♭	F	G
Fm	G♭	A♭	B♭m	Cm	D♭	E♭	B♭	C
B♭m	C♭	D♭	E♭m	Fm	G♭	A♭	E♭	F
E♭m	F♭	G♭	A♭m	B♭m	C	D♭	A♭	B♭
A♭m	B♭♭	C♭	D♭m	E♭m	F♭	G♭	D♭	E♭

235

TABLE 7: seventh chords in a major key

For a blues sound, play ♭VII, ♭III, and ♭VI as dominant 7s. For reasons of space IVm is omitted here (it would be a minor 7). The normal VII of the major key would occur as a half-diminished 7.

I	II	III	IV	V	VI	♭VII	♭III	♭VI	II^	III^
C#^	D#m7	E#m7	F#^	G#7	A#m7	B^	E^	A7	D#7	E#7
F#^	G#m7	A#m7	B^	C#7	D#m7	E^	A^	D7	G#7	A#7
B^	C#m7	D#m7	E^	F#7	G#m7	A^	D^	G7	C#7	D#7
E^	F#m7	G#m7	A^	B7	C#m7	D^	G^	C7	F#7	G#7
A^	Bm7	C#m7	D^	E7	F#m7	G^	C^	F7	B7	C#7
D^	Em7	F#m7	G^	A7	Bm7	C^	F^	B♭7	E7	F#7
G^	Am7	Bm7	C^	D7	Em7	F^	B♭^	E♭7	A7	B7
C^7	Dm7	Em7	F^7	G7	Am7	B♭^7	E♭^7	A♭^7	D7	E7
F^	Gm7	Am7	B♭^	C7	Dm	E♭^	A♭^	D♭7	G7	A7
B♭^	Cm7	Dm7	E♭^	F7	Gm	A♭^	D♭^	G♭7	C7	D7
E♭^	Fm7	Gm7	A♭^	B♭7	Cm	D♭^	G♭^	C♭7	F7	G7
A♭^	B♭m7	Cm7	D♭^	E♭7	Fm	G♭^	A♭^	F♭7	B♭7	C7
D♭^	E♭m7	Fm7	G♭^	A♭7	B♭m	C♭^	F♭^	B♭♭7	E♭7	F7
G♭^	A♭m7	B♭m7	C^	D♭7	E♭m	F♭^	B♭♭^	E♭♭7	A♭7	B♭7
C♭^	D♭m7	E♭m7	F♭^	G♭7	A♭m	B♭♭^	E♭♭^	A♭♭7	D♭7	E♭7

APPENDIX

TABLE 8: 20 song structures

In these suggested song structures, intros, links, solos, codas and repeat choruses are optional.

VERSE	VERSE	VERSE	VERSE	VERSE		
VERSE	VERSE	VERSE	VERSE	CHORUS	CHORUS	
VERSE	VERSE	VERSE	BRIDGE	VERSE		
VERSE	VERSE	BRIDGE	VERSE	BRIDGE	VERSE	
VERSE	VERSE	BRIDGE	SOLO	BRIDGE	VERSE	
VERSE	VERSE	BRIDGE	VERSE	BRIDGE	VERSE	
VERSE	CHORUS	VERSE	CHORUS			
VERSE	CHORUS	VERSE	CHORUS	VERSE	CHORUS	
VERSE	VERSE	CHORUS	VERSE	CHORUS		
VERSE	CHORUS	VERSE	VERSE	CHORUS		
VERSE	CHORUS	BRIDGE	CHORUS	VERSE	CHORUS	
VERSE	CHORUS	BRIDGE	VERSE	CHORUS		
VERSE	CHORUS	BRIDGE	VERSE	CHORUS	VERSE	CHORUS
VERSE	CHORUS	VERSE	CHORUS	BRIDGE	CHORUS	
VERSE	CHORUS	VERSE	CHORUS	BRIDGE	VERSE	CHORUS
VERSE	CHORUS	VERSE	BRIDGE	VERSE	CHORUS	
CHORUS	VERSE	VERSE	CHORUS			
CHORUS	VERSE	CHORUS	VERSE	CHORUS	VERSE	CHORUS
CHORUS	VERSE	CHORUS	VERSE	BRIDGE	VERSE	CHORUS
VERSE	PRE-CH	CHORUS	BRIDGE	PRE-CH	CHORUS	

EASY REFERENCE TABLE OF TECHNIQUES

#1: the primary three-chord trick
#2: playing with expectation
#3: the 12-bar
#4: the 16-bar section
#5: spotting the spoilers
#6: the dominant crescendo
#7: displacement
#8: the 'escalator' effect
#9: rate of chord change
#10: inversions
#11: inversions on a stepped bassline
#12: withholding
#13: the three-chord turnaround
#14: adding a fourth chord
#15: meet the 'sad twin' – simple chord substitution
#16: the secondary three-chord trick
#17: bar-sharing
#18: withholding a fourth (minor) chord
#19: inversions of minor chords
#20: the 'breather' bar
#21: the 'false rise' bassline
#22: 'walking on stilts' – inversions on an intro
#23: the four-chord turnaround
#24: meet the 'Big Three' – the primary turnarounds
#25: displacement in a turnaround
#26: the escalator turnaround
#27: the down escalator – descending turnarounds
#28: the turnaround with an inversion
#29: walking on stilts revisited – the inversion turnaround
#30: the 'trailer' bassline
#31: stretching a turnaround
#32: the truncated 3+4 turnaround
#33: the 'telescoped' turnaround
#34: secondary turnarounds
#35: the turnaround as link
#36: the through-composed verse
#37: reharmonizing
#38: chord substitution in a turnaround
#39: woke up this morning with an extra chord – the ♭VII
#40: ♭VII turnarounds
#41: introducing the ♭III and ♭VI
#42: inversions of ♭III and ♭VI
#43: the ♭VI-♭VII-I approach
#44: reharmonizing with ♭VII, ♭III, and ♭VI
#45: hard-rock songs
#46: the reverse-polarity turnaround
#47: the 'slush-maker'
#48: IVm and the lowered-degree chords
#49: common tones
#50: inversions of reverse-polarity chords

#51: the 'classical' minor key
#52: the minor three-chord trick
#53: the secondary minor three-chord trick
#54: the four-chord minor song
#55: minor-key blues
#56: the 16-bar minor section
#57: the minor turnaround
#58: the dominant 7
#59: the major 7
#60: the minor 7
#61: the major and minor 6
#62: suspended chords
#63: the added-ninth major chord
#64: the added-ninth minor chord
#65: the fifth chord
#66: the augmented chord
#67: the diminished chord
#68: methods for changing key
#69: using chords I, IV, and V to change key
#70 the reverse-polarity gate
#71: using IVm to change key
#72: key change to the dominant (V)
#73: key change to the subdominant (IV)
#74: key change to the supertonic (II)
#75: key change to the relative minor (VI)
#76: key change to the tonic minor
#77: the semitone key change
#78: changing key with a diminished 7
#79: the recycled intro
#80: the free-time intro
#81: the false intro
#82: the sus4 false intro
#83: the false intro (guitar version)
#84: the false keynote intro
#85: the turnaround bridge
#86: the bridge avoiding chord I
#87: the minor bridge
#88: the through-composed bridge
#89: the middle eight that isn't eight
#90: the coda
#91: the final cadence
#92: implied chords
#93: the implied dominant 11
#94: asymmetry
#95: duration – how long is your song?
#96: the enharmonic common tone
#97: pedal effects
#98: the prechorus
#99: descending basslines
#100: chromatic chords – the 'dark outriders'

APPENDIX

APPENDIX

GLOSSARY OF SONGWRITING TERMS AND CONCEPTS

Asymmetry: The opposite of something which is symmetrical and regular in form. In songwriting the principle of asymmetry is important because it prevents too much regularity, which can become boring and predictable. Asymmetry is unpredictable. Asymmetry is most useful when applied to the length of phrases, song sections, time signatures, the number of repeats, etc.

Augmented chord: A chord made up of two intervals of a major third; for example, C+ = CEG♯.

Bar-sharing: Refers to a bar in which there is more than one chord. This describes a rate of chord change. More specifically, the reharmonizing of half a bar from major to minor or the reverse.

Blue note: The flattened third, fifth or seventh of a major scale, as often heard in blues, jazz and rock music.

Blue chord: The ♭III or ♭VII chord in the major key.

Bpm: Beats per minute. A measurement of tempo (speed) that is used by songwriters to calculate the duration of a song.

Breather bar: A bar in which no melody is sung, usually at the end of a phrase, lyric line or song section, which gives the listener a pause before the next significant musical event. Breather bars sometimes naturally lead to asymmetry, because a song section becomes 4+1 or 8+1 or 12+1 bars.

Bridge: Also known as the 'middle eight', the bridge is the third important component section of a song, after the verse and chorus. It is traditionally placed after the second chorus to satisfy the aesthetic need for fresh material. It may open up new territory in the music and/or the lyric.

Cadence: The chord change that marks the end of a phrase, usually involving chord I and/or chord V. Traditional harmony recognises the perfect cadence (V-I), the imperfect cadence (I-V), the plagal cadence (IV-I) and the interrupted cadence (V-VI). Of these, the perfect cadence is the most significant for songwriting as it is used to change key and to end a song with finality.

Chorus: The song section which is usually the most memorable, the 'hook', which often has the title in the lyric.

Chromatic: The chromatic scale includes all 12 notes. When a note or chord is referred to as chromatic, it is one that does not belong in the home key.

Classical minor key: The minor key constructed from the harmonic minor scale (A B C D E F G♯), in which chord V is a major chord.

Coda: The final section of the song, after the last chorus. It can be a repetition of an earlier section such as a link, intro or chorus, with or without singing or instrumental soloing. In popular songwriting, the coda is often a fade.

Common tone: A note common to adjacent chords in a progression. F major (F A C) and C major (C E G) have one common tone; F major (F A C) and D minor (D F A) have two common tones; Fmaj7 (F A C E) and A minor (A C E) have three common tones. An enharmonic note (same pitch, different spelling) can disguise a common tone: E major is E G♯ B and F minor is F A♭ C, but G♯ and A♭ are actually the same pitch and therefore a common tone.

Composite harmony: A chord whose notes are played on more than one instrument – usually the bass and a harmony instrument, such as rhythm guitar. If the harmony instrument plays the chord Am and the bass plays F, the composite chord is F A C E = Fmaj7.

Curtailed phrase/form: Any song section or phrase which is expected to have a certain length but is unexpectedly shorter. An 11-bar section in a 12-bar blues song would be an example. Curtailed phrases often function to express asymmetry.

Dark outriders: The chromatic chords least related to a major or minor key.

Degree: Another term for referring to the notes of a scale. In the C major scale, E is the third degree.

Descending bass: A popular songwriting device in which a section's chords are built on a descending sequence of notes in the bass. The harmony is made subservient to this bassline. The harmony may also be static.

Diminished chord: A chord made up of two intervals of a minor third; for example, Cdim = C E♭ G♭. It occurs naturally as chord VII in the major key. If another minor third is added, it becomes a diminished 7 chord; Cdim7 = C E♭ G♭ B♭♭.

Displaced chord: A chord, usually I or V, pushed forwards or backwards of its usual position in a sequence. This technique is most easily applied to primary turnarounds where the position of I and V is predictable.

Dominant: The fifth note of the scale, the chord built on that note (chord V) and the key symbolized by that chord. In C major, G is the dominant and G major is the dominant chord – often played as the dominant 7 (G7).

Dominant crescendo: A traditional songwriting device in which the music gets louder whilst remaining on chord V. This is usually a drawn-out form of the perfect cadence, since the next chord is often I.

Dominant suppression: The deliberate avoidance of chord V in a song sequence or turnaround. A type of withholding.

Dreamer: A metaphorical name for a second-inversion chord.

Enharmonic note/chord: A note or chord that has two names but the same pitch; chiefly, the five black keys on the piano: A♯/B♭, C♯/D♭, D♯/E♭, F♯/G♭, G♯/A♭, and the major and minor chords built on those notes. B, F♯, and C♯ are the enharmonic equivalents of the keys C♭, G♭, and D♭.

Escalator effect: Powerful 'rising' feeling created by chords arranged in numerical sequence. The classic example, often found as a prechorus sequence, is II-III-IV-V.

False intro: A song introduction which arouses expectations in the listener that are unfulfilled. A false intro might start, for example, in a different tempo, key, time signature or style from the rest of the song.

False rise: A bassline that rises to end on an inversion where a root-note chord was expected. The chord sequence C-C/E-F-G7 with its rising bassline C-E-F-G would make us expect C or Am as the next chord. If the bassline moved instead to the note A harmonized by an F/A first-inversion chord, that would constitute a false rise.

Floating turnaround: A turnaround played over a pedal bass note, usually either the tonic or dominant of the home key. This technique is good for intros and bridges, or for making a turnaround's first chorus appearance less emphatic than its later ones.

Harmonic function: The role a chord plays in a major or minor key, as designated by a Roman numeral such as I, II, III, etc. The pitch identity (actual sound) of a chord stays the same regardless of its harmonic function in any context.

Hard-rock formula: A chord 'recipe' that involves using chords I, IV and V from the primary six and adding ♭VII, ♭III, and ♭VI. In C major this would be C F G B♭ E♭ A♭.

Inversion: A chord that does not have its root note as the lowest in pitch. A simple triad of C has a first inversion (C/E) and a second inversion (C/G). A Cmaj7 chord could have a third inversion (C/B) because there are four notes in the chord.

Implied turnaround: A turnaround in which the bass moves to the expected root notes but the chords are not sounded.

Keynote: The first note of the scale; also called the tonic.

Leading note: The seventh degree of the scale, one semitone (half-step) below the keynote in both the major and the classical minor scale. In C major, B is the leading note. Added to a major triad, it creates the major 7 chord; Cmaj7 = C E G B.

Major chord: A triad formed by an interval of two tones (whole-steps) and then one-and-a-half tones (steps): C major triad = C E G.

Major scale: The division of the octave into seven intervals on the pattern tone, tone, semitone, tone, tone, tone, semitone (whole-step, whole-step, half-step, whole-step, whole-step, whole-step, half-step). Playing the white notes of the piano from C to C produces the C major scale.

Mediant: The third note of the scale, the chord built on that note (chord III) and the key symbolized by that chord. In C major, E is the mediant and Em is the mediant chord.

Middle eight: Another name for the bridge section; so-called because it is often eight bars long and occurs roughly in the middle of a song.

Minor chord: A triad formed by an interval of one-and-a-half tones (steps) and then two tones (whole-steps): C minor triad = C E♭ G.

Modal minor: A set of chords derived from the natural minor scale (Aeolian mode): A B C D E F G. In popular songwriting, this is treated as a version of the key of A minor. It differs from the classical minor in that its chord V is minor.

Modulation: The process of changing key.

Pedal: A bass note that remains the same while chords change above it, creating differing amounts of harmonic tension. So-called because bass notes are played on the pedals of an organ. In guitar music, the pedal is usually E, A or D (the open lower strings). Not to be confused with a drone note – one which remains unchanging in the middle or at the top of the harmony above a changing bassline.

Perfect cadence: The chord change V-I at the end of a phrase or section.

Pitch identity: A chord considered by reference to its pitch name – C, G, Em, etc – in contrast to its harmonic function as chord I, V, III, etc. Pitch identity remains the same regardless of the harmonic role a chord is playing at any moment. See tables 1–4 above.

Primary three-chord trick: A song written using chords I, IV, and V of a key; in C major: C, F, and G.

Plus one: A technique in which one bar is added to a standard four-, eight-, 12- or 16-bar section. This is done to support a slightly longer lyric line, to increase the drama and suspense before a new section, to hold up the movement of chords, or to add a touch of asymmetry.

Rate of chord change: The frequency with which chords change from bar to bar or within a bar.

Relative chord/key: Every major chord/key has a relative minor to which it is closely related by virtue of having many of the same notes. A C major chord (C E G) is the relative major of an A minor chord (A C E). The relative minor is chord VI in a major key, chord III in a minor key: A minor is the relative minor of C major; C major is the relative major of A minor.

Reverse polarity: A songwriting technique which changes II, III and VI into major chords, and IV into a minor.

Root: The note in a chord after which the chord is named. The note C is the root of a C major chord. If this note is the lowest in the chord, the chord is in root position.

Sad twin: Metaphorical name for the relative minor chords of I, IV, and V: VI, II, and III respectively

Scale: The division of an octave into a series of notes (usually eight) from which chords, melody and a sense of key are generated. Blues and rock music also use modes and pentatonic scales (which have five notes).

Second-time option: A technique in which a song section is repeated but a change is made to its last bar or two bars, either by the use of different chords or by making the final bars the beginning of a new section.

Secondary three-chord trick: A three-chord song that omits chord V.

Secondary turnaround: A turnaround that omits chord V or I.

Spoiler: The appearance of a chord in a place or manner that prevents a later appearance from being as musically effective as it could be.

Subdominant: The fourth note of the scale, the chord built on that note (chord

IV) and the key symbolized by that chord. In C major, F is the subdominant and F major is the subdominant chord.

Submediant: The sixth note of the scale, the chord built on that note (chord VI) and the key symbolized by that chord. In C major, A is the submediant and A minor is the submediant chord.

Supertonic: The second note of the scale, the chord built on that note (chord II) and the key symbolized by that chord. In C major, D is the supertonic and D minor is the supertonic chord.

Telescoping: A technique in which a chord sequence is made to last twice as long as its regular length by doubling the number of beats for each chord. Telescoping is a mild form of disguise, so a songwriter can get away with using the same sequence for a verse and a chorus.

Tempo: The speed at which music is played, measured in beats per minute (bpm).

Three-chord trick: A song with only three chords, usually I, IV, and V.

Through-composed: A song or song section in which there are no repeated chord sequences.

Time signature: A numerical designation placed at the start of a piece of music which indicates the type of beat. It has nothing to do with tempo. The most common time signatures in popular music are 4/4 (four beats per bar; a quarter-note receives one beat) and 12/8 (12 beats per bar; an eighth-note receives one beat). Songs in such time signatures as 3/4, 6/8, and 2/4 occur less frequently.

Tonic: The first note of the scale; also called the keynote.

Tonic minor: The minor chord or key with the same root note as the tonic. C minor is the tonic minor of C major. Counter-intuitively, C minor is actually a more distant key than C's relative minor, A minor, because it has fewer notes in common, especially in its modal form.

Trailer bassline: A bassline that 'previews' the root notes of a chord sequence that will be heard in the song before those chords are actually played. It is a more general example of the bassline that makes an implied turnaround.

Triad: A chord made up of three notes; a C major triad is C E G.

Turnaround: A repeating chord sequence with three or four chords which last two, four, or eight bars each. For example, I-VI-IV-V or I-II-IV-V.

12-bar: A verse structure central to blues, rock'n'roll, R&B and rock, using chords I, IV, and V and containing its own hook.

Tyranny of four: A cautionary name for the habit among songwriters of letting the number '4' dominate – so you might have a four-chord song in 4/4 with four verse phrases and a chorus with a four-chord turnaround repeated four times and followed by a four-bar link … etc.

Walker: A metaphorical name for a first-inversion chord.

ABOUT THE AUTHOR

Rikky Rooksby is a guitar teacher, songwriter/composer writer on popular music. He is the author of the Backbeat titles How To Write Songs On Guitar (2000), Inside Classic Rock Tracks (2001), Riffs (2002), The Songwriting Sourcebook (2003), Chord Master (2004), Melody (2004), Songwriting Secrets: Bruce Springsteen (2005), How To Write Songs on Keyboards (2005), Lyrics (2006), Arranging Songs (2008) and How To Write Songs In Altered Guitar Tunings (2010). He contributed to Albums: 50 Years Of Great Recordings, Classic Guitars Of The Fifties, The Guitar: The Complete Guide For The Player, and Roadhouse Blues. He has also written The Guitarist's Guide To The Capo (Artemis 2003), The Complete Guide To The Music Of Fleetwood Mac (revised ed. 2004), 14 Fastforward guitar tutor books, four in the First Guitar series; transcribed and arranged more than 40 chord songbooks of music including Bob Dylan, Bob Marley, The Stone Roses, David Bowie, Eric Clapton, Travis, The Darkness, and The Complete Beatles; and co-authored 100 Years 100 Songs. He has written articles on rock musicians for the new Dictionary Of National Biography (OUP), and published interviews, reviews, articles and transcriptions in magazines such as Guitar Techniques, Total Guitar, Guitarist, Bassist, Bass Guitar ...ne, The Band, Record Collector, Playmusic, Sound On Sound, and Making Music, where he wrote the monthly 'Private Pluck' guitar column. He is a member of the Guild of International Songwriters and Composers, the Society of Authors, the Sibelius Society, and the Vaughan Williams Society. Visit his website at www.rikkyrooksby.com

AUTHOR'S THANKS

For their involvement in the preparation of this book's earlier and latest edition I would like to thank Nigel Osborne, Tony Bacon, John Morrish, Jim Roberts, Thomas Jerome Seabrook, Rod Fogg, Paul Cooper, Phil Richardson, and Kim Devlin. A special thanks to Holly Willis for all her work in publicising the original edition of this title – an author's texts never had a better friend. Thanks to Tim Turan of Tim Turan Audio, Oxford, who mastered the CD. Thanks also to Kay and Robin, and my wife Rhonda, for support during the writing of this book.

I would also like to thank readers who have posted online reviews of other books in this series.

The music on the CD remains copyright Rikky Rooksby. For commercial use in music libraries and similar please contact the author via the publisher.

APPENDIX